Sha

Related Palgrave titles

Shakespeare

Third Edition

KIERNAN RYAN

palgrave

First published 1989
Second edition published 1995 by Prentice Hall/Harvester Wheatsheaf
Third edition published by Palgrave 2002

PALGRAVE
Houndmills, Basingstoke, Hampshire RG21 6XS and
175 Fifth Avenue, New York, N.Y. 10010
Companies and representatives throughout the world

PALGRAVE is the new global academic imprint of
St. Martin's Press LLC Scholarly and Reference Division and
Palgrave Publishers Ltd (formerly Macmillan Press Ltd).

ISBN 0–333–78197–X hardback
ISBN 0–333–78198–8 paperback

This book is printed on paper suitable for recycling and
made from fully managed and sustained forest sources.

A catalogue record for this book is available
from the British Library.

Library of Congress Cataloging in Publication
data has been applied for.

10 9 8 7 6 5 4 3 2 1
11 10 09 08 07 06 05 04 03 02

Printed in China

For Rose and Tom Ryan

Contents

Preface to the Third Edition

A new edition and a new publisher have given me the opportunity not only to revise and update the text of the second edition, but also to add a great deal of new material, as a result of which *Shakespeare* has now expanded to twice the size of the first edition published in 1989. I have added a new final chapter, '"Dreaming on things to come": Shakespeare and the Future of Criticism', which spins its speculations out of the reception of Shakespeare by Wilde, Shaw and Joyce. Chapter 4, 'Shakespearean Comedy and Romance: The Utopian Imagination', has been enlarged to include two essays: 'Playing for Time: *The Comedy of Errors*' and '*Measure for Measure*: Double Trouble'. Throughout the book, I have inserted or extended footnotes to incorporate important recent criticism on particular plays or topics. And the list of Further Reading riding shotgun at the end of the book has more than doubled in length and is now divided into six sections: 'General Studies', 'Comedies', 'Histories', 'Tragedies', 'Romances' and 'Poetry'.

This book owes much to the many students at New Hall, Cambridge, and, more recently, on the Shakespeare MA at Royal Holloway, who have helped to shape its ideas. It owes special debts, for their kindness and encouragement at various stages in its evolution, to Heather Glen, Penny Wilson, Kate Belsey, James Wood, and above all Helga Geyer-Ryan. Heartfelt thanks are also due to Jackie Jones, who commissioned the first and the second editions of the book, and without whose patience and support neither would have seen the light of day. Margaret Bartley commissioned the present third edition for Palgrave, and Beverley Tarquini coaxed it expertly into print: I am deeply grateful to both of them.

Royal Holloway
University of London

Acknowledgements

Chapter 1 includes a brief excerpt from '*King Lear*: The Battle for the Bard', in *Critical Dialogues: Current Issues in English Studies in Germany and Great Britain*, ed. Isobel Armstrong and Hans-Werner Ludwig (Tübingen: Gunter Narr, 1995). Chapter 2 is a condensed and revised version of 'The Future of History in *Henry IV*', in *Theory in Practice: Henry IV*, ed. Nigel Wood (Buckingham: Open University Press, 1995). The section of Chapter 3 entitled '*Romeo and Juliet*: The Murdering Word' includes revised extracts from '*Romeo and Juliet*: The Language of Tragedy', in *The Taming of the Text: Explorations in Language, Literature and Culture*, ed. Willie Van Peer (London: Routledge, 1989). The section of Chapter 4 entitled 'Playing for Time: *The Comedy of Errors*' is adapted from 'Playing for Time: Improvising and Anachronism in Shakespearean Comedy', in *Die Wunde der Geschichte: Aufsätze zur Literatur und Ästhetik*, ed. Klaus Garber and H. Gustav Klaus (Cologne: Böhlau Verlag, 1999). The section of Chapter 4 entitled '*Measure for Measure*: Double Trouble' was first published, in a slightly different form, as part of '*Measure for Measure*: Marxism Before Marx', in *Marxist Shakespeares*, ed. Jean E. Howard and Scott Shershow (London: Routledge, 2001). Chapter 5 incorporates a brief extract from 'Shakespeare and the Future', in *Talking Shakespeare*, ed. Deborah Cartmell and Michael Scott (London: Palgrave, 2001). The author and publishers are grateful to Gunter Narr, Routledge, the Open University Press, and Böhlau Verlag for permission to reprint this material.

A Note on the Text

Textual references throughout are to *The Riverside Shakespeare*, ed. G. Blakemore Evans, 2nd edn (Boston: Houghton Mifflin, 1997).

1

Reinterpreting Shakespeare Today

New Critical Perspectives

The aim of this study is to further the development of fresh readings of Shakespeare's drama, readings designed to activate the revolutionary imaginative vision that invites discovery in his plays today. It is intended as a contribution to what remains a fundamental objective of radical criticism at the beginning of the twenty-first century: to contest and displace the established interpretations of canonical works, and thereby transform both the present function of past texts and the practice of criticism itself.

The closing decades of the twentieth century witnessed the terminal disillusionment of most students and teachers with traditional assumptions about the nature and point of literary criticism. English Literature is still, in both conventional and more modish versions, one of the most widely studied subjects in the school and university curriculum. But it is a subject which has long been recognized, even in conservative quarters, to be in dire disarray and in urgent need of reconstruction.[1] Alternative perspectives opened up by feminism, poststructuralism, psychoanalytic theory, new historicism and cultural materialism have thrown the rationale, and hence the interpretive authority, of once impregnable modes of criticism into serious question. It is now hard to resist the conclusion that the main function of orthodox criticism has been to bolster the beliefs upon which our patriarchal, class-divided culture depends.[2]

Nowhere has this argument been more convincingly advanced than in the case of Shakespeare, whose recruitment has played a crucial role in securing the objectives of the critical establishment since the eighteenth century. A history and a critique of this process of appropriation have been undertaken in a series of seminal studies, which provide the obligatory point of departure for any attempt to transform the prevailing perception of Shakespeare's significance.[3] I want to start, therefore, by summarizing the main points of the case that has been mounted by this groundbreaking body of work.

The reason why our perception of Shakespeare matters is that over the centuries his drama has come to constitute, as Alan Sinfield observes, 'an influential medium through which certain ways of thinking about the world may be promoted and others impeded'. Shakespeare has become, in other words, 'one of the places where ideology is made' and thus, inevitably, 'a site of cultural struggle and change'.[4] The problem is that so far most battles for the Bard have been won by forces intent on fabricating from his art a powerful apology for leaving the world the way it is.

Shakespeare's image has been endlessly refashioned and his works tirelessly redefined to ensure that they reflect the illusions underpinning the status quo. The Swan of Avon has been summoned as a star witness to the notion that the characters and fates of individuals are formed independently of their social milieu and historical conditions, whose seeming mutability masks an unchanging order of things. Generations of labourers in the vineyard of high culture have bent themselves to the task of constructing Shakespeare 'as the National Poet and as *the* example of the individual literary genius who transcends his period and produces texts of timeless value which reveal fundamental truths about a "universal human condition"'.[5] To reconsider in this light the most influential authorities on the plays, from the eighteenth century to the present, is to discern beneath the surface diversity of opinion a common, continuous 'effort of ideological containment, an attempt to harness the unruly energies of the text to a stable order of significance'. It is the effort, more specifically, 'to recuperate Shakespeare's text in the name of autonomous subjectivity and universal human experience. From Johnson to Leavis, a tradition grows up in which the plays are subjected to a powerful normative bias, an imposition of meanings and values as conceived by the dominant ideology.'[6]

Certainly, one of the chief kinds of criticism that have prevailed in Shakespeare studies is the sort in which 'history, if acknowledged at all, is seen as inessential or a constraint transcended in the affirmation of a transhistorical condition'.[7] There exists alongside this, to be sure, a venerable tradition of scholarship and commentary, which insists on returning and confining Shakespeare to his original historical habitat. But time and again such a move serves 'only to highlight in the foregrounded text preoccupations which turn out to be not historical at all, but eternal. History is thus recognized and abolished at one and the same time'.[8] These two apparently opposed styles of Shakespeare criticism reveal themselves, on sharper inspection, to be secretly complicit in the same enterprise. The formidable resilience of that enterprise owes much to the fact that 'the continuities of Shakespeare criticism and textual and historical scholarship all exert a powerful institutional brake upon any attempt to diverge from the order of concepts and methods they have sought to establish for themselves'.[9]

The institutional brakes have been applied most effectively in the sphere of education. Here the most cursory analysis makes it plain that Stratford's principal source of revenue 'has been made to speak mainly for the right', not only through the slanted paraphrase of what his works say, but also through his recurrent conscription 'to underwrite established practices in literary criticism and, consequently, in examinations'.[10] The overtly or implicitly reactionary presentation of Shakespeare is a vital component, in fact often the keystone, of school and degree courses in English Literature, not only in Britain but all over the world.[11] Indeed, in British secondary education today, as a result of drastic revisions of the curriculum, 'the importance of Shakespeare is perhaps greater than ever, for he is becoming the *sole vehicle* of high-cultural ideology and establishment literary criticism in schools'.[12]

Nor does the process of recuperating Shakespeare restrict itself to the academy and the classroom. An examination of the dominant directorial philosophies of the Royal Shakespeare Company (RSC) since the early 1960s, traced through the productions and pronouncements of Peter Hall, Peter Brook and Trevor Nunn in particular, exposes the pervasive and protracted influence of two critics above all: E. M. W. Tillyard, whose books *The Elizabethan World Picture* (1943) and *Shakespeare's History Plays* (1944) cast Shakespeare as a stout traditionalist rooted in his age, and Jan Kott, whose *Shakespeare Our Contemporary* (1965) depicts him rather as the modernist voice of a bleak, Beckettian vision. Despite their outward incongruity, both these conceptions of Shakespeare 'are really two sides of the same conservative coin – both predicated on the ideas of an essential human nature and the desirability of "order" and both hostile to positive political action'.[13] Film versions and television productions of Shakespeare's plays have generally fared little better. For, with a few honourable exceptions, where bold, inventive work has been achieved against the odds, the radical potentialities of Shakespeare on big screen and small screen alike 'are in practice systematically blocked, suppressed or marginalized by the conservatism of the dominant cultural institutions'.[14]

Given the sheer weight and global reach of the institutions that dictate how the world's most celebrated playwright and his works are reproduced in classes, theatres, lecture-halls, cinemas and livingrooms, the chances of reversing the current of interpretation seem slim, to say the least. But if there is one conclusion which the evidence of the radical scholars I have been quoting compels us to draw, it is that the canonized version of Shakespeare is a cultural creation, which has no intrinsic authority and whose validity is wide open to dispute. In short:

> Shakespeare does not have to work in a conservative manner. His plays do not have to signify in the ways they have customarily been made to . . . he does not have to be a crucial stage in the justification of elitism in education and culture. He has been appropriated for certain practices and attitudes, and can be reappropriated for others.[15]

Any serious venture to transform literary studies into an educational practice devoted not to maintaining but to changing the existing social order must undertake, as a major priority, the sustained reappropriation of Shakespeare's plays. The question, however, is what form this reappropriation should take, if it is to make his drama more disturbing in its impact on the institutions through which Shakespeare is reproduced, and more constructively alert to our most pressing problems and needs. The metaphysical premises on which most criticism of Shakespeare has proceeded are being dismantled, and the idealist interpretations that have entombed his plays for too long are crumbling away. But the kinds of reading that have emerged to take their place seem to me, for the most part, more questionable and less helpful developments.

Shakespeare's oeuvre is currently colonized by most breeds of new-historicist, cultural-materialist, feminist and poststructuralist criticism. The undoubted diversity of their approaches, however, disguises their engagement in a deeper argument between two basic critical strategies, neither of which proves persuasive. The one grounds the drama's objectives in the historical milieu from which it sprang; the other cold-shoulders past contexts, preferring to turn Shakespeare's text into a mirror of the critic's own method and present priorities.

The cultural materialist Jonathan Dollimore provides a characteristically grim and dispiriting instance of the former method at work. Dollimore's brand of historicism seeks to reveal 'the effectiveness and complexity of the ideological process of containment'[16] in which it presumes Shakespeare's drama to be embroiled. The progressive critic's task is to demystify Shakespeare's plays, by exposing them as elaborate devices employed by the repressive cultural machinery of his time to secure the status quo. Subversive impulses and flashes of resistance find expression throughout the plays, of course, but these are to be explained as ruses of the ruling ideology at its most cunning. Shakespeare only opens authority to question along the way in order to vindicate it more completely in the last analysis. Thus Dollimore's account of *Measure for Measure* maintains, despite abundant implications to the contrary, that the play is best fenced off as 'a reactionary fantasy, neither radical nor liberating ... the very disclosure of social realities which make progress seem imperative is recuperated in comedic closure, a redemptive wish-fulfilment of the status quo'.[17]

It is ironic that critics of Dollimore's bent confirm rather than dispute the coarse supposition of traditionalists like Tillyard that Shakespeare's plays enforce the political, moral and philosophical outlook of those who ruled his world. The (far from negligible) difference is that the Dollimore school offers a more complex diagnosis of the drama's conformity, and treats it as something to be smoked out and disarmed rather than sidestepped or celebrated. The plays can be studied and taught from a progressive modern viewpoint, but the idea that they themselves prefigure such a viewpoint is inconceivable. The possibility that Shakespeare's texts, once extricated from their conservative constructions, might be inclined to signify the opposite of what they have been induced to mean, is entertained only to be dismissed as an historically unwarranted delusion. Dollimore is anxious to reassure us that recognizing the power of the dominant ideology to turn even Shakespeare's imagination to its account 'by no means implies a fatalistic acceptance that it is somehow inevitable and that all opposition is hopeless'.[18] But, with scant textual evidence adduced to persuade us otherwise, it is hard to see what else it can imply, since it leaves merely negative or cynical reasons for studying such a contaminated Shakespeare at all.

It is consequently a relief, in many ways, to turn from this myopic rhetoric of gloom to Terry Eagleton's brazenly unhistorical 'exercise in political semiotics', *William Shakespeare*. Eagleton's book is an opportunistic attempt to read Shakespeare against the grain, to prove that 'this conservative patriarch' was actually a seditious postmodernist, whose plays exhibit a proleptic intimacy with the later revelations of 'Hegel, Marx, Nietzsche, Freud, Wittgenstein and Derrida'. As such, it constitutes a salutary assault on historicist pieties, wresting Shakespeare's drama from their fossilizing grasp to send it spinning into the late twentieth-century orbit of critical theory. The drawback is that the texts dwindle into anthologies of excerpts and allusions, whose real point is to validate Eagleton's poststructuralist thoughts on 'language, desire, law, money and the body'.[19] Moreover, the ostensibly liberating disregard for historical limits in fact renders the moments of illumination defenceless before the charge of being arbitrary and anachronistic, and thus incapable of arguing their advantage over rival readings.

Eagleton's eloquence and ironic verve make appealing what often becomes tediously predictable in most efforts to turn Shakespeare into a precocious poststructuralist – by showing, for example, 'how the Shakespearean self-reflexive forays of wit match, remarkably, the wit of the deconstructionist enterprise'.[20] This commonly means reading his plays in such a way as to demonstrate the abject impossibility of a coherent reading. The object is to leave us impaled 'on the problem of linguistic indeterminacy', floundering in 'the condition of interpretive uncertainty'.[21] As a strategy for breaking the stranglehold of arthritic interpretations, this certainly has its merits. But after the umpteenth exposition of the scandalous arbitrariness of the signifier and the ceaseless deferral of meaning, one begins to see the force of the complaint that deconstruction, when confronted with a text, 'can only endlessly rediscover its own first principles'.[22] Above all, the method leaves no ground on which cogent, stable accounts, however carefully qualified and provisional, might be built for practical use in education or the theatre. Deconstruction without reconstruction throws the potentially radical baby out with the metaphysical bathwater. For it kills the plays' urge to undo the credibility of the real world they represent, without pitching themselves or that reality into an abyss of verbal mediation in which nothing can be known or decided.

A fuller and sharper picture of the trends epitomized by Dollimore and Eagleton emerges if we survey the range of recent responses to the flagship of the canon, *King Lear*.[23] We can begin by looking more closely at the strain of criticism we have just glanced at: the sort that feels entitled to construe the Shakespearean text either as an allegory of its own procedure, or as a blank sheet transformed by the text's reception into a palimpsest of imputed meanings.

Thus deconstructive accounts of *King Lear* hail it as a coded confirmation of the absolute sway of *différance*. From this angle, the virtue of the tragedy resides in its refusal to tolerate not merely traditional Christian and humanist readings, but interpretive acts of any kind. As Gary Waller explains in 'Decentring the Bard: The Dissemination of the Shakespearean Text':

> Therein lies deconstruction's challenge to both orthodox and 'new historicist' Shakespeare criticism: that we approach his works as

language, not as vision, meaning, or thematizations of universal (or
even historically specific) concerns, and that we watch his plays
unravel our (and Shakespeare's) attempts to fix meaning in words.[24]

The deconstructive *King Lear* abandons us in a state of aporia, a
slough of uncertainty, which frustrates our craving for unity and
resolution, and which defies us to discern in the text anything but
the emptiness of language itself and the consequent vanity of representation.

For critics intent on proving Shakespeare a Derridean *avant la
lettre*, the *mise-en-abyme* of the Dover Cliff scene and an overt obsession with the word 'nothing' make *King Lear* a gift-horse in whose
mouth few are so foolish as to look. In *Signifying Nothing: Truth's True
Contents in Shakespeare's Text* Malcolm Evans pounces avidly on
Gloucester's pratfall, which in his view

> displays the gulf that exists between a mimetic 'referent' and the
> linguistic materials required for its production. Like the absence in
> the mirror of *Las Meninas*, the vertiginous drop into which Edgar's
> disguised voice can finally 'look no more,/ Least my braine turne, and
> the deficient sight/ Topple downe headlong' doubles as a topography
> of 'representation' itself.[25]

Evans does hint, intriguingly, that the vacuum at the heart of the
play might be an inverted expression of the festive state of plenitude
that the tragedy secretly covets. But no such crumbs of comfort are
scattered by Jonathan Goldberg's more ruthless pursuit of the same
theme in his essay 'Perspectives: Dover Cliff and the Conditions of
Representation'. Goldberg sternly turns his back on the soft-core
deconstruction that hankers after some founding presence or telos,
however flickering or virtual. To his eyes, even abject uncertainty
seems too cushy a condition to be left in, since it suggests the
residual delusion that there is still something left to be uncertain
about. Goldberg's *King Lear* accordingly contrives the suicidal dissolution of its own intelligibility: it dives off Dover Cliff after
Gloucester, vanishing into a truly unfathomable void in which no
ground of cognition survives: 'In *King Lear* nothing comes of nothing, and the very language which would seem (to us) solidly to locate

the world slides into an abyss, an uncreating, annihilative nothing-ness.'[26]

The same perception of the text as a void underwrites the treat-ment meted out to *Lear* by exponents of what might be called a cultural-materialist reception theory. In *Reinventing Shakespeare* Gary Taylor concludes his cultural history of the Bard's incarnations by stating that Shakespeare

> has become a black hole. Light, insight, intelligence, matter – all pour ceaselessly into him, as critics are drawn into the densening vortex of his reputation; they add their own weight to his increasing mass. . . . Shakespeare himself no longer transmits visible light; his stellar energies have been trapped within the gravity well of his own reputa-tion. We find in Shakespeare only what we bring to him or what others have left behind; he gives us back our own values.[27]

Thus Taylor is fascinated not by *King Lear*, but by A. C. Bradley's investment of the play with his own Victorian views on morality and politics. *Lear* may unfortunately have nothing to say for itself, but at least it affords Taylor the opportunity to contend that 'In Bradley's hands Shakespearian criticism became a philosophical novel.'[28] Indeed, what else but such constructions of *King Lear* can one ever hope to discuss, if Taylor is right to claim that recent scholarship has exploded the illusion of a primal text, obliging us to confront not a single play but a bewildering vista of revisions and rewritings?[29]

The standpoint favoured by Taylor has for some years found its wittiest champion in Terence Hawkes. Hawkes's endorsement of *Reinventing Shakespeare* in *The London Review of Books* (*LRB*) provoked the notorious 'Bardbiz' controversy, whose stormy exchanges in the 'Letters' pages of the *LRB* took some eighteen months to subside.[30] If anything, Taylor's line is a touch too tame for Hawkes, who detects a 'central weakness' in his stablemate's 'under-theorized commitment to a "real" (albeit unremarkable) Shakespeare lying underneath all the "reinventions"'.[31] Hawkes insists on Shake-speare's consisting entirely in the process of his reception, which 'has at the least made the "plays themselves" unreachable. At best, it may itself be more interesting and more revealing than they

could ever be'.[32] For Hawkes, there is little point ministering to
the congregation of words that convention has dubbed *King Lear*,
since

> we can have no immediate or objective access to the works of an
> 'essential' Shakespeare, to the 'plays themselves', or to what they
> 'really' mean. Nor could Shakespeare. Indeed, that is hardly the
> point of him or them. The point of Shakespeare and his plays lies in
> their capacity to serve as instruments by which we make cultural
> meaning for ourselves.[33]

Consequently, in his sarcastically titled study *Meaning By Shakespeare*, the chapter called 'Lear's Maps' is naturally not about the
tragedy as such, but about the politically loaded wartime production
of the play by Harley Granville-Barker, which Hawkes understandably finds 'more interesting and more revealing' than tackling a
merely imaginary text.[34]

After a tour round this critical realm, whose denizens regard *King
Lear* either as a play designed to self-destruct or as an obvious
hallucination, it might well seem like deliverance to travel to the
opposite pole, to the land ruled by critics confident that *King Lear*
exists and that it displays not only a determinate significance, but a
definable political purpose, which becomes plain when the tragedy is
returned to its Jacobean matrix. Here we find the founding father of
new historicism, Stephen Greenblatt, declaring in 'Shakespeare and
the Exorcists' that 'Deconstructionist readings lead too readily and
predictably to the void; in actual literary practice the perplexities
into which one is led are not moments of pure, untrammelled aporia
but localised strategies in particular historical encounters.'[35] He
then proceeds to show that the ambiguities of *King Lear* are built
into the play to clinch the bewitchment of the audience by the
rituals of drama. If the play works in part to unsettle official values,
it does so as a ploy devised by the theatre of the day to cultivate
compliance with the interests of the Crown. *King Lear* is rescued
from the shoreless seas of textuality only to be cabined and cribbed
in its historical role as a subtle buttress of the status quo. The
plausibility of Greenblatt's case depends, however, on his conspicu-

ous aversion to proving it on the play; his formidable ingenuity is invested instead in analysing one of its sources, Samuel Harsnett's *A Declaration of Egregious Popish Impostures*, whose logic supplies Greenblatt with the alleged motivation of the tragedy. This much at least unites Greenblatt with Taylor and Hawkes: a keenness to displace the discussion of *King Lear* into the discussion of some secondary or surrogate discourse.

The reading of *Lear* by Leonard Tennenhouse in *Power on Display: The Politics of Shakespeare's Genres* does possess the merit of engaging with the text. But Tennenhouse is even more anxious than Greenblatt to construe the play as a strategy of the stage, calculated to mystify and so sustain the authority of the Jacobean state. His argument takes its cue from Foucault's contention in *Discipline and Punish* that public executions reinforced the power of the state through the dramatic spectacle of punishment rather than the fact of execution itself. In the drama of Shakespeare, too, Tennenhouse maintains, 'stagecraft collaborates with statecraft in producing spectacles of power',[36] which are mounted likewise on a scaffold. So the pristine function of *King Lear*, once the centuries of misconstruction have been scraped away, turns out to have been the spectacular torture of the royal culprit himself: an exemplary theatrical display of the violence inflicted upon a king who violates the metaphysical taboos on which the mystique of the Crown depends.

As a cultural materialist, Kathleen McLuskie shares the new historicists' concern to unpack the complicities of *King Lear* with sovereignty and subjection. But as a feminist she is also intent on exposing the tragedy's collusion in perpetuating sexual injustice. *King Lear* stands accused by McLuskie of being a phallocratic morality play, whose female leads are saintly or demonic stereotypes, and whose finale marshals the full might of Shakespeare's dramatic poetry to wring compassion for this misogynistic monarch from even the hardest feminist heart. What further distinguishes McLuskie's cultural-materialist approach from that of her new-historicist cousins across the Atlantic is the use of contextualization as a ruse to radicalize the impact of the play today. To historicize *King Lear* is to dismiss its claim to be timeless and universal, to offer us 'the pleasure of understanding in place of the pleasure of emotional identification'.[37] Although the play itself is judged irredeemable, McLuskie exhorts the feminist critic not to abandon it, but to find ways of reading it against its historical grain, which will help break the spell of 'the patriarchal Bard'.[38]

Not all historicists, it must be said, are consistently inclined to find *King Lear* the sly secret agent or unwitting dupe of hegemony. In *Puzzling Shakespeare* Leah Marcus tightens the contextual focus about as far as it will go, isolating for scrutiny the performance of *Lear* before King James himself on St Stephen's Night in 1606.[39] In an attempt to pin down the play's original intention and effect, Marcus homes in on pointed topical allusions to the character and policy of James, and she considers how the story of St Stephen might have coloured the reception of the tragedy. But she is forced to conclude that Shakespeare's attitude to his Stuart sovereign in *King Lear* is at the very least ambivalent, and could have been tilted towards conformity or critique according to the audience. Annabel Patterson, on the other hand, has no doubt about where Shakespeare's true sympathies lie. Her relocation of the play in its time in *Shakespeare and the Popular Voice* leads her to contend that the author of Lear's apostrophe to the 'Poor naked wretches' of his realm (III.iv.28–36) speaks with the voice of the victims of power, mustering every obliquity at his command to deflect the censor's gaze.[40] Both Marcus and Patterson evince a refreshing readiness to address *King Lear* as the work of a dramatist whose orthodoxy is open to debate. But the play's scope for resistance is still restricted to the terms of its time. However dissident its posture is believed to have been, *King Lear* remains the past-bound expression of an obsolete world, the prisoner of a purely retrospective critical vision.

So our present understanding of the canon's crowning glory seems to be stalled between two equally uninviting alternatives. We can either consign *King Lear* to the dungeons of historicism, explaining its outmoded import as the product of the constraints under which it was originally composed; or we can sweep historical limits aside and wipe intrinsic meaning from the text, leaving it open to invasion by all comers. If we recoil from exhuming a *Lear* doomed to speak only of its origins, to own up to its enlistment by the ruler or the ruled, there seems little choice but to treat the play as the creation of its critics and study them instead, or accept it as a self-consuming artefact, a vessel from which meaning leaks as fast as we pour it in.

The longer one stares at these alternatives, moreover, the more they begin to resemble nothing so much as the old past-bound historicism and the old text-bound formalism – overhauled, updated and tricked out as the trailblazers of radical critical practice. In fact, recalling the earlier point about traditional historicism regularly dissolving into the timeless and universal line after all, one wonders whether the new-wave historicists and their poststructuralist rivals may not likewise share a closet kinship, an unwitting devotion to peddling the same defused Shakespeare they purport to have abolished.

The political implications of deconstruction would certainly seem to be the reverse of rebellious, since the passing of the Derridean angel leaves everything, bathetically, much the same as before. This is nowhere more persuasively argued than by Malcolm Evans, who concludes an exemplary disintegration of the comedies by proceeding, with the kamikaze consistency of his kind, to blow the gaff on his own methodology:

> Deconstruction permits a delirium of dissent which is also a babble of compliance, an equalising of all voices in the irreducibility of *écriture*. If the liberal subject 'man' knew no divisions of gender, race or class and the politics of criticism these divisions imply, the textual panoply of crazed signifiers, supplements at the source and subjects-in-process does little better.[41]

In sum, notwithstanding its boast of being the unruliest game in town, 'the deconstructive mode of criticism, particularly in its North American forms, appears to be a conservative rather than a progressive force'.[42] And in Francis Barker's view much the same charge can be levelled at new historicism, which

> tends at best to offer the political effect of leaving everything as it is, when it doesn't actually debilitate the very idea of opposition in the name of all subversion being a necessary condition of the functioning of power as such. The result is often, in the name of studying at least the poetics of power, a practical denial of the fact and poignancy of

domination, substituting notions of circulation for those of oppression, anxiety for terror.[43]

Barker for one is persuaded that in practice, 'despite their logical and philosophical incompatibility', both kinds of criticism frequently wind up mirroring each other. For new historicists are no less prone than deconstructionists to collapse history into textuality, reality into representation, and both breed 'a spectatorial passivity in respect of power' to gladden the heart of the most conservative humanist.[44]

Be that as it may, it ought to be possible to work towards a more productive way of reading Shakespeare's plays frankly but plausibly from a progressive modern viewpoint. This should not mean, of course, *carte blanche* to subject Shakespeare to whatever interpretive violence seems expedient, wrenching the texts to make them say whatever one wants them to say, regardless of textual or historical constraints on the process of interpretation. But nor should it mean burying them in an historicist vault, built from the categories and conflicts of their age alone.

What it should mean is that the key questions to be asked of a given play, the questions that will determine both the trajectory of the interpretation and the criteria by which the work is evaluated, are the following. How far, and in what specific ways, does the play succeed in challenging the principles of social, sexual and racial relationship governing Shakespeare's world and our own? To what extent, and again by what precise means, does it confirm and reinforce them? Or is the work divided against itself, challenging and confirming on different levels at the same time? And lastly, if the play does question rather than consolidate the status quo, past and present, is there any sense in which it foresees more desirable principles of human relationship, sited beyond the horizon of the age in which it was written, and perhaps beyond the horizon of our time, too? The answering of these questions, however, must meet appropriate standards of textual and contextual validation, if the readings that result are to be secured against the received accounts, whose authority they dispute. What I am advocating is not an arbitrary, rampant subjectivism, but a truly historical approach to the reclaiming of Shakespeare's drama.

The goal of this approach would be to break the disabling deadlock between a superseded Shakespeare fossilized in the past and a Shakespeare so drained of determinacy as to mean nothing for certain or whatever we like. The first step towards realizing that goal is to reject the false conception of history that sustains it. I mean the notion of history that severs the past from the present by treating history as an intractably previous state instead of as a process, which demands the ceaseless revising of what our past has been. Such a sealed-off, rear-view version of history paralyses the past. It robs it of its original fluidity and its potential to affect the making of the present and the moulding of the future.

The critical consequence is a propensity to freeze the function and meaning of Shakespeare in what is presumed to be the past, and thereby deprive his drama of its capacity to acquire fresh functions and ignite new meanings in the present. A Shakespearean text is not a final product of its age, but a productive practice of both its moment and our own. It is apt to intervene in quite unforeseen ways in the social process long after its initial occasion has vanished. Even if it were possible to prove beyond doubt that a given play was originally intended and perceived as the quintessence of conformity, its import and its impact need not be conservative now. Indeed the play may meanwhile have evolved a knowledge of its world beyond the grasp of its own author and first audience. As Walter Benjamin observes, the imprisonment of a work in its moment of genesis, whatever the political credentials of the critic, is always a reactionary manoeuvre, which has to be resisted. A literary text should be regarded, Benjamin believes, not as an immutable testament, but as a project to be strategically redefined in response to the altered needs created by new historical conditions. The strategic reappraisal of a work should proceed through a genuine dialogue, which permits our present situation to re-read itself in the light of the past, and the past to be construed anew in the light of the present.[45]

What I am suggesting is that Shakespeare could be read and taught in ways that bring the dimensions of past constraint and modern viewpoint – the moment of production and the moment of reception – into dynamic reciprocity. The idea is to generate accounts of his plays which are plainly provisional, because they must be open to revision and displacement by more relevant and competent readings; but which are also objective, in so far as they can be textually verified and historically legitimized within the adopted framework of critical understanding. For such interpretations could claim far greater validity and value in their endeavour to transform the perception of Shakespeare's world and our own in today's educational and cultural institutions.

This may well seem rather a tall order when put in such abstract, theoretical terms. So let me give a more concrete example of how this approach might apply to one of Shakespeare's most controversial plays, *The Merchant of Venice*. This play raises in the starkest form all the basic problems involved in the interpretation of Shakespeare's drama. For no work of Shakespeare's shows more vividly, through critics' repeated evasion of what it is disposed to reveal, the moral and political poverty of readings that fail to comprehend how the objective meaning and the value of a text can change historically as the conditions and perspective of its reception change.[46]

Re-reading *The Merchant of Venice*

The crux of *The Merchant* is, of course, Shylock and the significance of his revenge.[47] Conventional criticism has distorted or repressed the full implications of this problem, persisting for the most part in the romantic idealist conception of the play.[48] According to this, *The Merchant* is a tragically tinged but, in the end, delightful romantic comedy, in which the ruling-class Christians triumph, by virtue of their selfless love and merciful generosity, over the threat posed to their happiness by the pitiable but essentially evil Jew. In John Russell Brown's representative view: 'We cannot doubt that Shylock must be condemned. However lively Shylock's dialogue may be, however plausibly and passionately he presents his case, however cruelly the lovers treat him, he must still be defeated, because he is an enemy to love's wealth and its free, joyful and continual giving.'[49]

A telling endorsement of this position was provided several years later by the eminent Shakespeare scholar Samuel Schoenbaum. Reviewing a whole season of RSC productions, he singled out as the highpoint a production of *The Merchant* which had been 'rapturously received by an audience consisting almost entirely of Shakespeare scholars'. The virtue of the production, in Schoenbaum's eyes, was the director's 'refusal to be seduced by the opposing voice of the play' – the voice, that is, of Shylock. The production is applauded for not being 'sentimental', despite 'the holocaust and the history of European Jewry in this century'. It is acclaimed for its 'courage to be faithful' to what Schoenbaum regards as the historically fixed 'main thrust of the play' against 'the Devil Jew'.[50]

Conventional Marxist interpretations are in complete agreement with this standard view of the play's 'main thrust'. The only real difference is their negative evaluation of the play as the blind tool of whatever they take to be the dominant Elizabethan ideology. Hence Elliot Krieger's *A Marxist Study of Shakespeare's Comedies* reads *The Merchant* as having forged by the end an elaborate resolution designed to consolidate the sway of the aristocracy (Portia and Belmont) over the rising bourgeoisie (Venice and Shylock).[51] And in Christian Enzensberger's long, ambitious study the play is no less reductively diagnosed as an allegory of the triumph of merchant capitalism over the reactionary practice of usury, with Act V as the romantically refracted celebration of a merchant-capitalist utopia. For Enzensberger, the text cunningly dramatizes and solves a subordinate conflict of the period – mercantilism versus usury – as if it were the main conflict of society. It thus strives to conceal the really central contradiction between a racist capitalism and humanity.[52]

But this contradiction, I would argue, is precisely what the play exposes to the gaze of a fully historical reading. The cited critics are doomed, by their unhistorical idealism or their one-dimensional historicism, to remain deaf to the 'opposing voice' centred in Shylock, and therefore blind to the more valuable possibilities stored in the text. In responding to the play, we should not suppress the awareness we ought to have of 'the holocaust and the history of European Jewry in this century'. Nor should we resist the change in the angle of reception that such a consciousness creates. The extent to which the vision of *The Merchant of Venice* contradicts or corroborates the enlightened viewpoint of the present must be proved first

and foremost on the evidence of the text. But we should not fail to
take on board, too, the fact that the conditions of literary production
in Shakespeare's time made it possible for his drama to undermine
rather than underwrite the governing assumptions of his society. I
will say more about this later in the chapter. Suffice it for the
moment to suggest that, if one does allow these past and present
perspectives to converge upon the text, *The Merchant of Venice* turns
out to be dynamized by a profound struggle between conflicting
impulses. Its true achievement consists in its subversion of its own
conventional commitments.

This process of self-subversion is organized through Shylock. It
reaches its first explicit, devastating expression, of course, in his
speech rebuking the Jew-baiting Christians on the grounds of their
common constitution:

> Hath not a Jew eyes? Hath not a Jew hands, organs, dimensions,
> senses, affections, passions; fed with the same food, hurt with the same
> weapons, subject to the same diseases, heal'd by the same means,
> warm'd and cool'd by the same winter and summer, as a Christian
> is? If you prick us, do we not bleed? If you tickle us, do we not laugh?
> If you poison us, do we not die? And if you wrong us, shall we not
> revenge? If we are like you in the rest, we will resemble you in
> that.... The villainy you teach me, I will execute, and it shall go
> hard but I will better the instruction.
>
> (III.i.59–73)

With this speech there erupts into the play an irresistible egalitarian
attitude, whose basis in the shared faculties and needs of our physical
nature indicts all forms of inhuman discrimination. The speech
provokes a sharp shift of emotional allegiance, from which our
perception of the Christian protagonists never recovers. Through
Shylock, *The Merchant* proceeds to broach a perspective which cuts
through the received readings and transfigures our understanding of
the play.

The key line is the one that unsheathes the reasoning behind
Shylock's revenge: 'The villainy you teach me, I will execute.' The
consequences of this line are worth thinking through, for it makes it
clear that Shylock's revenge signifies much more than the usual evil

threat to the idyllic realm of romance. It explains that Shylock's bloodthirsty cruelty is not simply the result of the Venetians' abuse of him, but the deliberate mirror-image of their concealed real nature. The revenge is a bitter parody of the Christians' actual values, a calculated piercing of their hypocritical façade. The whole point of Shylock's demanding payment of 'a pound of flesh', and of Antonio's heart in particular (III.i.12 /), lies in its grotesque attempt to translate the heartlessness of Venice into reality.[53] Venice is a world where the human heart is literally a quantifiable lump of meat, a world where, as Shylock sardonically remarks,

> A pound of man's flesh, taken from a man,
> Is not so estimable, profitable neither,
> As flesh of muttons, beefs, or goats.
> > (I.iii.165–7)

The revenge uncovers the hidden reality of a money-centred society, which has created Shylock in its own avaricious image in order to project upon him its guilty hatred of itself.

The drive to demystify climaxes in the trial scene. Once again, it is a question of unpacking the full implications of the script, of spelling out completely in this case the meaning of Shylock's insistence on his bond, on his acknowledged legal right to his pound of flesh. Castigated by the Christians for his merciless bloodlust, Shylock reminds them that by their own principles, in the eyes of their own law – as they themselves explicitly concede – he is 'doing no wrong'. On the contrary:

> You have among you many a purchas'd slave,
> Which like your asses, and your dogs and mules,
> You use in abject and in slavish parts,
> Because you bought them. Shall I say to you,
> 'Let them be free! Marry them to your heirs!
> Why sweat they under burthens? Let their beds'
> Be made as soft as yours, and let their palates
> Be season'd with such viands'? You will answer,
> 'The slaves are ours.' So do I answer you:
> The pound of flesh which I demand of him

Is dearly bought as mine, and I will have it.
If you deny me, fie upon your law!
　　　　　　　　　　　(IV.i.90–101)

What the critical consensus has habitually repressed here is Shylock's irrefutable demonstration that his 'wolvish, bloody, starv'd, and ravenous' behaviour (IV.i.138) is the very foundation and institutionalized norm of Venice, whose inhumanity is ratified as 'justice' by its laws. The play as romantic comedy has nothing to say in reply that can compensate for this annihilating realization.

This is not to say that the play ends up justifying or excusing Shylock by turning its sympathy over to him. *The Merchant of Venice* operates at a level beyond the simplistic polarities of such sentimental moralism. To define the play in terms of which party deserves the blame and which the absolution, with readings and productions swinging now to Shylock and now to the Christians, is to miss the point. What is at stake is the deeper recognition that, through the revenge plot and the trial, through the ironies and contradictions they lay bare, an apparently civilized society is unmasked as premised on barbarity, on the ruthless priority of money values over human values, of the rights of property over the inalienable rights of men and women. The point lies not in the vindication of the Jew at the expense of the Christians, or of the Christians at the expense of the Jew, but in the critique of the structural social forces that have made them both what they are, for better and for worse.

What is fascinating, moreover, is the way the pressure exerted by this reappraisal of the Shylock plot throws further latent aspects of the play into unexpected relief.

It becomes evident, for example, that the casket-choosing plot at Belmont does more than test the moral competence of Portia's prospective husbands. It underlines the disparity between the visible and the veiled nature of people and things, between supposed worth and actual value: 'All that glisters is not gold,/ . . . Gilded tombs do worms enfold' (II.vii.65–9); 'So may the outward shows be least themselves' (III.ii.73). The casket scenes tune us to the frequency of the play's opposing voice. They school our expectations in the logic of inversion that runs through the play, reinforcing the discovery that the ruling ethos of this comedy is the shameful reverse of what its heroes and heroines suppose it to be.

Or take the intriguing first appearance of Lancelot Gobbo in Act II, Scene ii. The clown's monologue presents him as torn back and forth between his conscience's demand that he stay with his master the Jew and the devil's insistence that he abandon him. This apparently inconsequential scene can now be seen to convey much more than mere comic relief. As in other plays, especially *King Lear*, *As You Like It* and *Twelfth Night*, the fool acts as a personified index of the play's evolving viewpoint. Gobbo gives us a condensed comic version of the crisis of allegiance provoked by Shylock throughout *The Merchant of Venice*. What had hitherto lain submerged as a farcical interlude surfaces as a key strategy of estrangement, an internal objectification of the comedy's tormented subconscious.

We can now begin to decipher, too, the enigma of Antonio, the merchant of Venice himself. The opening scene fastens at once upon the mystery of Antonio's sadness, writing itself into a knot of frustrated interrogation, which is never untangled. The nominal hero of the play remains to the end a cryptically still and passive presence, the absent centre around which the action of the comedy revolves. But therein lies Antonio's true significance as the embodiment of the void at the heart of Venice. For it is in the play's rebellion against the expectations of its title, in its conspicuous refusal to project the merchant capitalist as hero, that Shakespeare's anguished rejection of the values invading Elizabethan England finds distorted expression.

Once a consciously modern grasp of the Shylock problem has awoken us to the authorized prejudice and inhumanity of Shakespeare's Venice, an equally undisguised concern with sexual injustice allows us to recognize *The Merchant*'s preoccupation with women as the alienated objects of men's vision, choice and possession. As Portia exclaims: 'O me, the word choose! I may neither choose who I would, nor refuse who I dislike; so is the will of a living daughter curb'd by the will of a dead father' (I.ii.22–5). For Bassanio, Portia is first and foremost the means 'to get clear of all the debts I owe' (I.i.135). She is 'a lady richly left' (I.i.161), imprisoned as her image in a leaden casket: 'I am lock'd in one of them' (III.ii.40). The freedom of thought, speech and behaviour she displays when alone with her maid Nerissa, or when disguised in male apparel as the lawyer Balthazar, only accentuates the constrictions of her normal identity as obedient daughter and, subsequently, submissive wife: 'Myself, and what is mine, to you and yours/ Is now converted' (III.ii.166–7).

Re-examined from this angle, the fifth-act closure in alleged romantic harmony is actually fraught with sinister insinuations. Even the first sweet, moonlit exchange cannot escape the shadow cast across the comedy by what Shylock's tale has taught us. Lorenzo's and Jessica's hymning of their love is infected by a rash of allusions to tragically doomed lovers: Troilus and Cressida, Pyramus and Thisbe, Dido and Aeneas, Jason and Medea (V.i.1–14). In the ensuing banter between the newly wed couples (Portia and Bassanio, Gratiano and Nerissa) disquieting doubts are raised about the quality of the men's love by their failure of the love-test in giving away their rings: 'You swore to me,' protests Nerissa, 'when I did give it you,/ That you would wear it till your hour of death' (V.i.152–3). The fact that the men unknowingly returned the rings to the disguised Portia and Nerissa does not override the nagging reproaches in which the women persist for a third of the entire act (V.i.142–246). The discord is amplified by Portia's and Nerissa's teasing threats of revenge through infidelity: 'Lie not a night from home,' warns Portia, 'Watch me like Argus' (V.i.230). And it is on a note of equivocally contained sexual anxiety that Gratiano ends the play: 'while I live I'll fear no other thing/ So sore, as keeping safe Nerissa's ring' (V.i.306–7).[54]

Perhaps most unsettling of all, though, is the moment shortly before this, when Antonio offers to heal the rift between the lovers by pledging himself once again as surety for Bassanio:

> I once did lend my body for his wealth,
> Which but for him that had your husband's ring
> Had quite miscarried. I dare be bound again,
> My soul upon the forfeit, that your lord
> Will never more break faith advisedly.
>
> (V.i.249–53)

These lines expose an ominous duplication in the sexual domain of the triangular financial bond upon whose implications the comedy has foundered, but with Portia now cast in the role formerly assigned to Shylock. The conscious parallel conveys a subliminal intuition of the symmetries that unite the racial oppression of the Jew and the sexual oppression of the female.

I have no space to do more than outline these embryonic insights into the changing meaning of *The Merchant of Venice*, all of which can be confirmed through close textual analysis. The point I want to stress is that the strategy responsible for these readings is neither arbitrary nor unhistorical. It postulates an historically implanted semantic potential,[55] a determinate range of verifiable readings genetically secreted by the play. The contexts and angles of the work's subsequent reception will dictate which veins of meaning will be mined and which remain undiscerned or neglected. What *The Merchant of Venice* means today depends as much on what we are disposed to make of it as it does on Shakespeare's text. The account I have privileged is a textually supported option inherent in the work, objectively encoded in the words that constitute the edition of the play being used. It is a demonstrably available interpretation, which could not be apprehended within the successive horizons of the play's previous reception, but which can be seized and elected to priority within the horizon of its reception now.

For those who share the values that define that horizon, a knowledge of the holocaust of the Jewish people, and a horror of that lethal juncture where capitalism and racism intersect, should not be suppressed as anachronistic or extraneous, as Professor Schoenbaum suggests. On the contrary, they ought to mark the point of departure for any unclouded engagement with *The Merchant of Venice* at this point in history, making it inconceivable to evade or refuse the vision that the work offers us today. To accept this vision is to learn that, all along, the play knew more about both its time and the times to come than historicist critics deemed it capable of knowing; that all along it was waiting to reveal uncharted shores of insight to the alien eyes of modern understanding.

The Historical Dimension

I

In order to secure the priority of such reinterpretations over prevailing views, it is clearly not enough to appeal to modern political relevance alone. The authority of that appeal is underwritten, however, not only by the textual verifiability of the readings incubating in the plays, but by a grasp of the contextual factors that conditioned their creation and endowed them with their untapped semantic potential.

To develop an interpretation on the strength of a detailed reading of a chosen edition, taking pains not to place anachronistic constructions upon the language of the play, is to be already engaged in an act of historical criticism. For any approach which professes respect for the words assembled on the page by modern textual scholarship,[56] the text exerts in practice a high degree of control over the spectrum of readings which it is prepared to tolerate as competent. A Shakespeare play does not roam free and innocent of history until it is pinned down and situated by an old or new historicist. It is already charged with the pastness and otherness of its own intrinsic historicity. The unique verbal configurations from which a given edition has been composed bear the hallmark of the local pressures under which the text was wrought, the imprint of its engendering, in every line. Stephen Greenblatt makes the general point here admirably, in an argument which cuts the ground from under the contextual archaeology he practises himself:

> Works of art are, to be sure, marked off in our culture from ordinary utterances, but this demarcation is itself a communal event and signals not the effacement of the social but rather its successful absorption into the work by implication or articulation. This absorption – the presence within the work of its social being – makes it possible, as Bakhtin has argued, for art to survive the disappearance of its enabling social conditions, where ordinary utterance, more dependent upon the extra-verbal pragmatic situation, drifts rapidly toward insignificance or incomprehensibility. Hence art's genius for survival, its delighted reception by audiences for whom it was never intended, does not signal its freedom from all other domains of life, nor does its inward articula-

tion of the social confer upon it a formal coherence independent of the world outside its boundaries. On the contrary, artistic form itself is the expression of social evaluations and practices.[57]

For the critic who takes for granted the work's necessary absorption of history, its constitutive 'inward articulation of the social', few things are less riveting than mountains of meticulous research documenting the parallels or incongruities between some sphere of Elizabethan reality and Shakespeare's depiction of it in his drama. Unearthing and wheeling forth stacks of scholarship on the situation of Jews or women, on the law, or on usury in late sixteenth-century England doubtless has countless merits, but equipping us to gauge the effect of their metamorphosis into *The Merchant of Venice* rarely proves to be one of them. All too often the primary documentation squats ponderously alongside its literary pretext in embarrassed irrelevance. Indeed, in the case of a work like *The Merchant*, treating the play as a reflection or distortion of a prior historical reality, which thus supplies the measure of the work's significance and success, is utterly misguided. For one of the most valuable properties of *The Merchant*, as we have seen, is its eagerness to put what has been posited as the relevant history into question. The text, far from being a passive product of its world, emerges as a creative act of investigation in its own right, compelling a searching reassessment of what the history that made it possible actually involved.

That Shakespeare's plays have their basis in the historical realities of his age hardly stands in urgent need of demonstration. What matters more, as I hope Chapter 2's account of the histories will confirm, is how those realities are perceived by the plays, and how we are induced to perceive the plays' depiction of those realities. But, if Greenblatt is right to maintain that 'artistic form itself is the expression of social evaluations', then we must also explain historically the means by which the plays mediate whatever materials they have chosen to transmute. In order to square a modern re-reading of Shakespeare with the demand for historical plausibility, we need first to contextualize the strategies of language and form that dictate how the plays conceive and judge their world.[58]

II

The Renaissance marks a moment of tremendous consequence in the history of English literature, because the sweeping cultural changes brought about by the establishment of a capitalist economy during this period made dissident plays, narratives and poetry a permanent possibility from this time on. The age of Shakespeare witnessed a seismic shift of concern towards mankind, whose members began to be viewed as dynamic individual and social beings, and towards life in this material world, grasped with unprecedented objectivity and realism as an immanent, secular history. This shift was generated by profound alterations in the nature of productive activity, and hence in people's fundamental sense of their relationship to each other and to the natural and social world. Of these transformations I want to single out two as crucial in creating the progressive potential of Renaissance literature and of Shakespeare's drama in particular.[59]

First, with the advent of the capitalist mode of production, the terms on which the life of society is reproduced become quite different from those that obtained under feudalism. The basic objective of the feudal system was to reproduce the existing conditions of production, to preserve traditional economic and social relations and the ideological framework that guaranteed them. But capitalism pursues the dynamic production of profit, which means production geared no longer to subsistence and the limited creation of use-value, but to exchange on the market and the ceaseless generation of surplus value. As a general result, under capitalism the reproduction of social life becomes a limitless rather than a circumscribed process: a process constantly changing people, things and relationships, demanding as it develops the dissolution of every precondition and preconception which would otherwise impede its expansion.[60] As Marx puts it in a celebrated passage:

> Constant revolutionising of production, uninterrupted disturbance of all social conditions, everlasting uncertainty and agitation distinguish the bourgeois epoch from all earlier ones. All fixed, fast-frozen relations, with their train of ancient and venerable prejudices and opinions, are swept away, all new-formed ones become antiquated before they can ossify.[61]

The point is that the effects of this phenomenon are equally apparent in the literary sphere. The transition from medieval to Renaissance culture involves a revolution in the nature and function of literature. To a degree hitherto inconceivable, people find themselves disposed to think, imagine, write and read on terms which are no longer determined by precedent, but which are apt to invalidate the presupposed in the light of a protean reality. The authors of this era begin to work a fresh seam of imaginative writing, calculated to resist the constraints imposed on expanding desires by the given structures of power and the received ideas that lock those structures down.

The second key factor in the cultural revolution of the Renaissance is indivisible from the first. For complex reasons rooted in the levelling spirit of the market economy, the Renaissance engenders an altogether new dimension of experience and awareness. The system of exchange-value is defined by Marx as 'a system of general social metabolism, of universal social relations, of all-round needs and universal capacities'.[62] On the foundations of this system there begins to rise a consciousness of the common humanity binding people across borders which can now be seen to be socially constructed and arbitrary rather than God-given or natural.

This recognition fosters an appreciation of the virtual equality and unanimity that transcend the economic, racial and sexual divisions between groups and individuals. In this respect the Renaissance signals nothing less than the modern materialist discovery of the human species, of the secularized concept of 'humanity'.[63] It is the discovery that, in Donne's famous formulation, 'No Man is an *Iland*, intire of it selfe; every man is a peece of the *Continent*, a part of the *maine*. . . . Any Mans *death* diminishes *me*, because I am involved in *Mankinde*',[64] or, as Montaigne puts it, 'chaque homme porte la forme entière de l'humaine condition'.[65] What starts to evolve is the understanding that every individual is also a *human* being, whose faculties, needs, experiences and aspirations are shared, or shareable, with the rest of the species. This is accompanied by an awakening appetite for forms of life able to accommodate the equitable satisfaction of common demands. The mounting sense of obstruction by the present and anticipation of the future finds its seminal imaginative embodiment in More's *Utopia* (1516) and momentous political

expression in the eruption of the English Revolution and the creation
of the Commonwealth only a few decades after Shakespeare's death.

This vision is made increasingly accessible to literature by the
dynamics of the capitalist economy. For the latter provokes a constant conflict between the changing forces of production and the
existing relations of production, between advancing collective
powers and a social order striving to preserve its divisive sway by
internalized constraint or by force. The recognition of this struggle
between legitimate new desires and their orchestrated repression
incites the most vigorous literature to undermine whatever restrains
people from becoming all that they might become under a more
equal distribution of rights and means. That the supreme capacity to
unleash such mutinous imaginings is to be found in the drama of
Shakespeare is what accounts for the massive investment of cultural
energy over the centuries in keeping his work muzzled. It is also
what makes the conscription of his work to help forge a truly
democratic culture both possible and imperative today.

III

The late Elizabethan and early Jacobean society that shaped the
theatre for which Shakespeare wrote belongs to an exceptional,
fleeting phase of English history.[66] It is a society poised between
two great epochs: a transitional formation which, considered as a
whole, is neither feudal nor bourgeois in character, but rather early
capitalist society coalescing within a moribund feudal world. Shakespeare's England has broken decisively with the feudal mode of
production; it has taken mighty strides towards 'shifting the hard
and fast lines that had divided the feudal estates with their rigid
hierarchical divisions';[67] and it has spawned in place of those divisions a 'babylonian confusion of classes'.[68] But the nation ruled by
Elizabeth and James does not yet represent modern bourgeois society
as such, which was to solidify only in the late seventeenth and
eighteenth centuries.

As a consequence, English Renaissance culture, and its literature
and drama in particular, typically display the same hybrid, unresolved quality. The dramatic productions of the public theatre
cannot be made to yield without distortion a purely feudal or a

purely bourgeois outlook on life. At their best, they furnish an eclectic medium for the compound articulation of a whole culture. As Walter Cohen points out, 'Elizabethan playwrights were able to mingle communal and individualist attitudes, to draw upon a pervasive and unique mixture of feudal, monarchical, humanist, bourgeois, and popular elements'; and 'they could often transform this multiplicity into a comprehensive and synthetic vision that was not simply reducible to any one narrow class orientation'.[69]

This transformation was made possible by the special nature of the public theatre, that 'unique, precarious product of a brief historical moment', which supplied the 'crucial mediation between drama and society'.[70] As Robert Weimann has shown, the drama's privileged standpoint is inseparable from the liminal phase in which it flourished:

> while growing capitalism and its related asceticism had *not yet* become a way of life for the masses, the new economic and corresponding social changes had *already* created conditions whereby a permanent public theatre, independent of the controlling influence of clergy and conservative guilds, could develop.[71]

Like the culture that nourished it, in other words, 'partly feudal, partly capitalist, the public theatre of the late sixteenth century was predominantly neither'. Indeed, 'the theatre's economic, social, political and ideological heterogeneity precludes any simple categorization. An emphasis on effective control of the stage – on patronage, licensing, censorship, and the like – points to the nobility and the monarchy, as do the thematic preoccupations of most of the plays.' At the same time, 'the large sums of money, the evident quest for profit, and the array of financial instruments integral to the operation of the public stage seem to indicate the dominance of the capitalist mode of production'. But shifting one's attention yet again to 'physical structures, audiences, dramatists, and especially actors reveals the popular dimensions of the theatre'. One can only conclude that the public theatre for which Shakespeare worked was indeed 'a socially composite organization'.[72]

The same blurring of origins and alignments, of plebeian and elite horizons, stamps the biographical profiles of most of the dramatists and actors, to both of whose brotherhoods the glovemaker's son and grammar-school boy from Stratford grew up to belong. 'Though often of comparatively humble origin, many of the playwrights managed to acquire a university education or its equivalent'; and in the lives of the players, too, we find inscribed 'the multiple and shifting class relationships that characterize English Renaissance society, theatre and drama'.[73] The enemies of the stage were outraged that the actors stood, 'like vagabonds and itinerant ped-dlers, on the bottom of the social ladder and yet had somehow become affiliated with its highest and most privileged spheres'[74] through the patronage of the Crown and great noblemen. Further-more, their performances at playhouses such as Shakespeare's Globe 'attracted virtually all urban strata',[75] shuffling 'every rank and class of society'[76] into 'a diverse and heterogeneous audience', whose diversity 'contributed to the complex elaboration of dramatic form'.[77]

To enter the Globe to watch *As You Like It* or *Antony and Cleopatra* was to cross into a licensed, ludic space marked off from everyday reality. As Michael Bristol reminds us, 'the public playhouses were "extra-mural" and therefore exempted from the formal jurisdiction of the city authorities'. Once inside the theatres, spectators found themselves in 'an ambiguous temporal situation outside the sched-ules of work and religious devotion':

> The time of performance is a festive time in which play and mimesis replace productive labour.... In the playhouse the audience has an experience that provides an alternative to regular social discipline: between periods of authorized activity an 'interlude' provides an escape from supervision and from surveillance of attitude, feeling and expression.[78]

This licensed public sphere encouraged playwrights to compose, and audiences to expect, an exploratory, improvising drama, constitu-tionally keen to transgress the accustomed boundaries of perception. Small wonder, therefore, that 'the playhouses were subjected to a virtually constant stream of criticism and official interference from various social and ideological communities'. Unlike most subsequent critics or, indeed, the drama's original patrons and apologists, the many virulent enemies of the theatre had it pegged from the start as 'a "school of abuse" or at least a setting in which authority may be radically interrogated'.[79] Those who felt their status, identity and beliefs most threatened by the stage had no trouble pinpointing the sources of its subversive potential. They instinctively knew that the trouble came from the confounding of social and sexual distinctions, from the uprooting and dispersal of discursive authority, and from a general subjection of the order of things to simulation, travesty and mutation.[80]

The extravagant multiplicity of Renaissance society, of the theatre itself, and of its audiences, converged with the extramural liberty of the playhouses and techniques inherited from popular stage tradition to shape the capacious perspective for which Shakespeare is remarkable among the Elizabethan and Jacobean dramatists who shared it. The self-conscious polyphony of their language and form plays a vital role in freeing his plays from the rival ideologies of the time by levelling the hierarchies that grip his world.

The urge to integrate multifarious class interests, cultural codes and dramatic conventions produced plays ripe to accommodate 'many of the popular, humanist and some of the courtly elements, together with their theatrical equivalents such as rhetoric, allegory, singing, dancing, clowning, dumb-shows, disguisings, and corresponding modes of speech, presentation and acting'.[81] The interplay of heroic, romantic or courtly protagonists with comic and serious figures from the lower orders and otherwise subordinate or marginal groups is a structural principle of Shakespeare's scriptwriting. In its most developed forms, the inclusion of usually excluded standpoints, of inverted or irreverent views of the action from below or beyond the realms of the ruling class, undercuts the residual and ascendant ideologies, creating a wider and longer perspective, more valid than either and independent of both. The roots of this independence reach down to the fact that, while cardinal principles of the feudal mentality were now being widely contested, the nascent priorities of capitalism were not yet viewed as the inevitable alternative. In neither social morality nor the conventions of the drama was their victory taken for granted:

> Older conceptions of honour were confronted by the new pride of
> possession, hatred of usury by the fervour for gold, the idea of service
> by the idea of profit, deeply seated community consciousness by
> passionate individualism.... In the late sixteenth and early seven-
> teenth centuries these heterogeneous ideas and attitudes jostled each
> other, and the resulting wealth and depth of conflict was reflected,
> more than anywhere else, in the Renaissance theatre, where the
> popular tradition was free to develop relatively independent of, yet
> in close touch with, the conflicting standards and attitudes of the
> dominant ideologies.[82]

Faced with the pretensions of both world views to exclusive,
universal authority, Shakespeare's 'perspective consciousness'[83] forces
them into mutually unmasking contradiction; or it confronts them
with versions of experience which they have suppressed in order to
command the status quo on their terms. These normally silenced
definitions expose the authorized accounts of experience as ideological,
and therefore of spurious or limited validity. They qualify them as
class-bound, masculine, racially biased or otherwise partial in their
interest and scope. They divest them of their inclusive finality,
betraying the socially constructed, vulnerable basis of their supremacy.

If we think again of *The Merchant of Venice*, it is plainly Shakespeare's propensity to push the available dramatic structures to their
limits, by bringing the most antagonistic values into violent conjunction, which compels him to embody the play's 'opposing voice'
in the despised Jew, Shylock; which clears a space for the publicly
shackled selves of Portia and Nerissa to act and speak more freely;
which exiles the play's official protagonist to the margins of the text
named after him; which promotes Lancelot Gobbo, clown-prince of
serious nonsense, to custodian of the play's self-knowledge; which
amplifies the animosities that sour the comedy's closing harmony;
and which generally thrives on turning comfortably enthroned views
and values upside down.

The process can be seen more strikingly at work in *King Lear*. There
both the service-bound pieties shared by Lear, Gloucester, Kent and
Edgar, and the aggressive individualism of Edmund, Goneril and
Regan, are contested by perspectives voiced by Cordelia, by the

Fool, by Poor Tom, by the mad Lear himself and the sightless Gloucester. A host of similar effects are achieved by figures such as Falstaff in *1* and *2 Henry IV*, Thersites in *Troilus and Cressida*, Apemantus in *Timon of Athens*, the witches and the porter in *Macbeth*, the gravedigger in *Hamlet* and Caliban in *The Tempest*; by wise fools like Touchstone in *As You Like It* and Feste in *Twelfth Night*, to say nothing of the motley crew of clowns from Launce and Speed in *Two Gentlemen of Verona*, through Dogberry and Verges in *Much Ado About Nothing*, to Autolycus in *The Winter's Tale*; by disguised, banished or demented female characters, such as Rosalind in *As You Like It*, Perdita in *The Winter's Tale*, Ophelia in *Hamlet* and Lady Macbeth; and by aristocratic protagonists who adopt plebeian viewpoints cast in the vernacular, as do Hamlet and King Lear in the throes of their antic dispositions.

The cynical critique of such accommodations as classic examples of repressive tolerance, whose aim is to boost the system's immunity to a full-scale assault, fails to see their true effect. That failure can be traced all too often to the critically crude practice of abstracting a play's supposed substance from its forms of expression. For the importance of Shakespeare's dissenting voices does not reside simply in the tenor of what they say (although, as Shylock shows, this may be formidable). It rises chiefly from the way their inclusion alongside the privileged voices, within the same dramatic frame, transfigures the relationship between them and their joint role in the play. The radical potential derives less from the insubordination of Falstaff or Feste as such, than from their collusion with their superiors to create a multivocal mode of dramatic perception. Hierarchy has far more to fear from the dispersal of authority across the full range of dramatis personae than from overt outbursts of irreverence.

Shakespeare's polyphony makes it impossible to invest any of the currently competing world views with exclusive legitimacy or self-evident sovereignty. Their mutual interrogation generates instead a synoptic vision, which overrides the imperatives of division and domination. The plays' roving impulse to displace the perspective across a spectrum of identities and attitudes creates their structural identification with the common interests of our kind rather than with one sector of society at the expense of the rest. It is a way of seeing which neither precedes, nor survives abstraction from, the total complex of dramatized acts and statements, in whose unfolding alone Shakespeare's vision is discovered and articulated.

IV

The plays' inbuilt awareness of humanity's potential to live more fully and freely than the present organization of life allows is reinforced by various verbal and theatrical devices. These are deployed to imply that the limited modes of experience and consciousness imposed by the social order are not unalterably fixed, but conditional and subject to change.

Every Shakespeare play confronts us not only with 'an anthology of generic principles',[84] but also with a miscellany of linguistic registers and literary styles, which complicates the plurality of characters and points of view. Shakespeare's scripts cross-cut varieties of verse with varieties of prose, braiding the demotic with the educated, high-flown rhetoric with the earthbound locutions of everyday usage, and not just in the play as a whole or through dialogue, but often in the discourse of the same character. In the Elizabethan playhouse we confront

> an actual heteroglot institution in which the exchange of speech crosses every social boundary, and the diversity of speech types traverses the genres of literature and of authoritative discourse.... Poetic language, rhetorical ornament and classical learning are compelled to share communicative space with vernacular speech and with vernacular misinterpretations of high culture.[85]

Shakespeare's multilingual drama forbids generic or stylistic monologue, the discursive enslavement of a manifold reality to a single viewpoint. The plays' dialogic disposition offers 'stubborn resistance to the entrenchment of any unifying language or code of representation',[86] which might nourish the illusion of a socially and morally united nation.

This display of linguistic diversity enhances our awareness of a play's language *as* language. By foregrounding the verbally mediated nature of its simulated action, the play revives our realization that the meanings it activates are not intrinsic to some pre-linguistic reality, but the effect of a written endeavour to make sense of an unstable world – a world which is as open to interpretation and revision as the play itself: 'I am a scribbled form, drawn with a pen/ Upon a parchment' (*King John*, V.vii.32–3).

Closely associated with this are the reflexive opportunities arising from the convention of male actors playing female characters, and the exploitation of disguise and mistaken identity throughout the plays: Portia as Balthazar in *The Merchant*, Edgar as Poor Tom in *King Lear*, Henry V as a common soldier at Agincourt, the confused twin masters and twin servants in *The Comedy of Errors*, and so on. These flagrantly theatrical devices enact the understanding enshrined in the motto traditionally ascribed to the Globe itself: *Totus mundus agit histrionem* ('The whole world plays the actor'). It is the understanding that, if 'All the world's a stage,/ And all the men and women merely players' (*As You Like It*, II.vii.139–40), then quite different productions can be mounted on the stage of history, and the parts being played at the moment can be not only swapped around, but also replaced by roles yet to be imagined. The degree to which identity should be regarded as arbitrary rather than innate becomes graphically evident in the bewildering manipulations of sexual disguise in characters such as Rosalind in *As You Like It* or Viola in *Twelfth Night*. This blurring of difference by cross-dressing grasps theatrically the modern feminist distinction between biologically defined sex and culturally devised gender. It articulates in concrete, dramatic terms Montaigne's contention that, beyond the imposed discriminations dividing the sexes, 'les masles et femelles sont jettez en mesme moule; sauf l'institution et l'usage, la différence n'y est pas grande'.[87]

Shakespeare's self-conscious insistence on the play as play is not restricted to remarks such as Antonio's 'I hold the world but as the world, Gratiano,/ A stage, where every man must play a part' (*The Merchant of Venice*, I.i.77–8); or Duke Senior's 'This wide and universal theatre/ Presents more woeful pageants than the scene/ Wherein we play in' (*As You Like It*, II.vii.137–9). Nor is it exhausted by the dizzying self-mirrorings involved in the play-within-a-play in *A Midsummer Night's Dream* or *Hamlet*, to cite only the most prominent examples.[88] It is a deeply ingrained feature of Shakespeare's drama, inscribed in the spatial dynamics of the platform stage itself. For 'a platform stage capable of sustaining both illusionistic and non-illusionistic effects was indispensable to the interplay between realistic and stylized modes of expression, and between a new consistency of *mimesis* and traditional audience awareness'.[89] By switching from more naturalistic dialogue to plainly artificial monologue (in soliloquies, asides, or direct audience address); by bracketing or interrupting the action with prologues, epilogues, choruses and songs; or by disrupting the illusionistic flow of blank verse or prose with couplets, proverbs, wordplay and other heightened speech-patterns, the plays recall the audience from their engrossment in an imaginary world to the reality of the theatre in which they sit. They are invited to collaborate in redefining the relations between the real and the written, to work out for themselves 'the similarities and differences between dramatic illusion and Elizabethan reality. The world is seen as a stage, the stage, in turn, as an image of the world,'[90] without erasing the objectivity of either domain.

The effect is far from fulfilling the postmodern fantasy of a purely linguistic universe, divorced from the material world of history. The ceaseless shuttling between immersion and detachment ensures that the play is framed and qualified as only one version of things. The validity of that version, however persuasive the fiction may seem, is no more permanent than the reality it presupposes and transcribes. By distancing and estranging his drama, Shakespeare defamiliarizes and problematizes the reality it refracts. The audience is discouraged from surrendering to the representation of life before them, because to do so would be to become the prisoner of the play rather than its creative accomplice in opening the world and the text, and the relationship between them, to constant sceptical scrutiny.

These basic techniques of Shakespearean composition have always been inherent, objective features of his plays. The difference is that now, as a result of advances in literary and linguistic theory, we can identify them more clearly and explain them more fully than ever before. They should not be dismissed as imputed properties, extorted from the plays in an anachronistic effort to redeem them for an alien political cause. The techniques I have singled out are the historically prescribed terms in which the subversive potential of Shakespeare's plays was originally encoded. They are thus the vital means by which radical critics can activate that potential in the present.

Shakespeare's drama harbours the capacity to realize what Brecht saw as the aim of all progressive art. It is the capacity to depict reality in ways which make it clear that it is not the only reality possible; that how things have been until now is not how they have to be; that other forms of life are desirable and imaginable; and that men and women have had, and still have, the power to make them real. It is Brecht, too, who points to the importance of releasing this faculty of Shakespeare's plays in our reception of them today. For by recognizing the transience of the culture in which the plays were written, we can also comprehend the impermanence of our own, and look to the future with the hope that is inseparable from aesthetic pleasure.[91]

Shakespeare's refusal to become obsolete springs from the fact that it became historically and technically possible for him to dramatize the future possibilities stored in stubborn actualities. It became possible for him to judge life in the England of Elizabeth and James on the strength of prospective values, which are directly opposed to those on which modern British society is still constructed. In the chapters that follow I want to show some of the ways in which Shakespeare's histories, tragedies and comedies use the powers vested in their language and form not only to indict his own divisive world, but also to sharpen our need to forge a world from which division has been purged.

2

The Future of History:
1 and *2 Henry IV*

The Politics of Interpretation

As dramatizations of the fate of Crown and nation two centuries
before the time of Shakespeare and his audience, the *Henry IV* plays
pose explicitly the key questions facing radical criticism today.
What is the relationship between the reality of history and its
creative representation, between the world of the past and the work's
account of it? What is the political role of the work in its own world:
to shore up or shake the foundations of power? Can the literature of
the past speak only of the past, or has it secrets to reveal to the
present and appointments to keep with the future?

No attempt to answer these questions in recent years has been
more ambitious or compelling than Fredric Jameson's *The Political
Unconscious* (1981), which seeks to construct nothing short of a new
Marxist hermeneutics, a comprehensive political theory of interpretation.[1] My own proposals in Chapter 1 for a fresh approach to the
interpretive task find much in that theory with which to concur.
Part of my purpose in this chapter, therefore, is to show how
Jameson's sharpest initiatives can help carve out a more searching
account of the *Henry IV* plays than the most influential criticism to
date has delivered. Jameson's basic view of literature, however, is
fatally flawed by the tunnel vision to which so much radical criticism seems to be congenitally predisposed. So by reappraising these

plays I also want to establish the power of Shakespeare's drama to confound such misconceptions through its superior imaginative grasp of the problems Jameson addresses.

But let me begin by underscoring those ideas of Jameson's, developed both in *The Political Unconscious* and in his essay 'Marxism and Historicism' (1979), which point towards a more plausible way of engaging with literary texts, and which consolidate some of the arguments I have advanced so far. The first concerns the claims of the literature of the past on the critical practice of the present. As I have already observed, contemporary criticism offers two main strategies for dealing with a work that confronts us from the temporally remote and culturally estranged past that first housed it. One is the retrospective route followed by both the traditional and the newer kinds of historicist response: the restoration of the work to some apposite original context, in which its meaning may be more authentically, and hence more securely, moored. The other path leads in the opposite direction, towards the colonization of the past by modernity: the collapsing of historical distance, and hence the erasure of difference, by an act of appropriation which makes the author of the text our contemporary. At the extremes, the work is either embedded in a past world which excludes modern consequence, or absorbed into current categories from which historicity has been drained.

Jameson's response to 'the question of the claims of monuments from distant and even archaic moments of the cultural past on a culturally different present' is to reject 'this unacceptable option, or ideological double bind, between antiquarianism and modernizing "relevance" or projection'. Interpretation can be released from this disabling impasse only by implementing a view of history 'capable of respecting the specificity and radical difference of the social and cultural past while disclosing the solidarity of its polemics and passions, its forms, structures, experiences, and struggles, with those of the present day'.[2] But this should not mean merely a revamped, politicized historicism, which continues to submit texts to the superior gaze of belated comprehension. The ideal relationship is one of genuine dialogue rather than a fake exchange between a dummy version of the past and the modern critical ventriloquist. If we can achieve such a dialogue,

> We will no longer tend to see the past as some inert and dead object
> which we are called upon to resurrect, or to preserve, or to sustain, in
> our own living freedom; rather, the past will itself become an active
> agent in this process and will begin to come before us as a radically
> different form of life which rises up to call our own form of life into
> question and to pass judgement on us and through us on the social
> formation in which we exist. At that point the very dynamics of the
> historical tribunal are unexpectedly and dialectically reversed: it is not
> we who sit in judgement on the past, but rather the past . . . which
> judges us, imposing the painful knowledge of what we are not, what
> we are no longer, what we are not yet.[3]

It is in the sense implied in that last phrase that Jameson believes
the past 'speaks to us about our own virtual and unrealized "human
potentialities"'. The attempt to initiate an authentic dialogue between history and modernity through literature is indivisible from
the quest to restore to interpretation the dimension of futurity: 'the
hermeneutic contact between past and present . . . cannot fully be
described without the articulation within it of what Ernst Bloch
has called the Utopian impulse'. The mode of interpretation Jameson envisages should involve 'a hermeneutic relationship to the past
which is able to grasp its own present as history only on condition it
manages to keep the idea of the future, and of radical and utopian
transformation, alive'.[4]

Jameson proposes an equally valuable revision of the way in which
the relationship between the world and the work, between literature
and history, is commonly perceived. His reappraisal of this relationship makes it easier to break another basic critical deadlock I have
already touched upon, a deadlock wrought once again by the antagonism of two powerful but lopsided positions. To take the line toed
by old-fashioned practical critic and daredevil deconstructionist
alike, and treat the literary work as a largely autonomous textual
event, whose meaning owes few debts to biographical and social fact,
is plainly unsatisfactory. But to espouse an approach that reduces the
work to no more than a symptom or suffix of its age, which alone can
illuminate its significance and value, is scarcely less problematic.
Jameson's thesis endeavours to do justice both to the text's aesthetic
integrity, its seeming independence of history, and to its power to

animate through language and form a version of that lived world in which it is rooted, but to which it cannot be reduced. Far from being a mere echo or imprint of history, the literary text in Jameson's view 'always entertains some active relationship with the Real'. It comes equipped to 'draw the Real into its own texture', to select and incorporate its own indispensable contexts, and thus 'carry the Real within itself as its own intrinsic or immanent subtext'.[5] On this point Jameson is at one with Greenblatt, whose remarks about 'the presence within the work of its social being' allowing it 'to survive the disappearance of its enabling social conditions' I quoted in Chapter 1.[6]

If it is true that significant literature absorbs and transports through time whatever circumstances it requires to make sense to its readers or spectators, then the kind of criticism that labours to 'restore' text to context by exhuming the world to which it refers is labouring to little purpose. For those who still regard literature as a distinct, privileged enterprise, not to be confused with or subordinated to history, there is no point turning the text into a pretext for unpacking backgrounds and expanding contexts which the work itself has already looted, or which it has ruled out as redundant from the outset. Indeed the current drive to dissolve literary into cultural and historical studies might strike the cynic as the fashionable resort of those who have failed to recognize the literature of the past as an imaginative historiography in its own right. Whatever the truth of that may be, this part of Jameson's argument can be recruited to tighten the focus on 'the transformations of form'[7] to which the work submits whatever materials it has chosen to translate from the discourse of history into the language of literature.

The trouble is that Jameson's lack of faith in literature's powers of vision and resistance scuppers the positive potential of his argument from the start. No sooner has the work been sprung from its incarceration in mere subsequence than it is flung back in the airless slammer of ideology with slim prospects of reprieve. What might have blossomed into a hermeneutics of hope withers into the hermeneutics of suspicion routinely practised by more disenchanted political critics. Thus Jameson allows literature the agency to submit reality to the transformations of form, but purely in the interests of the ruling account of that reality: 'the aesthetic act is itself ideological, and the production of aesthetic or narrative form is to be seen as an ideological act in its own right, with the function of inventing imaginary or formal "solutions" to unresolvable social contradictions'.[8] Jameson shares with most devotees of new historicism and cultural materialism 'a manipulatory theory of culture'[9] – a kind of cultural conspiracy theory, which compels them to treat the work of literature as a seductive technique of containment, historically programmed to prop up the status quo and delay or disguise the advent of liberating change.

But how can such a craven tool of reaction speak so trenchantly of its time as to rattle the complacency of the present and spark premonitions of an expansive future? The answer for Jameson is that it can be made to do so only in spite of itself. Once the text has been lured onto the psychiatrist's couch to deliver an account of its intent, the critical analyst's role is to tease from that account clues to the undeluded understanding the text has repressed, to coax its political unconscious to the surface. The best the radical modern critic can do with a past masterwork is to read it with hindsight against the grain, forcing its symptomatic slips and silences to betray the secret truths of history it has contrived so ingeniously to efface. The utopian aspect of the work can likewise be wrested from its reactionary grasp only by an act of hermeneutic violence, which construes the ideology of the text as a travesty of the ideal condition it unwittingly predicts. For, in as much as they thrive on creating illusions of unanimity, on feeding us intimations of a true, classless community, 'even hegemonic or ruling-class culture and ideology are Utopian, not in spite of their instrumental function to secure and perpetuate class privilege and power, but rather precisely because that function is also in and of itself the affirmation of collective solidarity'.[10]

In other words, even the most powerful feats of the poetic mind are doomed to conceal the conflicts of their world behind façades of formal harmony and structural unity; but these fantasies of reconciliation and closure cannot help symbolizing the very dispensation whose arrival in reality they were designed to forestall. It may readily be admitted that this might prove a fruitful way of tackling works that are plainly transfixed by the legitimating myths of their day. What is questionable is the need to stifle at birth the possibility that literature may not always be so completely beguiled by ideology as Jameson presumes, but may prove intent on exposing the current map of experience to critique from a utopian standpoint which is irreducible to ideology of any sort.

The strengths and the drawbacks of Jameson's theory emerge clearly when it is brought to bear on the *Henry IV* plays and put to the test of textual analysis. Both works are directly engaged with history, politics and ideology. They are as preoccupied as Jameson with the relationship of the past to the present, with the implications of converting historical realities into verbal fictions, and with the role of language and representation in preserving and contesting power. To what extent do these history plays not only speak to us of what our world once was, but also challenge us to confront what it remains and what it has yet to become? If the relation of Shakespeare's writing to reality is indeed one of active formation rather than supplementary expression, then to answer that question we need to examine how the plays' formal resources and dramatic effects organize our perception of their version of history. This in turn will enable us to determine to what degree both parts of *Henry IV* seek to ratify the power-structures they portray, and in what ways they foreshadow the extinction of hierarchy itself.

'From a prince to a prentice'

On the face of it, it might seem hard to imagine drama more eager to comply with Jameson's expectations than *1* and *2 Henry IV*. Here, surely, is a perfect instance of art in the frank service of the reigning ideology, dramatizing the central contradictions of society in order to forge their imaginary resolution in a final vision of personal and political unity. Why else devote two plays to the triumphant defeat of rebel forces by the incumbent monarch, and the inseparable victory of Prince Hal over the mutinous impulses destroying his credibility as heir to the throne of England? The divisions in the kingdom parallel the divisions in its future king, and their reciprocal suppression allows *Part 2* to culminate in the prospect of a renewed nation unified by a transfigured sovereign, poised to divert the collective aggression of his people upon the French. Jameson's notion of literature imposing a spurious harmony on intractable social conflicts, but projecting through that illusion the true reconciliation anticipated from a classless community, appears to fit *Henry IV* like a gauntlet. Even without Hal's subsequent consecration as glorious warrior-king in *Henry V*, *1* and *2 Henry IV* arguably achieve a sense of closure strong enough to invest their history of bloodshed and guilt with the retrospective sanction of providential design.

What binds both plays into this reading is, of course, the myth of the Prodigal Son. The opening scene of *Part 1* reveals Hal's sire as so ashamed of the 'riot and dishonour' visited upon the House of Lancaster by his offspring that he wishes himself the father of Northumberland's boy, Hotspur, instead: 'a son who is the theme of honour's tongue' (*1 Henry IV*, I.i.85, 81). Hal has betrayed his identity as Prince of Wales and heir to the realm by preferring the idle fellowship of thieves, drunkards and whores to the resolute pursuit of his royal vocation. As his father puts it in their taut confrontation in Act III, Hal has, like 'the skipping King' Richard, 'mingled his royalty with cap'ring fools'; he has diluted his latent sovereignty in wanton familiarity with his inferiors, whose vision of him is consequently 'sick and blunted with community', when it should be awestruck: 'For thou hast lost thy princely privilege/ With vile participation' (*1 Henry IV*, III.ii.60, 63, 77, 86–7). The most scandalous effect of Prince Hal's delinquency is this erasure of the line dividing the ruler from the ruled, the ultimately metaphysical distinction on which not only his own right to rule, but also the whole social hierarchy, depends.

The conflict between 'vile participation' and the enforcing of regal distance is central to Hal's story and the shaping of both plays. It is vitally entwined with the concern to preserve the fragile difference between the regicidal usurper Henry IV and the rebellious lords who helped him seize the throne they now seek to hijack in their turn. It is to defend this discrimination, upon which the legitimacy of the Lancastrian line relies, that the climactic battle at Shrewsbury is fought in *Part 1* and Prince John dupes the rebels at Gaultree at the end of *Part 2.* The twin peaks of Hal's battle with his own wayward drives coincide dramatically with these victories over insurgence on the national plane. That the prodigal prince will return to the royal fold seems, however, a cast-iron bet from the start. The soliloquy with which he concludes his first scene with Falstaff notoriously charts the exact course his life will follow over both parts of *Henry IV.* The agile ease with which he divorces himself from the alehouse intimates of a moment before, reduces them to terms of unequivocal contempt, and swaps spontaneous banter for the calculated scripting of his public image, proves his father's anxieties to be unfounded:

> Yet herein will I imitate the sun,
> Who doth permit the base contagious clouds
> To smother up his beauty from the world,
> That, when he please again to be himself,
> Being wanted, he may be more wonder'd at
> By breaking through the foul and ugly mists
> Of vapours that did seem to strangle him.
> If all the year were playing holidays,
> To sport would be as tedious as to work;
> But when they seldom come, they wish'd for come,
> And nothing pleaseth but rare accidents.
> So when this loose behaviour I throw off
> And pay the debt I never promised,
> By how much better than my word I am,
> By so much shall I falsify men's hopes,
> And like bright metal on a sullen ground,
> My reformation, glitt'ring o'er my fault,
> Shall show more goodly and attract more eyes
> Than that which hath no foil to set it off.
> I'll so offend, to make offence a skill,
> Redeeming time when men think least I will.
>
>   (*1 Henry IV,* I.ii.197–217)

This prince needs no lessons from the king on how to impress the singularity and exclusiveness of his identity upon his people.

The dramatic interest is created, therefore, not by a genuine, unpredictable conflict in the 'sword-and-buckler Prince of Wales'

(*1 Henry IV*, I.iii.230), but by the suspense of his deferral of the
inevitable. We are constantly reminded that we are dealing with a
strategic postponement rather than a purely feckless refusal of his
appointment with history. Hal's sobering assurance at the end of the
'play extempore' that one day he will indeed 'banish plump Jack, and
banish all the world' (*1 Henry IV*, II.iv.280, 479–80) foretells the
chilling dismissal of Falstaff for real in the final scene of *2 Henry IV*:
'I know thee not, old man, fall to thy prayers' (V.v.47). Sharply
upbraided by the father Hotspur calls 'this king of smiles' (*1 Henry
IV*, I.iii.246), Hal responds by reiterating the pledge framed in his
earlier monologue, thus reinstating between himself and his future
subjects the crucial disparity that he has allowed to evaporate:

> I will redeem all this on Percy's head,
> And in the closing of some glorious day
> Be bold to tell you that I am your son,
> When I will wear a garment all of blood,
> And stain my favours in a bloody mask,
> Which wash'd away shall scour my shame with it.
>   (*1 Henry IV*, III.ii.132–7)

At the Battle of Shrewsbury with which *Part 1* concludes, where
he saves his father's life and defeats his extravagant rival Hotspur,
Hal heroically proves himself to be a man of his word and a monarch
in the making. His affectionate indulgence of Falstaff on the battlefield confirms, nevertheless, that the narrative of redemption is still
incomplete when the curtain falls on Act V. The story can therefore
be picked up in *Part 2*, which recycles the pattern of disaffection and
delay finally expiated by the promise fulfilled, only this time with a
resounding sense of sublime culmination:

> My father is gone wild into his grave;
> For in his tomb lie my affections,
> And with his spirits sadly I survive,
> To mock the expectation of the world,
> To frustrate prophecies, and to rase out
> Rotten opinion, who hath writ me down
> After my seeming. The tide of blood in me

Hath proudly flow'd in vanity till now;
Now doth it turn and ebb back to the sea,
Where it shall mingle with the state of floods,
And flow henceforth in formal majesty.

(*2 Henry IV*, V.ii.123–33)

This tailoring of history to fit the moral myth of the Prodigal Son, of the sinner's salvation, works powerfully in *Henry IV* to rationalize hierarchy, glorify royalty, and disguise contingency as destiny. From Jameson's point of view, the radical critic's job would be to expose the plays' obfuscation of political reality by reading them against the drift of their orthodox import, by deciphering the undoctored version of the situation secreted between their lines. Their conformity could then be turned inside out to disclose the prophecy of collective emancipation and true unity concealed in the very instrument of divisive misprision. But to return to the texts of *Henry IV* with this dual objective in mind is to recognize its redundancy in the light of a closer reading. The account of the plays I have given so far can only survive through the neglect of formal techniques, structural implications and dramatic parentheses, whose import changes the meaning of the narrative they articulate. By abstracting the double tale of Hal's redemption and the royal victory over rebellion from the syntax of its dramatization, and thus from the way we are induced to understand it, *1* and *2 Henry IV* are reduced to the ideology they are intent on unravelling. But a refusal to sunder what the plays say from how they say it restores to us more fascinating texts, which do not need to be read against the grain in order to be saved from themselves.

Let us consider just two of the many scenes and passages in *Henry IV* that are commonly skipped over or marginalized in critical accounts, but whose function is to punctuate and inflect what is said and done in ways that transmute the meaning of the drama.

In the first scene of Act II of *1 Henry IV* there is an intriguing exchange between Gadshill and the chamberlain of the inn near which the robbery involving Hal is to proceed. It is ushered in by the complaints of the two carriers, who are preparing their day's labours. One observes: 'This house is turn'd upside down since

Robin ostler died' (II.i.10–11). The line suggests, perhaps, a plebeian parallel with the state of the kingdom following the death of
Richard: the previous scene has witnessed the conspiracy of the
rebels. The other echoes his abuse of the flea-pit they have just
slept in: 'there is ne'er a king christen could be better bit than I
have been since the first cock' (II.i.16–18). Fleas observe no distinctions of rank. Gadshill's badinage with the crooked chamberlain
accentuates the scene's awareness of the play's key concerns. Chamberlain and pickpurse are interchangeable titles, quips Gadshill, 'for thou
variest no more from picking of purses than giving direction doth
from labouring: thou layest the plot how' (II.i.50–2). The collapsing
of distinctions between those who give the orders and those who obey
them clears the way for Gadshill's assurance that the participation of
the powerful makes their criminal enterprise impregnable:

Gadshill.	. . . I am join'd with no foot land-rakers, no long-staff sixpenny strikers, none of these mad mustachio purple-hu'd malt-worms, but with nobility and tranquillity, burgomasters and great oney'rs, such as can hold in, such as will strike sooner than speak, and speak sooner than drink, and drink sooner than pray; and yet, 'zounds, I lie, for they pray continually to their saint, the com-monwealth, or rather, not pray to her, but prey on her, for they ride up and down on her, and make her their boots.
Chamberlain.	What, the commonwealth their boots? Will she hold out water in foul way?
Gadshill.	She will, she will, justice hath liquor'd her. We steal as in a castle, cock-sure; we have the receipt of fern-seed, we walk invisible.

(*1 Henry IV*, II.i.73–87)

The common thieves are conflated with their more elevated breth-
ren, whose ransacking of the commonwealth differs only in the
legitimacy which renders its criminality 'invisible'. The prince's
role in the robbery creates the occasion for this illuminating identification, which pivots in turn on the more fundamental reflection
with which Gadshill bows out of the scene: '*homo* is a common name
to all men' (II.i.95).

Comparable implications can be quarried from otherwise pointless remarks made by Falstaff in *Part 2*. During his evasive encounter
with the Lord Chief Justice in the second scene of the play, Falstaff
pleads the malady of deafness as his reason for not responding to the
Justice's admonitions, and he attempts to distract the latter by
snatching up the topic of the king's ill-health: 'And I hear, moreover,
his Highness is fall'n into this same whoreson apoplexy.' This
apoplexy is 'a kind of lethargy', Falstaff informs the exasperated
magistrate, 'a kind of sleeping in the blood'; in short, according to
Galen, 'it is a kind of deafness'. 'I think you are fallen into the
disease,' retorts the Lord Chief Justice, 'for you hear not what I say to
you' (I.ii.107–8, 111–13, 117). The full value of these lines, in
which the lord of the land and the lord of misrule are subject to
the same affliction, becomes apparent if we turn to Falstaff's meditation on the peculiar affinity between Shallow and his servants:

> It is a wonderful thing to see the semblable coherence of his men's
> spirits and his. They, by observing him, do bear themselves like
> foolish justices; he, by conversing with them, is turn'd into a just-
> ice-like servingman. Their spirits are so married in conjunction with
> the participation of society that they flock together in consent, like so
> many wild geese. If I had a suit to Master Shallow, I would humour
> his men with the imputation of being near their master; if to his men,
> I would curry with Master Shallow that no man could better com-
> mand his servants. It is certain that either wise bearing or ignorant
> carriage is caught, as men take diseases, one of another...
>
> (*2 Henry IV,* V.i.64–77)

The revelation of consanguinity crossing the threshold of social
difference is conveyed this time by an appeal to the democratic
impartiality of infection, which holds the privileges of birth and
blood in contempt. But here there is a further glimpse of the utopian
potential of such benign confoundings of rank through 'the participation of society' (what Henry IV in *Part 1* denounced in Hal as 'vile
participation'): an idyllic condition, in which spirits normally seg-
regated by the antagonistic principle of subordination become 'so
married in conjunction...that they flock together in consent, like
so many wild geese'.

Such passages provide the keys to decode more sustained enact-
ments of improvised irrelevance, whose liberty from the burden of
advancing the historical plot permits them to explore the cost and
consequences of that history, to reinstate the exclusions and suppres-
sions that made it possible. In Act II of *Part 1* Hal confesses wryly to
Poins: 'I have sounded the very base-string of humility. Sirrah, I am
sworn brother to a leash of drawers, and can call them all by their
christen names, as Tom, Dick, and Francis' (II.iv.5–8). The witty
substitution of the tapster's name for the expected 'Harry' invites the
equation of the former's plight with the prince's in the practical joke
that follows. Francis is torn between the temptation 'to play the
coward with [his] indenture and show it a fair pair of heels' (II.iv.47–
8) and the immediate obligation to answer the call of a customer,
which he postpones with 'Anon, anon, sir', the parroted watchword
of his trade. Simultaneously hailed by vocation and desire, *'the
Drawer stands amazed, not knowing which way to go'* (II.iv.79, s.d.),
the plebeian epitome of the future king's suspension in a limbo of
delay. Hal's jest fleetingly lifts the barrier between the destinies of
both men, and dissolves Hal's aristocratic identity in the broad
stream of humanity through the ages: asked by Poins for the upshot
of the gulling of Francis, he replies, 'I am now of all humours that
have show'd themselves humours since the old days of goodman
Adam to the pupil age of this present twelve a' clock at midnight'
(II.iv.92–5).

The intensity of this compulsion to lose himself in the soul of a
subordinate by projection or displacement is confirmed by his
obsessive return to the theme in *Part 2*. The price of the prince's
elision of difference by deferment is anxiety, guilt and melancholy.
'Before God, I am exceeding weary' (II.ii.1), he laments to Poins at
the opening of Act II, at once disenchanted with his royalty and
ashamed of his abandonment of eminence: 'But indeed these humble
considerations make me out of love with my greatness. What a
disgrace is it to me to remember thy name, or to know thy face
to-morrow' (II.ii.11–14). The sense of a character caged in his own
myth, stranded in a trance of procrastination until the cue to pace
the stage of history breaks the spell, is insistent. But the whole point
of forcing open such lacunae, in which history is put on hold, is to

create the space to demolish the foundations on which that reading of history is built.

The Prince of Wales strives stoutly to drive the wedge back between his heritage and the 'vile company' he blushes to acknowledge, appealing to his script for ultimate vindication: 'Let the end try the man' (II.ii.49, 47). It requires, however, rather less than 'A crown's-worth of good interpretation' (II.ii.92) to see that urge vanquished by the need for communion in the hoax that springs from this scene. The path to the jape is paved by quips haunted by more of the same demarcation disputes. Poins glances at those who 'never prick their finger but they say: "There's some of the King's blood spilt"' as a prelude to claiming themselves to be 'the King's poor cousin'. 'Nay,' Hal chimes in, 'they will be kin to us, or they will fetch it from Japhet' (II.ii.112–13, 117–18) – Japhet being the son of Noah from whom all Gentiles were thought to be descended. The pressure to dilute the prince's blue blood also dictates the ironic speculation about Hal marrying Poins's sister, Nell (II.ii.127–41). And by the end of the scene, the frail dyke of convention dividing Hal from the common tide of humanity has been breached by his compliance with Poins's scheme to disguise themselves in the 'leathern jerkins and aprons' of Francis's calling: 'From a god to a bull? a heavy descension! it was Jove's case. From a prince to a prentice? a low transformation! that shall be mine' (II.ii.171, 173–5). The reincarnation of the heir apparent is complete two scenes later, when the prince-prentice answers Falstaff's 'Some sack, Francis' with his surrogate's remorseless 'Anon, anon, sir' (II.iv.281–2), directly echoing the corresponding scene in *Part 1*.

Nor is the razing of hierarchy the only effect sought by such confusions of identity. In the 'play extempore' of *Part 1* Falstaff plays Henry IV, reproving Hal 'in King Cambyses' vein' (II.iv.387); then he swaps places to play Hal to the prince's own impersonation of his father. The conscious theatricality of this parodic performance highlights both the rootlessness of the roles and the staged nature of the historical realities being burlesqued. The majesty of the English throne dwindles to a few tawdry props stripped of mystique: 'Thy state is taken for a join'd-stool, thy golden sceptre for a leaden dagger, and thy precious rich crown for a pitiful bald crown!'

(II.iv.380–2). Falstaff's caricature of the admonishing monarch deploys an obsolete theatrical rhetoric, which is persuasive enough to captivate his tavern audience: 'O Jesu, he doth it as like one of these harlotry players as ever I see!', cries the delighted Hostess (II.iv.395–6). But more important for the audience beyond the footlights is the scene's preemptive ironizing of the serious clash of royal father and reprobate son in Act III. Their characters and their dialogue are marked out in advance as scripted creations, so that their impassioned appeals and protestations are mocked by their conformity to recognized postures and patterns of exchange.[11]

The spectators are encouraged to recognize majesty as a rehearsed production and reminded of the gulf between the performed events before their eyes and the remote past realities they presuppose. Henry IV activates this awareness by his frank confessions of using theatrical simulation and diversion as instruments of power:

> And then I stole all courtesy from heaven,
> And dress'd myself in such humility
> That I did pluck allegiance from men's hearts,
>   (*1 Henry IV*, III.ii.50–2)

> For all my reign hath been but as a scene
> Acting that argument . . .
>   . . . Therefore, my Harry,
> Be it thy course to busy giddy minds
> With foreign quarrels, that action, hence borne out,
> May waste the memory of the former days.
>   (*2 Henry IV*, IV.v.197–8, 212–15)

The very battle fought at Shrewsbury to bolster the sovereign's unique authority involves the subterfuge of fielding noblemen 'Semblably furnish'd like the King himself' (*1 Henry IV*, V.iii.21). Advised by Hotspur that 'The King hath many marching in his coats,' Douglas swears: 'Now by my sword, I will kill all his coats;/ I'll murder all his wardrop, piece by piece,/ Until I meet the King' (V.iii.25–8). But, when he encounters the monarch in person, he remains understandably sceptical:

Douglas.	Another king? they grow like Hydra's heads.
	I am the Douglas, fatal to all those
	That wear those colours on them. What art thou
	That counterfeit'st the person of a king?
King.	The King himself, who, Douglas, grieves at heart
	So many of his shadows thou hast met
	And not the very King. I have two boys
	Seek Percy and thyself about the field,
	But seeing thou fall'st on me so luckily,
	I will assay thee, and defend thyself.
Douglas.	I fear thou art another counterfeit,
	And yet in faith thou bearest thee like a king.

(1 Henry IV, V.iv.25–36)

The action contrived to clinch the exclusive legitimacy of Boling-broke's claim to the throne breeds a multiplicity of sovereigns. The ploy disperses Henry's singularity and blatantly insinuates that to bear oneself like a monarch and don the robes of royalty may be all there is to being royal for real – as Sir Walter Blunt discovers to his mortal dismay.

Detail and structure conspire throughout parts *1* and *2* to dismantle the scaffolding of dominion and unmask the fictive status of authorized social distinctions and moral oppositions. The coincidence of king and prince sharing their Christian name with the rebel Earl and his son is played up to the full in Shakespeare's phrasing to stimulate our apprehension of their covert equivalence:

> O that it could be prov'd
> That some night-tripping fairy had exchang'd
> In cradle-clothes our children where they lay,
> And call'd mine Percy, his Plantagenet!
> Then would I have his Harry and he mine.

(1 Henry IV, I.i.86–90)

> Harry to Harry shall, hot horse to horse,

(1 Henry IV, IV.i.122)

Two stars keep not their motion in one sphere,
Nor can one England brook a double reign
Of Harry Percy and the Prince of Wales.
                                    (*1 Henry IV*, V.iv.65–7)

Like Hal and Francis, or Hal and Falstaff when the latter takes the
prince's part in the tavern, or ironically appropriates his promise of
eventual contrition, the royal and the regicidal turn out to be
Siamese twins. Indeed, as John Kerrigan has shown, both plays are
obsessed with doubling and replication at every turn: from Falstaff
with the dead Hotspur on his back, denying himself to be the 'double
man' he seems (*1 Henry IV*, V.iv.138), or Shallow's cryptic query 'And
is old Double dead?' (*2 Henry IV*, III.ii.43), down to the fine grain of
speech rhythms, where duplication reigns in the mouths of foolish
judge: 'Certain, 'tis certain, very sure, very sure' (*2 Henry IV*, III ii.36)
and majesty alike: 'Not Amurath an Amurath succeeds,/ But Harry
Harry' (*2 Henry IV*, V.ii.48–9). The rhetorical term for this figure of
speech is *geminatio* or 'twinning'; and, as Kerrigan points out, quoting
Thomas Wilson's definition in *The Arte of Rhetorique* (1553), 'In Tudor
rhetoric, "doublet" translates *geminatio*: "when we rehearse one and the
same word twice together", as in "Anon, Anon, sir!"'.[12]

This local instruction in the art of *geminatio* finds its global
counterpart in the scenic composition of the plays. The structural
trick of switching to and fro between king and conspirators, and
from both to the Eastcheap empire of Falstaff, or the rural domain of
Shallow and Silence, and back again, begins by underlining points of
contrast and discrimination. But its cumulative impact transforms
our initial acceptance of disparity into a dawning realization of
resemblance. By commuting between diverse ranks and value
systems the plays disclose an appetite for consensus eating away at
the ideology of difference and duality. The official scale of social
worth, graphically codified in the descending list of dramatis personae that still fronts modern texts, is scrambled by these oscillations
as surely as shuffling a new deck of cards confounds the decorum of
each suit. The kaleidoscopic vision of *1* and *2 Henry IV* forges a
prospect of egalitarian community, which exposes the national and
royal principles of union as frauds.

Nor can the teleological view of history conscripted by those principles survive the sabotaging to which *Part 2*, as the expected resolution of questions left dangling in *Part 1*, is especially subject. A refusal of deterministic historiography is declared at the outset in the remarkable Induction and opening scene of the play. In a direct address to the audience, the personification of Rumour introduces himself as one upon whose tongues 'continual slanders ride,/ The which in every language I pronounce,/ Stuffing the ears of men with false reports' (*2 Henry IV*, Ind. 6–8). His present purpose, as he stands before the castle of Northumberland, is

> To noise abroad that Harry Monmouth fell
> Under the wrath of noble Hotspur's sword,
> And that the King before the Douglas' rage
> Stoop'd his anointed head as low as death.
> (*2 Henry IV*, Ind. 29–32)

The first scene then thrusts us into the midst of enacted history, as Lord Bardolph repeats Rumour's false account to Northumberland as 'certain news from Shrewsbury' (I.i.12). Northumberland needs convincing: 'How is this deriv'd?' (I.i.23). But the 'certain news' is rapidly unseated by Travers's revised report, which Morton's no less breathless arrival confirms: young Harry Percy's spur is cold indeed, and

> The sum of all
> Is that the King hath won, and hath sent out
> A speedy power to encounter you, my lord,
> (*2 Henry IV*, I.i.131–3)

For a moment the closed book of historical fact is reopened and rewritten. The fixity of the past surrenders to the supposition that all might have been otherwise, that the chronicles could quite plausibly have been obliged to tell another tale. We are forewarned that this rival version is unfounded, and the upstart is, of course, swiftly deposed; but it is entertained and elaborated for long enough to stake its claim to likelihood and so restore the original fluidity of frozen events. History is rewound and replayed with the different direction it might have taken spliced back in. We are called upon to witness the translation of once vital experience into a vulnerable narrative, refracted through this dramatic reconstruction in the lived present of performance: 'Open your ears; for which of you will stop/ The vent of hearing when loud Rumour speaks?' (Ind. 1–2). History, it is plain, is not simply what happened, but what gets made, misconstrued, disputed and remodelled.[13]

Part 2 is riddled with double-takes, false starts and stops, rewrites and reversals of expectation. Their purpose is to resist, and thereby transform, the ultimate course things must take in order to climax in the defeat of the rebels and the coronation of the prodigal redeemed. The infectious doubling of identities is matched by a doubling of incident, in which what actually happens is unsettled by the imagination of another possibility. Thus the achievement at Gaultree of a bloodless and just resolution, whereby the rebels' grievances will find redress and both sides enjoy the concord of 'restored love and amity' (IV.ii.65), is acted out convincingly up to the very last moment; at which point the apparent meaning of events is abruptly turned on its head by Prince John's icy duplicity. A similar effect is produced when King Henry envisions a persuasive future ruled by Hal's 'headstrong riot':

> The blood weeps from my heart when I do shape,
> In forms imaginary, th'unguided days
> And rotten times that you shall look upon,
> When I am sleeping with my ancestors.
> (*2 Henry IV*, IV.ii.58–61)

But these bleak predictions prove as mistaken as the abandoned future under Hal that excites Falstaff's fantasies, or the prophecy of the king's death in a Jerusalem which turns out to be the name of a palace chamber, far from the Holy Land he had hoped to wrest from the infidel.

Most disconcerting of all is the way the play trips Hal up on the brink of his accession and moral resurrection. Having diagnosed his father's death with exemplary alacrity, he seizes the crown from the pillow and ceremoniously sets the 'polish'd perturbation' (IV.v.153) on his own head:

> My due from thee is this imperial crown,
> Which, as immediate from thy place and blood,
> Derives itself to me. [*Puts on the crown.*] Lo where it sits,
> Which God shall guard; and put the world's whole strength
> Into one giant arm, it shall not force
> This lineal honour from me. This from thee
> Will I to mine leave, as 'tis left to me. [*Exit.*]
>   (2 *Henry IV,* IV.v.41–7)

Seconds later, the conclusive resonance of this speech is shattered as the king revives, denounces his son's precipitate, callous theft, and forces Hal to crawl back, crown in hand, to convince him of the innocence of his motives and the genuineness of 'The noble change' (IV.v.154) he keeps promising. Shakespeare's dramatization of the episode exploits its disruptive impact to the full, compelling the denouement to double back and restart from revised assumptions about Hal, with a refreshed feeling for the unpredictability of experience before the fact.

These backtracking devices allow the blood to flow once more through the veins of chronicled history, flushing act and incident with the indeterminacy that providential narrative denies them. It comes as no surprise to find the question of history on the overt agenda of 2 *Henry IV,* in which characters speculate continually on the relation of the past to the future and on the possibility of foreknowledge:

> *King.*   O God, that one might read the book of fate
>   And see the revolution of the times
>   Make mountains level, and the continent,
>   Weary of solid firmness, melt itself
>   Into the sea, and other times to see
>   The beachy girdle of the ocean
>   Too wide for Neptune's hips; how chance's mocks
>   And changes fill the cup of alteration
>   With divers liquors! . . .

Warwick.   There is a history in all men's lives,
                Figuring the natures of the times deceas'd,
                The which observ'd, a man may prophesy,
                With a near aim, of the main chance of things
                As yet not come to life, who in their seeds
                And weak beginning lie intreasured.
                Such things become the hatch and brood of time...
                            (*2 Henry IV*, III.i.45–53, 80–6)

'Jesus,' exclaims Shallow, 'the days that we have seen!', confirming
in his nostalgia for 'the times deceased', when he heard 'the chimes at
midnight' (*2 Henry IV*, III.ii.219, 215), that a predilection for edited
highlights of the past is not exclusive to great lords. Such gentle
guying of selective retrospection ('Lord, Lord, how subject we old
men are to this vice of lying!' (III.ii.303–4)) calls the whole project
of the *Henry IV* plays to account. For it keeps alive in the spectator's
mind the distortions inevitably entailed in the process of historiography, the gap which must always divorce long-gone realities from
the discursive representations in which alone they become intelligible. Not the least virtue of the Epilogue's appearance at the close of
Part 2, to promise that 'our humble author will continue the story'
(Epil. 27–8), is its oblique insistence that *as* a story, to quote Samuel
Daniel's *Defence of Rhyme* (1603),

> an Historie...is but a Mappe of Men, and dooth no otherwise
> acquaint us with the true Substance of Circumstances then a super-
> ficiall Card dooth the Seaman with a Coast never seene, which always
> prooves other to the eye than the imagination forecast it...[14]

Both power and history are demystified, even as the plays complete their supposed contract with the presiding ideology. The
prescribed royal reading of history dictates the narrative shape of
1 and *2 Henry IV*. But the strategies of disenchantment built into the
dramatization rob that narrative of its supremacy, breaking its
monopoly on what is thought to have happened. This critique of
the approved account is anchored in the utopian assumptions of an
anticipated world. At the end of *Part 1* and *Part 2* monarchy,

hierarchy and the illusions that sustain them emerge intact, even strengthened, *within* the world of the plays; but our understanding and judgement of them has been changed completely by the way they have been portrayed. What the protagonists persist in believing, and what the spectators are encouraged to conclude from the standpoint they are obliged to adopt, are two quite different things. The perspectives of the denizens of *Henry IV* – high and low, urban and rural alike – remain bound by the limits of the imagined universe they inhabit; our assessment of them, however, is released from that bondage by our standpoint as audience or readers, whose vision of their universe is filtered through the formal lens of defamiliarization. As a result, the plays liberate us to decipher 'the main chance of things/ As yet not come to life', which is encoded in their depiction of 'the times deceas'd'. They afford us a proleptic glimpse through their eyes of the future in the past.

'of things/ As yet not come to life'

Reading the *Henry IV* plays in the light of Jameson's theory of interpretation explodes the common misconception of literary texts that prevents his most fertile insights from releasing the full potential of literature from the past. Jameson begins by blazing a trail towards viewing texts as active transfigurations of vanished realities, capable of vexing modern preconceptions and signposting the end of oppressive institutions. But this admirable enterprise soon shrivels into the extortion of progressive significance from works whose instinctive commitment to the legitimation of class society is taken as read. *Henry IV* testifies, however, to the historically evolved capacity of poetic language and dramatic form to undo the ideology of division from a standpoint beyond the reach of subjection. Jameson remains trapped in the historicist hermeneutics of suspicion from which his own sharpest insights offer an escape-route. To demonstrate this, moreover, is to pull the plug on a range of critical responses and a long tradition of theatrical productions, which have diminished or denied the power of the *Henry IV* plays to undercut the hegemonic narratives they stage.

Scott McMillin has traced the British performance history of *1* and *2 Henry IV* from the 1945 Old Vic production, starring Olivier and Richardson, to the 1986 touring version by the English Shakespeare Company, under the direction of Michael Bogdanov. His survey dwells on three benchmark productions, all of which put the plays on as part of a cycle sequence: the staging by the Shakespeare Memorial Theatre Company in 1951, directed by Anthony Quayle, which established the cycle mode as the standard modern format for the histories, and the RSC productions of 1964 and 1975, under the direction of Peter Hall and Terry Hands respectively. McMillin discerns an uncomfortably direct relationship between the politics of the institutionalized theatre and the political message all too predictably read into Hal's reformation:

> The modern subsidized theatre helps cycles be staged and cycles make Falstaff a figure to be rejected. This is what happens to *1 Henry IV* in its modern cycle-oriented treatments: the Prince grows into royal authority by turning aside the old fat man, and it is government subsidy that provides the wherewithal . . . to let this lesson be drama-tized.[15]

These productions seem to have swallowed the hierarchical as-sumptions and the fusion of personal and national destiny which the plays are not fooled by for a moment. For Peter Hall the world view affirmed by the plays was plain: 'all Shakespeare's thinking, whether religious, political, or moral, is based on a complete acceptance of this concept of order. There is a just proportion in all things: man is above beast, king is above man, and God above king'; rebellion is monstrous because it 'destroys the order and leads to destructive anarchy'.[16] Terry Hands's production bent the drama into an ageless study in the growth of majesty, traced through the exemplary evolution of the adolescent male from callow disaffection to respon-sible maturity. For Hal, according to the programme note for the production, the stage 'is always the blank slate on which life writes its lessons', 'the bare metaphysical arena in which the soul of a royal Everyman discovers his destiny and true friends'.[17] As McMillin remarks: 'So long as Prince Hal is said to be caught up in such timeless and essential experience, his career will seem purified of the political and all the more agreeable to the managers of our affairs.'[18]

Given the opportunities for inculcating conformity afforded by suitably slanted productions, it is less than astounding to learn that 'More than any other play, *1 Henry IV* is swung into position on occasions of dignity and ceremony in Stratford.'[19] After baptizing the new Stratford Memorial Theatre in 1932 on the Bard's birthday, it was the birthday play during the history cycles of 1951, 1964 and 1975; and when the RSC opened at the Barbican in 1982 with another inevitable cycle of histories, the birthday production was once more *1 Henry IV*. 'The thinking of the RSC', remarks McMillin wryly, 'had become so accustomed to taking the *Henrys* as curtain-raisers for occasions of wealth and power that the venture could be predicted before some of the actors in the eventual production were out of secondary school.'[20] It is the cultural centrality and enormous influence of these imaginatively stunted versions of the *Henry IV* plays that make the development of readings that can do them justice so important. And this endeavour demands an approach fuelled by quite different assumptions about the relation of poetic writing to the enthroned prescriptions and stereotypes of the age.

That Tillyard's study of *Shakespeare's History Plays* (1944) directly and indirectly shaped the 1951 and 1964 cycle productions of *1* and *2 Henry IV* is no surprise. Tillyard's work has remained the cornerstone of the conventional view of the histories to this day, and the automatic antagonist of those seeking to contest the nationalistic and authoritarian attitudes he found sanctioned by these plays. According to Tillyard, Shakespeare

> expressed successfully a universally held and still comprehensible scheme of history: a scheme fundamentally religious, by which events evolve under a law of justice and under the ruling of God's Providence, and of which Elizabeth's England was the acknowledged outcome.[21]

For Tillyard, therefore, the two parts of *Henry IV* exemplify the ideal education of the Christian prince for the office destiny has prepared for him. Tillyard's Hal 'is a man of large powers, Olympian loftiness,

and high sophistication, who has acquired a thorough knowledge of
human nature both in himself and in others. He is Shakespeare's
studied picture of the kingly type.'[22] Hal's tormenting of Francis in
Part 1 clouds Tillyard's admiration for a moment, but the perfection
of Hal's portrait is swiftly restored by the historian's appeal to the
principle of degree: 'The subhuman element in the population must
have been considerable in Shakespeare's day; that it should be treated
almost like beasts was taken for granted.'[23] It is perhaps too easy to
feel superior now to that telling rationalization, whose offhand
inhumanity has been highlighted in a recent study of the histories.[24]
But it gives the measure of Tillyard's commitment to reading
Shakespeare in *1* and *2 Henry IV* as the unquestioning advocate of
a rigidly stratified society.

Reinforced by similar views of the histories promoted in John
Dover Wilson's *The Fortunes of Falstaff* (1943), G. Wilson Knight's
The Olive and the Sword (1944), and Lily B. Campbell's *Shakespeare's
Histories: Mirrors of Elizabethan Policy* (1947),[25] this conception of
1 and *2 Henry IV* as a defence of the divine necessity of order and
authority controlled discussion of the plays for decades. Its survival,
in a subtly adapted, more appealing form, was guaranteed by C. L.
Barber's classic study, *Shakespeare's Festive Comedy* (1959). Barber
allows the saturnalian zest of Falstaff and the Eastcheap world
much more play and purchase than most of the Tillyard camp tend
to, but only because of its ulterior role as the negative pole in the
moral schooling of the budding ruler. The temporary reign of
misrule under Falstaff functions here as a kind of safety-valve, a
cathartic release of anarchic energies and appetites, which Hal must
finally reject to qualify as the governor of a stable, disciplined
kingdom. The lawless threat to propriety is introduced in order to
enhance the triumphant return of dutiful decorum with Hal's fulfilment of his royal vocation: 'the misrule works, through the whole
dramatic rhythm, to consolidate rule'.[26]

Thirty years on, the same angle is still going strong: recycled in a
still more sophisticated form and yoked now to a dissenting critical
politics, but fundamentally unchanged. Thus, in the course of constructing his new-historicist Shakespeare in *Power on Display*,
Leonard Tennenhouse maintains that

the various confrontations between licit and illicit authority compris-
ing the *Henriad* more firmly draw the distinction between aristocracy
and populace even as they appear to overturn this primary categorical
distinction.... Criminalizing the popular figures of inversion is as
necessary to the poetics of power as incorporating a certain popular
vigor within the legitimate body of the state.... Legitimate order can
come into being only through disruption...[27]

This is also the position endorsed by Stephen Greenblatt, whose
celebrated essay 'Invisible Bullets' takes *1* and *2 Henry IV* as ideal
texts with which to bolster his belief that 'Shakespeare's plays are
centrally, repeatedly concerned with the production and containment of subversion and disorder.'[28] In Greenblatt's view, power
feeds off the transgression and sedition it needs in order to define
its identity and authority. And, by inoculating itself with a controlled symbolic dose of realizations that could destroy it, the body
politic helps ward off actual insurrection. Hence, as theatrical instruments of the power of the Elizabethan state, 'the Henry plays
confirm the Machiavellian hypothesis that princely power originates
in force and fraud even as they draw their audience toward an
acceptance of that power'.[29] Greenblatt's account of the relationship
between drama and domination is more intricate than Tillyard's or
Barber's, and its objective is demystification rather than occlusion,
but the bottom line is the same: the *Henry IV* plays are the voice of
Elizabethan orthodoxy, and never more so than when they mimic the
accents of dissent.[30] This approach dovetails perfectly with Jameson's presumption that the masterpieces of the past cannot earn
political salvation by their own merits, but must depend for redemption on the grace of the modern critic.

In *Shakespeare Recycled: The Making of Historical Drama* the cultural
materialist Graham Holderness has attempted to overturn conservative readings of *1* and *2 Henry IV* by tying Falstaff into Bakhtin's
concept of the carnivalesque and stressing his function as

> a constant focus of opposition to the official and serious tone of
> authority and power: his discourse confronts and challenges those of
> king and state.... His world is a world of ease, moral licence, appetite
> and desire; of humour and ridicule, theatricals and satire, of community,

freedom and abundance; a world created by inverting the abstract society, the oppression and the hierarchy of the official world.[31]

But Falstaff can indeed merely invert; he cannot transcend that official world, which beholds in him its mirror image, its secret sharer, not its negation or displacement. Exhilarating as Holderness's sketch of him sounds, to champion the cause of Falstaff against the dour disciplines of authority and historical necessity simply reverses the poles of the orthodox view. Defecting to Eastcheap and elevating a sentimental idealization of its ethos over the imperatives of duty and national destiny sells the plays short, because it leaves them caged within the system of social differences and moral dichotomies they seek to dismantle. To privilege the liberties of 'headstrong riot' (*2 Henry IV*, IV.iv.62) over 'The majesty and power of law and justice' (*2 Henry IV*, V.ii.78) is to repress the reciprocity of the royal and plebeian realms, whose values are in practice identical, and so leave the entrenched disparities of the status quo intact. This strategy plays straight into the hands of the new-historicist paradox that the upshot of subversion is the consolidation of dominion and the rule of law.

As long as criticism of *Henry IV* keeps shuttling between the claims of the Crown and the lure of the taproom, it remains tangled in the spurious dilemma forged by Hal as he hesitates between his father and plump Jack. Whether the rejection of Falstaff is applauded, regretted or safely construed as ambivalent, the critic accepts the characters' perception of their world and the alternatives they confront at face value, as the terms on which we are supposed to interpret and evaluate the plays. But such readings must block out all the devices deliberately constructed to colour our vision and complicate our judgement, because the plays are designed to withdraw through formal implication what they avow through overt statement and action. Both parts of *Henry IV* employ techniques of framing, interruption and conflation, which weave a counterfactual perspective into their dramatization of history. By preventing our submersion in the mentality of the cast, they unravel the rationale of the standard interpretations. Far from enclosing the spectator in an Elizabethan perception of late medieval England, the *Henry IV* plays invalidate the hierarchical terms in which the problems of the protagonists are posed and solved, even as they concede the factual force and historical triumph of subjugation.

The inhabitants of *1* and *2 Henry IV* are doomed to dwell forever in 'the times deceas'd' (*2 Henry IV*, III.i.81) which, as one of them laments, 'Crowd us and crush us to this monstrous form' (*2 Henry IV*, IV.ii.34). But the plays' perspective on their lives reaches forward 'to sound the bottom of the after-times' (*2 Henry IV*, IV.ii.51) and anticipate the transfigured shape the 'hatch and brood' (*2 Henry IV*, III.i.86) of history might take. The opening speech of *Part 1* tunes us subliminally to this dual vision informing both plays:

> Those opposed eyes
> Which, like the meteors of a troubled heaven,
> All of one nature, of one substance bred,
> Did lately meet in the intestine shock
> And furious close of civil butchery,
> Shall now, in mutual well-beseeming ranks,
> March all one way, and be no more oppos'd
> Against acquaintance, kindred, and allies.
> (*1 Henry IV*, I.i.9–16)

The *Henry IV* plays are written in a way that allows us to behold a world ruled by fierce oppositions through the eyes of a world which has surrendered such barbarism to the cooperative sway of human solidarity.

Older and newer forms of historicist criticism share a notion of literature as the incurably anterior expression of an extinct reality. They evince a chronic aversion to the conjecture that Shakespeare's drama might be drawn as much towards a future beyond our own apprehension as back to its place of origin in the past. It is the virtue of Jameson's theoretical stance that it argues so effectively against such sterile historicism and so passionately for the activation of the utopian dimension of literature. Jameson's error, however, is to arrogate to the interpretive act alone that potent blend of critique and prescience which, as *Henry IV* attests, the most exacting literature of the past has always possessed, but which will remain inert and ineffectual if the prevalent accounts of that literature go unchallenged.

It is an error which Ernst Bloch, a major influence on Jameson, never made, mistaking as it does the power of the critic for the power of the work. For Bloch,

> Every great work of art, above and beyond its manifest content, is carried out according to the latency of the page to come, or in other words, in the light of a future which has not yet come into being, and indeed of some ultimate resolution as yet unknown.[32]

And what lifts a work 'above and beyond its manifest content' and into the light of the future is the lever of form. As Adorno puts it: 'Perspectives must be fashioned that displace and estrange the world, reveal it to be, with its rifts and crevices, as indigent and distorted as it will appear one day in the messianic light.'[33] It is precisely such distortions that the *Henry IV* plays inflict on their age, which we are invited to see not as it was, but as it one day *will have been* for those no longer walled up in that kind of world. In these works we perceive Elizabethan realities transposed into the history of Henry IV, then filtered through the lens of futurity, which twists the plays out of line with convention and into their proleptic form. Parts *1* and *2* of *Henry IV* afford us nothing less than a preview of the past. They project us forward to a point where we can grasp Shakespeare's version of his times as the eventual past of a still unfolding future.

3

Shakespearean Tragedy: The Subversive Imagination

Questioning the Consensus

Viewed through the eyes of most orthodox and most radical critics of Shakespeare, the vision of his tragedies appears to be profoundly conservative. In the two dominant, complementary manoeuvres, the tragedies are presented either as endorsing the established order of things by vindicating conventional values, or as reconciling us to our intractably flawed human nature, and thus to the necessity of our generic plight, however monstrous and unbearable its cruelty and injustice may be. At their most blinkered, radical historicists treat these texts as insidious tools or dupes of hegemony, ripe for dispassionate exposure.[1] Even Francis Barker, one of new historicism's sternest left-wing critics, concedes that 'it would take massive rewriting to make this kind of tragedy radical',[2] and believes that the best we can do is read between the lines for involuntary flickers of disaffection. But the traditional critical response, with which I will chiefly be concerned in this chapter, has been keener to surrender to the sway of the awesome and ineffable:

> What do we touch in these passages? Sometimes we know that all human pain holds beauty, that no tear falls but it dews some flower we cannot see. Perhaps humour, too, is inwoven in the universal pain, and the enigmatic silence holds not only an unutterable sympathy, but

also the ripples of an impossible laughter whose flight is not for the wing of human understanding.

This is G. Wilson Knight in a relentlessly reprinted account of *King Lear*.[3] The rapturous rhetoric may no longer be quite so fashionable in Shakespeare criticism, but the substance of the passage remains representative of the position from which a depressingly large number of books and essays on the tragedies continue to be written. It is a position which applauds Shakespearean tragedy for confirming that 'human pain' is universal, and therefore permanent and un-avoidable; that the reasons for this pain are beyond human compre-hension; and that the pain is somehow beautiful and necessary in a sense we cannot fathom.

A more sober statement of the same ideas is furnished by H. B. Charlton's likewise much anthologized study, *Shakespearian Tragedy*. The tragic hero's fate, we are told, 'springs irresistibly from the ultimate nature of things'. Shakespeare 'simply reveals his hero's death as the inevitable outcome of primary universal law. That is, indeed, the fundamental note of tragedy.' Moreover, as far as the effect on the audience or reader is concerned,

> intellectual acquiescence is all that is immediately required; one is aroused to feel that the action is inevitable, but reason cannot formu-late the ultimate principles which make it inevitable. The riddle of the universe remains; and mystery is still one of the major threads in the web of human destiny.[4]

Nor is this stance peculiar to critics of Knight's and Charlton's generation. In Michael Long's *The Unnatural Scene*, for example, the author's distinctly modern critical idiom serves to deliver the same basic punchline: 'Shakespearean tragedy sees the delimiting structuration of social and mental life as being *absolutely necessary and yet necessarily reductive*' (Long's emphasis).[5]

The notion that Shakespeare's tragedies depict as fixed and inexor-able the destructive forces to which individuals find themselves subject, and that the wisdom they preach is submission to conditions human beings cannot change, crops up in a wide variety of critical guises. Its most common application turns the tragedies into religious or secular morality plays. The success of this stratagem is borne out year after year in examination scripts at all levels. Shakespeare's tragedies are twisted into timeless spiritual narratives of fall, sacrifice and redemption, or temptation and damnation; or they are pressganged into labouring as secular parables, dramatized cautionary tales, which stress the prudence of obeying, and the folly of flouting, the overt or unspoken rules that secure the way things are.

However sophisticated the phrasing, it is remarkable how much criticism boils down to this reductive, moralistic kind of reading. The myopic banality of such an approach is nowhere more apparent than in its infliction on *Hamlet*. Harry Levin has called *Hamlet* 'the most problematic play ever written by Shakespeare or any other playwright',[6] although critics seem to have had few qualms about recycling the same old solution to the problem decade after decade. Maynard Mack's essay of 1952 winds up with a Hamlet who at last 'accepts the world as it is, the world as a duel, in which, whether we know it or not, evil holds the poisoned rapier and the poisoned chalice waits; and in which, if we win at all, it costs not less than everything'.[7] And, thirty years later, Harold Jenkins concludes the introduction to his Arden edition of *Hamlet* in exactly the same vein:

> Johnson is well known to have said that Shakespeare 'seems to write without any moral purpose'; but this is perhaps a play in which a moral is implicit, both simple and profound. For it commends a man who, after questioning the meaning of creation, comes to accept a design in it beyond our comprehending, and who therefore, after seeking to withdraw from life through an abhorrence of all that is ugly and vicious in it, is finally – though tragically not until death approaches – content to live life as it is, able to acknowledge, in word and deed, 'The readiness is all'.[8]

Hamlet's task is seen here as the restoration of the status quo by exposing and killing Claudius, and thus executing the revenge commanded by the ghost of his father. The tragedy of the situation is construed as Hamlet's possession of moral and psychological flaws, however virtuous their origin, which prevent him from fulfilling his obligation without delay. 'We are forced to make the conclusion', as Willard Farnham puts it, 'that [Hamlet] might have escaped catastrophe if he had had narrower nobility', and had remained uncontaminated by 'a sort of deadly sin of sloth'.[9] If only, Jenkins clearly suggests, Hamlet had been able to perceive earlier the inescapable necessity of accepting one's appointed fate, of resting content with the mysterious way things are, no matter how 'ugly and vicious', the normal course of life might have been re-established and the tragedy need not have occurred.

But this misses the point of Shakespearean tragedy, which is to devise predicaments that cannot be accounted for, let alone resolved, by pinning the responsibility on the protagonist alone. Shakespeare's greatest tragedies compel us to probe beyond moralism, to analyse the attitudes that could trap such an individual in such a predicament in the first place. For the moralistic critic, the tragedy of Hamlet consists in his unfortunate, enigmatic failure to conform to the prescribed codes of behaviour from the start, although he is congratulated on seeing the need for resignation too late rather than never seeing it at all. But what if one proceeds on the opposite assumption? What if Hamlet's tormented reluctance to surrender to the role of revenging prince expresses a legitimate rejection of the whole way of life that festers in the 'prison' (II.ii.243) Denmark has indeed become? In that case the tragedy turns out to be something quite different. It is the tragedy of having to live and die on the 'rotten' (I.iv.90) terms of such a place at all, despite the knowledge that life could and should be otherwise, that human beings are not forever doomed to become the scoundrels, pawns and parasites that this sort of society moulds most of them into. Hamlet's belligerent withdrawal into the dramatic limbo and licensed discourse of his 'antic disposition' (I.v.172) functions, in fact, as a sustained estrangement-effect. It sabotages the revenge-play formula and thereby strikes at the social order whose validity that formula presupposes, and whose axioms it would otherwise smuggle through unchallenged. Only critics for whom compliance with convention is the plainest common sense could find Hamlet's failure to capitulate more promptly a source of endless puzzlement, and make this tragedy 'the most problematic play ever written'. But, once one has grasped that it is truly the time that is out of joint (I.v.188) and not Hamlet, the supposed central problem of the play melts away.

Most of the interpretations canonized in the standard editions and critical casebooks strive to defuse Shakespeare's tragedies. They habitually bleach out the plays' depiction of life as a changing social situation made, and hence transformable, by men and women. Time and again the tragedies' dynamic, concrete account of a particular person's history is obliterated. The plays are forced to testify instead to the underlying uniformity of human experience, which mocks social differences and historical development as delusions. Such criticism drains the tragedies of their power to expose the alterable causes of injustice, violence and despair, and expand our awareness of alternative fates hovering in the wings of what happens.

But if the tragedies are read from the position this study adopts, it becomes impossible to claim that their aim is to reconcile us to the purposeful pain and necessary defeat of the heroic figures they portray. Bradley's classic study discerns in Shakespeare's tragedies reassuring fables, in which virtue finally celebrates a Pyrrhic victory over evil, and 'what remains is a family, a city, a country, exhausted, pale, and feeble, but alive through the principle of good which animates it'.[10] And countless critics take refuge in the belief that Shakespeare 'purges our emotions of pity and fear by making us acquiesce without bitterness in catastrophe'.[11] But I would maintain that precisely the reverse is the case. Shakespeare's tragic vision affords us no therapeutic catharsis, no soothing consolation or compensation for the anguish and death it dramatizes. It furnishes every reason for resisting the complacent conclusion that this is how things were meant to be, that such agonies and devastations must be endured to appease spiritual forces beyond our ken, or because they are rooted for some obscure, enriching reason in the nature of mankind.

The present value of the tragedies stems from their refusal to resolve the contradiction between justified desires and their unjustifiable suppression: the heartbreaking contradiction between what men and women could be, and what time and place condemn them to become, in spite of the superior selves and fuller lives struggling within them for realization. Shakespearean tragedy is organized by its awareness of alternative potential; it demonstrates that what happens in these plays results from a specific constellation of conditions and pressures, and thus that human lives could take quite different paths under other conceivable circumstances. It is the contestable nature of the plight that grinds down the protagonists, regardless of merit or their capacity to live otherwise, that defines the tragic quality of the drama.

Shakespeare's tragedies oblige us to confront without illusions the appalling cost of beliefs that doom people to destroy not only others but themselves, making a cruel farce of their conscious intentions. Shakespeare's great tragic protagonists are indeed 'fools of Time' (Sonnet 124),[12] but in the sense that they are hoodwinked by history. They are overpowered by the prevailing tides of their moment, which sweep them unawares out of their depth, rather than by some metaphysical misfortune or by some flaw, whether culpable, haphazard or innate, in the composition of their characters. Romeo and Juliet, Hamlet, Othello and Desdemona, King Lear, Macbeth, Antony and Cleopatra: all of them resonate in retrospect as figures born before their time, citizens of an anticipated age whose values their suffering discloses, pointing us towards more desirable storylines yet to be scripted by history. Their tragedy is to find themselves stranded back in time, far from that foreshadowed future; marooned in a hostile, alien reality which has already contaminated their hearts and minds, and eventually crushes them completely.

Romeo and Juliet: The Murdering Word

Conventional criticism has mustered all the standard ruses to prevent *Romeo and Juliet* from being read in this way. The lovers' fate is most commonly ascribed to the rigidities of natural or supernatural law. J. W. Draper goes so far as to suggest that they are the literally 'star-cross'd' victims of astral determinism, 'the puppets of the stars and planets and of the days and times of day'.[13] A more typical tack, however, is pursued by John Lawlor, who believes that Romeo and Juliet are conquered by the 'unchanging limits' of life and love, the inflexible imperatives of human existence.[14] As Frank Kermode puts it: 'just as [love] is in its very nature the business of the young, with passions hardly controlled, so is it in its very nature associated with disaster and death'.[15] Norman Rabkin, too, regards the lovers as inherently doomed by 'the self-destructive yearning for annihilation that we recognize as the death-wish'.[16]

Another school of critics spotlights the failure of Friar Lawrence's message to reach Romeo in Mantua and the calamitous timing of events at the tomb. From these facts it concludes that the play's emphasis 'seems to be, rather more than we should like, on chance', and that perhaps 'we understand the play better if we think of it as a tragedy of "bad luck"'.[17] To such critics, as Franklin Dickey observes, the tragedy seems to be deeply flawed, because the catastrophe is 'embarrassingly fortuitous ... the accident of chance to which all human life is subject'.[18] For yet another group, however, there is little doubt that 'the causes of the tragedy lie in the sufferers themselves', whose 'dangerous fault ... is their extreme rashness'.[19] Virgil Whitaker locates the chief authority for this judgement in the Friar, who underscores 'the irrational violence, and therefore the culpability, of the haste with which Romeo acts'.[20] In this kind of account *Romeo and Juliet* depicts the penalty paid by those who demand too much too soon, who refuse to let their desires be bridled by the reasonable rules of their society.

By explaining the torments and suicide of Romeo and Juliet as a perennial tragedy of 'the human condition',[21] as the random result of misfortune, or as the protagonists' just deserts, these critics have obscured the true significance of their love and the play's disclosure of the forces that destroy it. Appeals can, of course, be made to the evidence of the text. The moralistic interpreter can invoke Friar Lawrence's warning that 'these violent delights have violent ends' (II.vi.9). Romeo himself can be subpoenaed to confirm that he is the victim of 'some consequence ... hanging in the stars' (I.iv.107). Nor could anyone dispute that accidental factors play a crucial role in sealing the lovers' final doom. But it is a mistake to equate one character's viewpoint with the perspective formed by the play, or to construct from isolated incidents an explanation of the entire pattern of events. For *Romeo and Juliet* creates a concerted vision more searching than such methods are equipped to discern.

Not that recent feminist and psychoanalytic approaches have proved less problematic. The deep-seated urge to distil from the play an enduring human plight seems determined to survive the transformation of Shakespeare studies ushered in by the advent of theory. In *Tales of Love* Julia Kristeva reads the tragedy as Shakespeare's displaced lament for the death of his son Hamnet, as a chapter in the Bard's psychobiography, which betrays 'the intrinsic presence of hatred in amatory feeling itself'.[22] Irene Dash drops de Beauvoir for Dr Johnson to prop up her view that Juliet's adolescent bind 'has a universality not limited to a particular place' or period.[23] Edward Snow's suggestive essay on the tragedy cannot resist freezing male and female mentalities into primal states of being, purged of circumstance and historicity.[24] Coppélia Kahn detects in the cultural conflict between two styles of manhood 'the all-embracing opposition of Eros and Thanatos',[25] whose rapprochement the lovers' death alone can effect. And Dympna Callaghan offers a bleak critique of the play's supposedly innate 'ideological propensity to posit desire as transhistorical', and thus lock women into 'apparently unchangeable structures of oppression, particularly compulsory heterosexuality and bourgeois marriage'.[26]

What all these interpretations screen off are precisely the qualities that account for *Romeo and Juliet*'s profound hold on the hearts of generations of spectators and readers down through the centuries. The source of the play's abiding power lies in the way it foreshadows a more satisfying kind of love, freed from the coercions that continue to drive men and women apart and prevent their meeting each other's emotional needs. Not the least remarkable feature of the text, moreover, is its revelation that the crippling constraints on the lovers are largely enforced through the language that binds them to a world with which they cannot compromise, and which they would therefore rather relinquish.

Throughout Act I, while he is still fixated on Rosaline and before he has met Juliet, Romeo is trapped inside the hackneyed role and ossified verse of the Petrarchan lover. His rhyming speech is paralysed by the dead weight of clichéd paradoxes and inert metaphors, exiled from actual experience and emotions:

> She is too fair, too wise, wisely too fair,
> To merit bliss by making me despair.
> She hath forsworn to love, and in that vow
> Do I live dead that live to tell it now.
>
> (I.i.221–4)

Romeo speaks more truly than he knows, when he describes himself as 'Shut up in prison, kept without my food,/ Whipt and tormented' (I.ii.55–6). For he is indeed the prisoner of an abject attitude, which turns the woman into a sadistic goddess and the man into a tortured slave, condemning both sexes to a degrading charade of domination and subjection. Even here, however, Romeo seems aware that his true identity exists beyond the confines of his masochistic role: 'I have lost myself, I am not here:/ This is not Romeo, he's some other where' (I.i.197–8).

Mercutio's cynical mockery travesties Romeo's posturing and punctures his inflated speech:

> Romeo! humours! madman! passion! lover!
> Appear thou in the likeness of a sigh!
> Speak but one rhyme, and I am satisfied;
> Cry but 'Ay me!', pronounce but 'love' and 'dove',
> Speak to my gossip Venus one fair word,
> One nickname for her purblind son and heir,
> Young Abraham Cupid, he that shot so trim,
> When King Cophetua lov'd the beggar-maid!
>
> (II.i.7–14)

But it is soon clear that Mercutio's disillusionment offers no valid alternative. On the contrary, he shares with the belligerent servants in the opening scene a reductive, aggressive conception of sex, which is the inverted mirror-image of what he satirizes in Romeo: 'If love be rough with you, be rough with love;/ Prick love for pricking, and you beat love down' (I.iv.27–8). From Mercutio's equally stale standpoint, love means nothing more than male penetrating female in a stark gratification of animal appetite: 'O, Romeo, that she were, O that she were/ An open-arse, thou a pop'rin pear!' (II.i.37–8). Romeo and Mercutio are steered by the same ubiquitous disposition, which denies men and women the option of love unfettered by subjugation.

Juliet's domestic subjection to this mentality is more blatant. The first we hear of her is in Act I, Scene ii, where her father is wondering whether to give her in marriage to Paris: even before she enters, she is defined as an object of male choice and negotiation. The following scene shows Juliet being pressed by her mother to accept Paris's suit and persuade herself to love him. The terms in which Lady Capulet strives to secure her daughter's compliance are revealing:

> Read o'er the volume of young Paris' face,
> And find delight writ there with beauty's pen;
> Examine every married lineament,
> And see how one another lends content;
> And what obscur'd in this fair volume lies
> Find written in the margent of his eyes.
> This precious book of love, this unbound lover,
> To beautify him, only lacks a cover,
> The fish lives in the sea, and 'tis much pride
> For fair without the fair within to hide.
> That book in many's eyes doth share the glory,
> That in gold clasps locks in the golden story;
> (I.iii.81–92)

The elaborate book metaphor points to the correspondence between Juliet's situation and Romeo's. Romeo's Petrarchan bondage to his mistress is matched by the projected binding of Juliet to 'the golden story' of her husband's destiny. The husband is assumed to be the author and the subject of the 'precious book of love', whose 'content' the wife is expected to digest and simply embellish with a glamorous 'cover'. The prospective marriage submits Juliet, like Romeo, to a set text dictated by the sexual conventions of their society, which forbids them to invent their own script, create their own roles or speak lines of their own devising.

Because words are the chains that bind the lovers to the sexual norms and social imperatives of Verona, their struggle for fulfilment expresses itself as a struggle to free themselves from the way Verona has taught them to speak. It is no accident that Romeo and Juliet meet and fall in love (I.v.) while Romeo is masked and before they learn each other's name. For, while they are nameless, they are untrammelled by their given identities, which would prevent their meeting purely as a man and a woman. For a moment the festive licence of the masquerade relieves them of their obligations and inhibitions as Montague and Capulet, waiving the strict codes of courtship that would normally make such a direct and intimate first encounter between any man and woman of their class unthinkable. Before long the outraged Tybalt will identify Romeo's voice, triggering again the mindless machinery of the feud, which drives its lethal wedge between the lovers in Act III. But this privileged interlude allows them to touch and kiss with frank immediacy, and their fragile love unfurls.

Their entire exchange (I.v.93–110), initiated by Romeo, is enclosed in the contrived form and idiom of the love-sonnet, whose artifice still constricts Romeo's emotions and imagination. They complete their first sonnet together with a kiss (I.v.93–106), and at once begin a second (I.v.107–10). But, having played his language-game so far, Juliet sabotages this sonnet in the fourth line, begun by Romeo, turning its second half back against the speaker in playful mockery of his textbook courtship:

Romeo.	Thus from my lips, by thine, my sin is purg'd.
	[*Kissing her.*]
Juliet.	Then have my lips the sin that they have took.
Romeo.	Sin from my lips? O trespass sweetly urg'd!
	Give me my sin again. [*Kissing her again.*]
Juliet.	You kiss by th' book.

Juliet's teasing quip reflects the gap already divorcing undefined feelings from this formal literary discourse, which distorts and stuns those feelings in the act of voicing them. Seconds after their exchange, however, each discovers the name of the other, and instantly, with the pronouncing of the words 'Capulet' and 'Montague', the licence of the moment is cancelled and the tragic conflict between the lovers and their world begins. From now on they are forced, as the Chorus foretells, 'to steal love's sweet bait from fearful hooks' (II.Chorus.8).

The linguistic dimension of the tragedy becomes explicit in the balcony scene of Act II. Believing herself to be alone, and thus relieved of the burden of self-censorship that a public statement would impose, Juliet soliloquizes on the problem at the heart of the play:

> O Romeo, Romeo, wherefore art thou Romeo?
> Deny thy father and refuse thy name;
> Or, if thou wilt not, be but sworn my love,
> And I'll no longer be a Capulet ...
> 'Tis but thy name that is my enemy;
> Thou art thyself, though not a Montague.
> What's Montague? It is nor hand nor foot,
> Nor arm nor face, nor any other part
> Belonging to a man. O, be some other name!
> What's in a name? That which we call a rose
> By any other word would smell as sweet;
> So Romeo would, were he not Romeo call'd,
> Retain that dear perfection which he owes
> Without that title. Romeo, doff thy name,
> And for thy name, which is no part of thee,
> Take all myself.

And Romeo replies:

>   I take thee at thy word.
> Call me but love, and I'll be new baptiz'd;
> Henceforth I never will be Romeo ...
>   ... By a name
> I know not how to tell thee who I am.
> My name, dear saint, is hateful to myself,
> Because it is an enemy to thee;
> Had I it written, I would tear the word.
>   (II.ii.33–6, 38–51, 53–7)

These passages spell out the stifling contradiction between being a man and being a Montague, between a potentially unshackled self and the disabling controls and commitments inscribed in such a family name. The designations 'Capulet' and 'Montague' fix Romeo and Juliet within a patriarchal power-structure, whose demands frustrate their self-sanctioned needs as human beings. 'The tradition of the dead generations,' as Marx memorably observed, 'weighs like a nightmare on the minds of the living.'[27] *Romeo and Juliet* makes plain the extent to which that tradition is felt as the weight of words, the discursive gravity that pins individuals to involuntary lives.

It is not only their names from which the lovers are straining to cut themselves loose. As the balcony scene attests, Romeo's love for Juliet has begun to transmute his language into a mode of expression which is much more direct, personal and sincere. The transmutation is far from sustained, and traces of the old Petrarchan diction, with all that it implies, cling to his phrasing and to Juliet's to the end. A complete break with the accepted idioms of their world is impossible. But they have already leaped far enough beyond them to define the gulf that yawns between their dawning identities and their former selves.[28]

Thus Juliet rejects the impulse to bury the intensity of her desire beneath the decorum of polite public speech: 'Fain would I dwell on form, fain, fain deny/ What I have spoke, but farewell compliment!' (II.ii.88–9). She turns down the part of the devious courtly mistress, with its obligation to be reserved and 'strange' (II.ii.101–2), 'to frown and be perverse, and say thee nay' (II.ii.96). And she forbids Romeo to cast himself in the corresponding role of devoted worshipper at her shrine. When he threatens to slip back into the routine pose of submissive suitor by swearing an elaborate oath to his lady, she cuts him off with 'Do not swear at all' (II.ii.112). To succumb to these stances and the locutions that confirm them would be to linger in a realm of assumptions which Romeo and Juliet have abandoned. 'Love goes toward love,' remarks Romeo, 'as schoolboys from their books' (II.ii.156). The new kind of union developing between them means tossing aside the obsolete texts of the school of love in which they have been educated and finding fresh answers elsewhere.

What they fleetingly discover is a form of love which propels them not only beyond the divisive social formation epitomized by the feud, but also beyond the established sexual order, and thus beyond the scope of the discourse that helps perpetuate that order. The verbal horizon that once circumscribed them cannot contain

what they are now experiencing and their revised sense of themselves. A way of life which had seemed unquestionable is exposed as a
prison-house, whose walls are built of words. For Romeo and Juliet
those walls prove in the end too strong, but their struggle to
demolish them affords the audience a prospect of release, by confirming that what Verona enforces as normal is neither pervasive nor
impregnable.

The innovative character of their love is stressed from the opening
of Act II. Its utopian impact is produced by the fact that it is
founded on reciprocity rather than subservience. As the Chorus
puts it: 'Now Romeo is belov'd and loves again,/ Alike bewitched
by the charm of looks . . . / And she as much in love' (II.Chorus.5–6,
11). Romeo himself employs symmetrically balanced syntax and
diction to express the perfect equivalence of attraction and power
that distinguishes their relationship: 'one hath wounded me/ That's
by me wounded' (II.iii.50–1); 'As mine on hers, so hers is set on
mine' (II.iii.59); 'Her I love now/ Doth grace for grace and love for
love allow;/ The other did not so' (II.iii.85–7).[29] It is, moreover, a
mutually enhancing, limitless love, whose value defies selfish quan-
tification. In Juliet's wonderful words:

> My bounty is as boundless as the sea,
> My love as deep; the more I give to thee,
> The more I have, for both are infinite.
> (II.ii.133–5)

> They are but beggars that can count their worth,
> But my true love is grown to such excess
> I cannot sum up sum of half my wealth.
> (II. vi. 32–4)

Romeo and Juliet's 'true-love passion' (II.ii.104), as Juliet calls it,
goes much further than dramatizing the pernicious effects of the
family feud. That the play vindicates the emergent right to love
whoever one chooses, regardless of arbitrary prohibitions or prejudice, has long been recognized. What has not been appreciated is its
still vital quest to envision beyond that a bond uncontaminated by

the urge to use and dominate, which perverts love into an instrument of pain. Romeo and Juliet's real tragedy is that they are caged in a culture which precludes the survival of such emancipated love. This is 'the true ground of all these piteous woes' (V.iii.179), not some flaw in the fabric of young love, and not some preternatural fiat, whatever the Friar may say or Romeo believe. Moreover, the accidental confusions that result in the double suicide spring from the institutional pressures that split and isolate the lovers, leaving them prey to such chance adversities. The question is not whether their fate might have been averted if only their luck had held, but why they should have been driven to the point where their lives are at the mercy of mere luck at all.

A long stride towards disaster is taken when Mercutio's death compels Romeo to shoulder again the name he had shed for Juliet, re-enter the arena of the family feud and kill Tybalt in revenge (III.i). As a consequence, the lovers must undergo the agonies of separation, inflicted once again by a single word:

> *Juliet.* Some word there was, worser than Tybalt's death,
>   That murd'red me ...
>   'Tybalt is dead, and Romeo banished.'
>   That 'banished', that one word 'banished',
>   Hath slain ten thousand Tybalts ...
>   'Romeo is banished': to speak that word,
>   Is father, mother, Tybalt, Romeo, Juliet,
>   All slain, all dead: 'Romeo is banished'!
>   There is no end, no limit, measure, bound,
>   In that word's death, no words can that woe sound.
>   (III.ii.108–9, 112–14, 122–6)

> *Romeo.* No sudden mean of death, though ne'er so mean,
>   But 'banished' to kill me? 'Banished'?
>   O Friar, the damned use that word in hell;
>   Howling attends it. How hast thou the heart,
>   Being a divine, a ghostly confessor,
>   A sin-absolver, and my friend profess'd,
>   To mangle me with that word 'banished'?
>   (III.iii.45–51)

A word can maim or kill as surely as poison or a bullet. But, even as they reel from this realization, Romeo and Juliet insist on the rift between their secretly evolving selves and the intolerable identities that the language of their world weaves round them:

> *Juliet.*   Hath Romeo slain himself? Say thou but ay,
> And that bare vowel *I* shall poison more
> Than the death-darting eye of cockatrice.
> I am not I, if there be such an ay,
> Or those eyes shut, that makes thee answer ay.
>   (III.ii.45–9)

> *Romeo.*   As if that name,
> Shot from the deadly level of a gun,
> Did murther her, as that name's cursed hand
> Murder'd her kinsman. O, tell me, friar, tell me,
> In what vile part of this anatomy
> Doth my name lodge?
>   (III.iii.102–7)

The tragic sense of being turned into a character in a script beyond one's control suffuses Juliet's poignant line, 'My dismal scene I needs must act alone' (IV.iii.19). It also informs Romeo's compassion for his dead rival, Paris, in whom he perceives a fellow victim of the same remorseless narrative: 'O, give me thy hand,/ One writ with me in sour misfortune's book!' (V.iii.81–2). The final chapter of that text is penned by Capulet's demand that Juliet obey the word of her father and marry the husband he has chosen. The drug plot is a last vain attempt to convert their tale into a truly 'precious book of love'. Its denouement is aptly staged in the Capulet crypt, repository of the dead generations and symbol of the patriarchal family, whose legacy of repression has gripped Romeo and Juliet from the start. In this sense both of them have been all along a 'Poor living corse, clos'd in a dead man's tomb' (V.ii.30), and their self-inflicted deaths transform that virtual entombment into a fearful reality.

Romeo's total dislocation from the matrix of their doom emerges in his bitter words to the impoverished apothecary, from whom he seeks the means of death in the closing act:

> Famine is in thy cheeks,
> Need and oppression starveth in thy eyes,
> Contempt and beggary hangs upon thy back;
> The world is not thy friend, nor the world's law,
> The world affords no law to make thee rich . . .
> There is thy gold, worse poison to men's souls,
> Doing more murther in this loathsome world,
> Than these poor compounds that thou mayest not sell.
> I sell thee poison, thou hast sold me none.
>   (V.i.69–73, 80–3)

Romeo and Juliet lays siege to the legitimacy of a world that deprives men and women of boundless love as surely as it deprives the poor of their share in the world's wealth. The reconciliation of the families and the promise of golden memorials cannot redeem the brute fact that Romeo and Juliet were trapped in their fatal impasse by the injustice of 'the world's law', by the tyranny of its customs and prescriptions. But by sundering the lovers from the discourse that defines them, Shakespeare shows their plight to be man-made and mutable, the local imposition of a transient culture. The crude radical critic indicts the play for colluding in 'the cultural produc- tion of desire required by the rise of absolutism, the centralization of the state, and the advent of capitalism'.[30] But *Romeo and Juliet* in fact foretells the demise of the dispensation that produced it. In the estranged idiom of the lovers can be read the tragedy's estrangement from its era, the imprint of its commerce with futurity.

'That's he that was Othello'

The destruction of Othello and Desdemona lays bare the barbarity of a culture whose preconceptions about race and gender cannot allow a love like theirs to survive and flourish. The modern significance and value of the play are rooted in this revelation. In loving and marry- ing each other, Othello and Desdemona instinctively act according to principles of racial equality and sexual freedom which are far from generally accepted and practised in our own day, let alone in Shake- speare's. As a result they find unleashed on them, through Iago, the fury of a society whose foundations are rocked by the mere fact of their relationship. Like *Romeo and Juliet*, *Othello* has acquired in our time the power to prefigure a kind of loving beyond the corrosive prejudice and entrenched injustice bequeathed us by the world that shaped its words.

The critical consensus blocking the route to such a reading remains, however, formidable. Examples of the standard way of masking or repressing the play's visionary dissidence lie ready to hand in the introductions to two of the most widely studied editions of the tragedy. Alvin Kernan's account in the Signet edition of *Othello* maintains that

> The vision of human nature which the play offers is one of ancient terrors and primal drives – fear of the unknown, pride, greed, lust – underlying smooth, civilized surfaces ... a formal vision of all life that comprehends and reaches back from man and nature through society and history to cosmic powers that operate through all time and space.

Kernan confesses without embarrassment to having 'schematized *Othello*' into 'a morality play, offering an allegorical journey between heaven and hell on a stage filled with purely symbolic figures'.[31] This chimes perfectly with Frank Kermode's introduction in *The Riverside Shakespeare*, where *Othello* is finally abstracted into

> an enactment of the Fall ... a psychomachia, with Iago as the bestial parts of man, and Othello as the higher.... The greatness of *Othello* lies, in the end, there – in the beautiful complexity with which it renders an individual instance of generic Pascalian man, repository of truth, sink of uncertainty and error.[32]

These still staple, widespread views of *Othello* distort the play beyond recognition in their anxiety to dissolve it into a reassuringly eternal tragedy of our global condition. But there is nothing ageless or universal about the tragedy as Shakespeare represents it. Its stubbornly specific causes are all too painfully clear. Despite promising developments in recent alternative readings,[33] it is still necessary to insist that the critic begin from the simple proposition most convincingly advanced by G. M. Matthews: that the tragedy arises first from the fact that Othello is black, and thus racially and culturally an alien – an intensely vulnerable alien – within 'a hierarchical, predatory and therefore not yet fully human society'.[34] One can hardly imagine Desdemona suffering quite the same fate if she had married a suitable white man, more in line with the expectations of her father and her class.

It is worth restating the main points of Matthews's argument. A close reading of the text makes it perverse to resist the evidence that Iago persecutes Othello essentially because he is black, a 'Moor' as he repeatedly refers to him. Into the figure of Iago is condensed all the mindless fear, hostility and malice which, in a more naturalistic play, would be focused on the couple by society at large. Iago's warped response to Othello is not an idiosyncratic aberration (except, perhaps, in its neurotic intensity), but the attitude shared by Brabantio and Venice in general: Othello is contemptuously cartooned by Roderigo, for example, as 'the thicklips' (I.i.66). The pervasiveness of that contempt is solidly established in the opening scenes, when the scandalous news of the couple's elopement is first noised abroad by Iago and Roderigo.

Iago's improvised reasons for loathing Othello carry no weight at all. Their chief role seems to be to veil the true reason from Iago himself. Indeed, it is the transparent inadequacy of his motives that provokes us to search beyond them, to discover the obsessive source of his malignity betraying itself in his language from the beginning of the play. 'Even now,' he cries, as he announces the marriage to Brabantio,

> Even now, now, very now, an old black ram
> Is tupping your white ewe. Arise, arise!
> Awake the snorting citizens with the bell,
> Or else the devil will make a grandsire of you.
> (I.i.88–91)

And again:

> you'll have your daughter cover'd with a Barbary horse, you'll have
> your nephews neigh to you; you'll have coursers for cousins, and

> gennets for germans … your daughter and the Moor are now making
> the beast with two backs.
>
> (I.i.111–13, 115–17)

For Iago, the Moor is not a man at all. He is an animal: a ram, a
horse, an ass. In loving and marrying Desdemona, Othello acts in a
manner which outrageously presumes his human identity with the
ruling-class whites of Venice. He thus triggers in Iago the racist
compulsion to reduce him to a gibbering beast in order to sustain
belief in his own superiority, in order to rebuild the pyramid of
difference that the couple have demolished at a stroke.

The tragedy is not a study of a thinly civilized noble savage, who
reverts under pressure to the primal self that pulses beneath the
surface all along, although this is the view underpinning much
orthodox criticism of the text. Arthur Kirsch, for instance, writing
as recently as 1981, concludes without a blush that Othello is a hero
'because he enacts for us, with beautiful and terrifying nakedness,
the primitive energies that are the substance of our own erotic
lives'.[35] But *Othello* is more uncomfortably engaged in the exposure
of a white barbarian, who tries to turn an infinitely more civilized
black man into his image of the kind of creature a Moor should be.
Not the least disquieting feature of the play is the way it encourages
us, through the villain's downstage intimacy with the audience, to
identify more with the viewpoint and values of Iago than with
Othello. The effect of this should be to compel us to confront our
own collusion in Othello's tragedy, a collusion confirmed by our
involuntary attraction to Iago's self-interested cynicism, and by
our tacit acquiescence in the degrading mentality that finds in
him such a seductive spokesman. The most distinguished critics,
however, continue to walk blindly into this telling trap.[36]

Reading *Othello* in this way, as a socially conditioned tragedy
which is inexplicable without a grasp of racial injustice, is the
point from which any meaningful modern engagement with the
text should set forth. But, once this dimension of the play's significance has been secured, we can set about quarrying the further layers
of meaning unearthed when a complementary feminist concern is
brought to bear on the tragedy.[37]

I wish to consider in particular the extraordinary exchange between Emilia and Desdemona in the final scene of Act IV. Most
critical accounts have failed to register the full ramifications of the
passage – not least, no doubt, because it vexes the critics' most
vulnerable prejudices. With Othello now possessed beyond dissua-
sion by murderous jealousy, on the very threshold of the catastrophe
of Act V, the two women fall to talking about the rights and wrongs
of adultery. The scene closes with this trenchant, impassioned speech
by Emilia on the injustice built into marriage:

> But I do think it is their husband's faults
> If wives do fall. Say that they slack their duties,
> And pour our treasures into foreign laps;
> Or else break out in peevish jealousies,
> Throwing restraint upon us; or say they strike us
> Or scant our former having in despite:
> Why, we have galls; and though we have some grace
> Yet have we some revenge. Let husbands know
> Their wives have sense like them; they see, and smell
> And have their palates both for sweet and sour,
> As husbands have. What is it that they do
> When they change us for others? Is it sport?
> I think it is. And doth affection breed it?
> I think it doth. Is't frailty that thus errs?
> It is so too. And have not we affections,
> Desires for sport, and frailty, as men have?
> Then let them use us well; else let them know,
> The ills we do, their ills instruct us so.
>
> (IV.iii.86–103)

The speech directly echoes Shylock's lines upbraiding his Christian persecutors and warning them that 'The villainy you teach me, I
will execute' (III.i.71–2). It transforms our understanding of the
nature of the tragedy, especially because of the climactic moment at
which the scene takes place – just before Othello, consumed by his
own 'peevish jealousies', executes Desdemona on behalf of his sex for
her supposed adultery: 'Yet she must die, else she'll betray more
men' (V.ii.6). Emilia's speech explains that the real problem lurks

deeper than the fact that Othello's jealousy is groundless and mistaken. To trace the sources of the tragedy no further than that fact, at which most readings prefer to stop short, is to come to rest on the alarming assumption that the killing of Desdemona would have been justified if Othello had been right and his wife *had* been cuckolding her husband with Cassio. This startling passage invites us to recognize that the true sexual tragedy springs from Othello's thraldom to the male version of marital jealousy and the male presumption of dominion and possession of which such jealousy is the outcome.

Emilia's argument leaves us no room to doubt that sexual deceit and vengeful jealousy, whether justified or not, are the predictable products of organized inequality and oppression, and that they cannot be understood, never mind judged, as transgressions attributable solely to the individual in question. The whole scene derails what would otherwise remain the unrivalled male view of events. Its egalitarian female perspective defines and brackets the play as a specifically masculine tragedy: a tragedy produced not only by Iago's prejudiced hatred of the Moor, but by Othello's own allegiance to the prevailing sexual ideology. To put it another way: in so far as Othello is a black outsider, he is the tragic victim of the poisonous racist mentality embodied in Iago; but, in as much as he is a man, acting in unconscious obedience to the norms of patriarchy, he is also the complicit agent of his own derangement and demise.

Othello himself apprehends this in the enigmatic last speech he makes before he commits suicide. Asking that those responsible report truthfully what has happened and why, he concludes:

> Set you down this;
> And say besides, that in Aleppo once,
> Where a malignant and a turban'd Turk
> Beat a Venetian and traduc'd the state,
> I took by th' throat the circumcised dog,
> And smote him – thus.   (V.ii.351–6)

And with that he stabs *himself*. What we have in this passage is nothing less than a compressed definition of the whole tragedy.

Othello portrays himself both as the servant and instrument of the Venetian state and as the Turk, 'the circumcised dog' whom Venice feels threatened by and whom it despises. He correctly perceives himself to have been both the alien victim of Venetian society and the active, though unwitting, accomplice of its destruction of him.

The fully realized effect of these lines is of decisive importance, for they frame and objectify the story of Othello, and thus identify the tragedy as a socially scripted production, in which Othello now sees himself to have been cruelly miscast. A few moments before he kills himself, to Lodovico's question, 'Where is this rash and most unfortunate man?', Othello has replied: 'That's *he* that was Othello; here *I* am' (V.ii.283–4; my italics). The entire tragedy is contained in the gulf that divides those two pronouns. By insisting on the distinction between the self disclosed by the catastrophe and the fatal part he has had to play as the noble Moor and jealous husband 'Othello', Shakespeare drives home the revelation that destinies such as this are neither natural nor inevitable, but the resistible result of living in a world that can be changed.

Macbeth: 'For mine own good'

In the introduction to his Arden edition of *Macbeth*, Kenneth Muir cites and underwrites a selection of critical conclusions, which define the firmly ensconced consensus on the play:

> *Macbeth* is Shakespeare's 'most profound and mature vision of evil'; 'the whole play may be writ down as a wrestling of destruction with creation'; it is 'a statement of evil'; 'it is a picture of a special battle in a universal war, and the battleground is in the souls of Macbeth and his wife' ... the contrast between light and darkness is part of a general antithesis between good and evil, devils and angels, evil and grace, hell and heaven.[38]

With that, the abstraction of *Macbeth* into an allegorical map of mankind's pathway to perdition, tellingly exemplified by the fate of a regicidal usurper, is complete. The unpredictable specificity of the tragedy evaporates under the pressure exerted to flatten it into the familiar archetypal narrative.

Such a reading, however, does not survive a closer textual examination, guided both by historical knowledge of what Shakespeare's drama was prone to perceive, and by the present objectives of radical criticism. When *Macbeth* is re-read at the point where these perspectives coincide, it crystallizes afresh as a fierce arraignment of one of the mainsprings of modern Western society. I mean the ideology and practice of individualism: a way of feeling, thinking and behaving which has become, since its rise to predominance in Shakespeare's time, so finely woven into modern subjectivity as to seem the quintessence of the human animal. Hence the instinctive impulse of conservative critics to displace or efface the main thrust of a work that is primed to imperil the values they are committed to protecting.[39]

The witches notwithstanding, *Macbeth* does not add up in the end to a tale of a man possessed by some nameless, supernatural 'evil', devoured by impenetrable 'powers of darkness'. *Macbeth* is the tragedy of a man driven, despite the resistance of a new kind of self awakening within him, to become a savage individualist, whose defiant creed is: 'For mine own good/ All causes shall give way' (III.iv.134–5). The play affords an unflinching demonstration of the cost of that creed, with whose less eloquent, latter-day slogans ('me first', 'look out for number one', 'every man for himself') most of us are all too familiar.

There is no need to reduce the weird sisters and the whole supporting cast of apparitions to figurative phenomena. Their objective independence of Macbeth's perception does not have to be explained away. Because, however awesome and inconceivable their origins may be, it is they who acquire their point and purpose from their role in the human drama of Macbeth, and not the other way round. Lady Macbeth may well attribute the course of events to 'fate and metaphysical aid' (I.v.29). But what the play actually shows is an experience explicable in the sublunary, man-made terms of this world alone. When the witches first greet Macbeth with his forthcoming titles, he is observed by Banquo to 'start' in evident 'fear' at what should be marvellous news, becoming strangely 'rapt withall'

(I.iii.51, 57). It rapidly becomes apparent that what has thrown him is the open voicing of the 'black and deep desires' (I.iv.51) already brewing secretly in his heart before the encounter. The witches can foresee 'the coming on of time' (I.v.9) and thus offer Macbeth an inkling of 'the future in the instant' (I.v.58). But the veracity of each prophecy is only retrospectively manifest to Macbeth. Before the promised event nothing can be certain, and the uncertainty is only compounded by the increasing 'equivocation of the fiend/ That lies like truth' (V.v.42–3). Whether the prophecies come to pass always depends on Macbeth's deliberate complicity, although their full significance and consequences are cruelly closed to him. The 'imperfect speakers' (I.iii.70) of the heath can predict, but they cannot coerce. Within the historical bounds of his situation, as he is culturally constrained to perceive it, Macbeth's fate is the work of his own mortal hands.

The qualification logged in the last sentence is crucial, however. It points to the way the witches complicate the play's tragic vision by confounding the moralistic view of Macbeth as an inhuman 'hell hound' (V.viii.3), who brings his mental torture and extermination by the rightful ruler upon himself. The 'secret, black, and midnight hags' (IV.i.48), who haunt and taunt Macbeth, give visible form and cryptic expression to his aspirations and anxieties, his wishful delusions and actual options, at the points where personal choice and the unseen laws of necessity are about to intersect. The witches personify the external and internalized pressures that trap the appalled Macbeth in his harrowing dilemma. The handmaidens of Hecat underscore the fact that Macbeth does indeed fashion his own doom, but does so under conditions which he has neither created nor chosen himself, and over whose ultimate ramifications he has no control at all.

The entire action of *Macbeth* is prefaced and punctuated by the apparition of 'the weird women' (III.i.2). Their uncanny interruptions of human reality and conventional discourse clarify the parameters of the tragedy even as they violate and erase them. As Terry Eagleton puts it: 'Androgynous (bearded women), multiple (three-in-one), and "imperfect speakers", the witches strike at the stable social, sexual and linguistic forms which the society of the play needs in order to survive.' As their teasing riddles and deadly nonsense-rhymes make plain, they 'scorn male power and lay bare the hollow sound and fury at its heart. Their words and bodies mock rigorous boundaries and make sport of fixed positions, unhinging received meanings as they dance, dissolve, and re-materialize.'[40] These elusive creatures of between and beyond betray the flimsiness of the cultural fictions by which Macbeth becomes 'cabin'd, cribb'd, confin'd, bound in' (III.iv.23). Their gibing jingles, their tantalizing prophecies, and the spectral dynasty of future kings they summon to torment his eyes, target the violent male fantasies of supremacy fostered in 'Bellona's bridegroom' (I.ii.55) by the cut-throat ethos that surrounds him. The witches isolate Macbeth's thoughts and deeds as symptoms of the life he has learned to lead, thwarting the urge to accept them without questioning their causes.

Sceptical detachment is also stimulated by the jocular intrusion of the porter, which breaks the emotional tension immediately after the murder, when the knocking at the gate begins. This wry plebeian figure's self-portrait as the 'porter of Hell Gate' (II.iii.2), who 'had thought to have let in some of all professions that go the primrose way to th' everlasting bonfire' (II.iii.17–19), switches us into an abruptly contrasting view of Macbeth's plight. It brings the damnable consequences of his master's crime into vivid focus, while keeping a crude, morality-play reading parodically at bay. The riddling, quibbling patter of the 'devil porter' (II.iii.17), for whom 'much drink may be said to be an equivocator with lechery: it makes him and it mars him' (II.iii.31–2), supplies a comic prose paraphrase of Macbeth's self-destructive double-bind. By playing back 'the imperial theme' (I.iii.129) in an irreverent, vulgar key, the passage nails the nightmare engulfing Macbeth as the tragedy of a man of the ruling class, whose experience defies allegorical abstraction.

The witches and the porter prise into relief a tragedy which arises from the struggle in Macbeth between sharply opposed value-systems and versions of masculinity. There is an obvious antagonism between his feudal obligations as a nobleman to his king, 'the Lord's anointed temple' (II.iii.68), whose 'sacrilegious murther' (II.iii.67) will make 'a breach in nature' (II.iii.113), and the ravenous imperatives of 'vaulting ambition' (I.vii.27). The latter find a formidable advocate in Lady Macbeth, whose masculine ideal demands that

Macbeth shoulder aside whatever qualms inhibit him from seizing outright everything he wants: 'When you durst do it, then you were a man' (I.vii.49). But the overt moral conflict of the play is swiftly eclipsed by the more profound battle that flares up within Macbeth: the battle between the rapacious individualism he senses to be futile from the start, and an as yet embryonic form of manhood, which exposes both the feudal and the self-seeking styles of masculinity as tyrants.[41]

Lady Macbeth points us towards the source of this alternative early on, when she voices her justified fear that her husband is not the stuff of which ruthless individualists are made, because he is 'too full o' th' milk of human kindness/ To catch the nearest way' (I.v.17–18). As J. K. Walton points out in an illuminating analysis of the much-quoted key phrase:

> 'Human' (which was usually spelt 'humane', as it is, in fact, in the Folio text) could mean 'belonging or pertaining to a man or mankind' but also 'befitting a man, kindly ... kind, benevolent' – that is to say, it combined the meanings now usually given to 'human' and 'humane'. On the other hand, 'kindness' could mean both 'kinship' and the 'natural affection arising from this' as well as its more limited present day sense of 'kind feeling ... affection, love'.[42]

The phrase 'th' milk of human kindness' suggests a tender, nurturing attention to others, sustained by a sense of shared identity with one's fellow human beings, and by a sense of the obligations attendant on this feeling of community with one's kind. The idea achieves its most potent expression towards the end of Act I, in the electrifying soliloquy in which Macbeth reviews all the arguments against murdering Duncan. It is clear from this speech that he is curbed less by the fact that Duncan is his divinely ordained king than by his fear of the apocalyptic wrath of 'pity, like a naked new-born babe,/ Striding the blast' (I.vii.21–2). This image embodies a moral code which overrides all others, because it is grounded in a recognition that the claims of other humans on one's 'kindness' are as compelling as those imposed by the needs of 'a naked new-born babe', regardless of its gender, race or rank.

Hence Macbeth's immediate dread after killing Duncan is not that he now bears the guilt of regicide, of having betrayed 'the service and the loyalty' that he owed his monarch's 'throne and state' (I.iv.22, 25) as 'his kinsman and his subject' (I.vii.13). He is horrified because he 'hath murther'd sleep' (II.ii.39), which Lady Macbeth calls 'the season of all natures' (III.iv.140), and thus has severed himself from this 'innocent' (II.ii.33) common blessing which linked him to his kind. What tortures Macbeth and his wife above all, though, is their obsession with having shed blood – not the blood of the king as such, but the vital substance that courses through the veins of kings and commoners alike, and that exerts its own moral authority, independent of its owner's status: 'It will have blood, they say; blood will have blood' (III.iv.121). When the sleepwalking Lady Macbeth recalls Duncan, as she frantically strives to wash her hands clean of their crime, his royalty has been erased from her memory as an irrelevance: 'Yet who would have thought the old man to have had so much blood in him?' (V.i.39–40).

The moral vision that circulates through these potent words and images rests on principles utterly alien to those around which feudalism and individualism revolve. At the end of the tragedy the action moves, of course, towards the restoration of the traditional feudal order under Malcolm; but not before that order and that ending have been eclipsed by the values forged in the conflict that tears Macbeth apart. The superiority of these values is secured by the play's demonstration that the individual's true interests and those of the human community are ultimately identical. To destroy another man or woman merely 'for mine own good' is in the end to destroy oneself, or at least any self worth having: 'Thriftless ambition, that will ravin up/ Thine own live's means!' (II.iv.28–9). Macbeth's complete incorporation of this all-consuming principle, and his smothering of that quite different Macbeth acknowledged in the line, 'To know my deed, 'twere best not know myself' (II.ii.70), result in his winding up isolated and hopeless, cornered and cut down like some rabid cur: the hero not of the glorious royal chronicle he might have imagined, but of 'a tale/ Told by an idiot, full of sound and fury,/ Signifying nothing' (V.v.26–8).

Composed at the dawn of our self-centred capitalist culture, *Macbeth* has now become a resonant modern parable, in which that culture's competitive aggression can be seen driving it to a suicidal finale in a blind rush of male violence. This makes it even more important to grasp that Macbeth's fate is dramatized as this man's subjection to these vicious imperatives, rather than as proof of our collective enslavement to some malign, metaphysical statute, which we are powerless to repeal. For by this means *Macbeth* creates a space in which a whole new kind of society begins to be imaginable: a society in which the claims of self and the needs of others are no longer incompatible, and the 'milk of human kindness' flows freely.

King Lear: 'men/ Are as the time is'

Shakespeare's revelation of the chasm that divides how people could live from the lives they are doomed by their time to endure receives its most compelling dramatization in *King Lear*. Given that our world is one that swarms far less forgivably with millions more 'houseless heads and unfed sides' (III.iv.30), that has truly ushered in an age when 'Man's life is cheap as beast's' (II.iv.267) and 'Humanity must perforce prey on itself,/ Like monsters of the deep' (IV.ii.49–50); and granted that we ourselves are the cast of what may yet be a factual tragedy of apocalyptic proportions – 'the promis'd end' for sure and no mere 'image of that horror' (V.iii.264, 265) – the urgent bearing of *King Lear* on our own predicament, and hence the critical priorities which that relevance dictates, should scarcely need spelling out.

Nor would they, were it not for the lingering spell cast by the adepts of obfuscation cited at the start of this chapter, and the dead ends to which, as I have already suggested, more recent accounts of *King Lear* have led us.[43] The *Riverside* introduction to the play enshrines a salutary instance of the sterile historicism that has no idea why *Lear* might be worth studying by people who are living now. The opening gambit contracts the play into an allegorical enactment of Renaissance legal and political theories, which exemplify the doctrine of 'the King's two bodies'. The dense, complex experiences incarnate in the tragedy recede before these schematic abstractions, which misplaced scholarship exhumes and passes off as the real protagonists of the play. Thus Lear 'appears in the opening scene as Justice itself, illustrating ... the two main branches of Justice according to Aristotle: Distributive, as when he portions out his kingdom, and Retributive, as when he punishes Cordelia for her lack of compliance'.[44]

The sclerotic effect of this antiquarian approach is compounded by critics who force the tragedy to fit the formula of pride humbled into charity by a purgatorial trial, which culminates in the sublime reward of spiritual salvation. (Bradley thought the play might more aptly be entitled *The Redemption of King Lear*.[45]) This is the persistent conception of the play promoted, for example, in the Arden edition by Kenneth Muir, who regards Shakespeare's 'religious attitude' in *King Lear* as self-evident. This *Lear* is the story of a man who 'loses the world and gains his soul', and the main Christian message run by the tragedy emerges, with dreary inevitability, as the divine wisdom of passive endurance.[46]

But the illusion that what happens in *King Lear* mirrors some ultimately beneficent, supernatural plan, which 'shows you are above,/ You justicers' (IV.ii.78–9), is expressly invoked by the play itself in order to be shattered time and again by fresh horrors, the last and most excruciating being the gratuitous deaths of Cordelia and her father. At the same time, the opposite idea of *Lear* (popularized by Jan Kott[47]) as an existentialist vision of mankind abandoned in a meaningless universe, as the supreme text in the repertoire of the theatre of cruelty, gets equally short shrift. Gloucester's celebrated absurdist reading of events – 'As flies to wanton boys are we to th' gods,/ They kill us for their sport' (IV.i.36–7) – is ironically framed and deliberately disqualified within the tragedy. It is demolished not only by Edmund's caustic parody of his father's philosophy right at the start (I.ii.118–49), but also by the whole play's confirmation that its calamities stem from the fact 'that men/ Are as the time is' (V.iii.30–1) rather than as nature or the gods direct, whatever the characters may blindly assert to the contrary.

In *King Lear* the assault on traditional structures of domination by a pitiless, voracious individualism – the war staged inside Macbeth's mind – is refracted through the generational conflicts that rip the families of Lear and Gloucester apart. In the course of these conflicts, both the old code based on service and the new self-serving realism undergo a searching dramatic evaluation, which faithfully registers the admirable and appealing as well as the ugly and pernicious qualities of the rival ideologies. The plot is obviously pulled towards a reaffirmation of the feudal ethos by the formal chivalric triumph of 'Legitimate Edgar' over 'the bastard Edmund', who holds 'the plague of custom' in contempt (I.ii.16, 17, 3). But the play ultimately urges us to reject both the waning and the waxing world views it explores, and to adopt instead an implicit perspective, whose purchase on our imagination and moral sense is far more powerful.

Lear's violent dislocation from the society and the ideology that defined him as king makes the growth and discovery of this standpoint possible. The meaning of that dislocation cannot begin to be fathomed by the countless interpretations, including George Orwell's stunningly uninspired reading,[48] which assume that the tragedy consists in Lear's being driven, by the flaws in his temperament, into the pure folly of ditching his sovereignty. To take this line is to block out the entire point of *King Lear*, which subjects an all-powerful monarch to a traumatic experience, whose consequences throw into question kingship as such and the unequal distribution of wealth and power on which it is predicated. The tragedy confounds conventional expectations by obliging us to reach beyond the facts of Lear's personal fate to examine the codes that determine the shape his fate takes. It compels us, once again, to delve deeper than a moralistic critique of the characters allows, to indict the unconscious exactions that deny them the option of being otherwise.

Thus we watch Lear being stripped of his status and power, and hounded to the stark extremities of mental anguish. In his encounter with Poor Tom on the heath, he is disabused of any remaining fantasy that his robes conceal something other than the same 'unaccommodated man' and 'poor, bare, fork'd animal' (III.iv.106–8) that shivers beneath the rags of his most wretched former subjects. The scene enforces the arresting realization that distinctions of rank

('Off, off, you lendings!' (III.iv.108)) have no natural or intrinsic authority at all. Lear's disillusioning 'madness' expels him into a licensed space outside the perceptual enclave contrived by class society. In this space he is soon joined by the blind Gloucester, once he too has learned to 'see ... feelingly' (IV.vi.149). It is the space briefly sprung open in the play's first scene by Cordelia, whose rebellious refusal to express her feelings in the language of her father's world summons the might of the unspoken to reject that world's coercive, quantified definitions of love and relationships: '[*Aside*] What shall Cordelia speak? Love, and be silent' (I.i.62).[49] And it is the space continually inhabited by the classless and timeless figure of the Fool, with whom Cordelia is subliminally identified at the end in Lear's line, 'And my poor fool is hang'd!' (V.iii.306).

Like Gobbo in *The Merchant*, and like Touchstone and Feste in their plays, as we shall see in Chapter 4, the Fool activates our awareness of the momentous issues at stake in *King Lear*. This is most apparent at the close of Act III, Scene ii, at the turning point of the tragedy, as Lear moves off with Kent to the hovel in the storm and the Fool tarries to address the audience directly:

> I'll speak a prophecy ere I go:
>> When priests are more in word than matter;
>> When brewers mar their malt with water;
>> When nobles are their tailors' tutors;
>> No heretics burn'd, but wenches' suitors;
>> Then shall the realm of Albion
>> Come to great confusion.
>> When every case in law is right;
>> No squire in debt, nor no poor knight;
>> When slanders do not live in tongues;
>> Nor cutpurses come not to throngs;
>> When usurers tell their gold i' th' field,
>> And bawds and whores do churches build;
>> Then comes the time, who lives to see't,
>> That going shall be us'd with feet.
> This prophecy Merlin shall make, for I live before
> his time.   [*Exit.*]
>
>   (III.ii.80–95)

In these enigmatic, colloquial couplets, delivered in the ambivalent zone between the illusionistic play world and the reality of the audience, the Fool sardonically shuffles together bitter actualities and millennial possibilities, challenging us to turn our minds to the tragic contradiction between history and utopia that pulses at the heart of *King Lear*. The Fool's teasing prophecy, which is cast – like Gower's narrative links in *Pericles* – in an obsolete idiom, dislocates and complicates our temporal perspective. In a modern production of *Lear*, a late twentieth-century audience is confronted by an enigmatic figure in a Renaissance play about ancient Britain, who enlists mock-Chaucerian verse to deliver a prediction not scheduled to be made until the mythical reign of King Arthur several centuries later. Present, past and future are conflated in a manner which solicits their convergence in our response to the play. The Fool's speech accentuates the wilful anachronism of the tragedy's construction: its employment of every resource at its command to stay out of step with its time, to wrench itself free from the grip of the given.

The 'all licens'd Fool' (I.iv.201) disappears into the text once Lear has made the wise fool's role his own and invested himself with motley. Out on the heath in the storm, Lear learns to feel what 'Poor naked wretches' feel (III.iv.28ff), to identify physically and emotionally with the 'houseless poverty' (III.iv.26) of the dispossessed and discounted, embodied before him in the figure of Poor Tom. In the process, however, he does not break through to some primordial bedrock of human nature, persisting unchanged beneath the surface of history. He stumbles instead into a way of seeing which enables *us* to apprehend the need to rebuild our social life upon beliefs diametrically opposed to those responsible for this tragedy.

King Lear edges us into an understanding which turns the class-divided view of society, then as now, on its head. Lear's moving prayer that the rich and powerful may suffer a change of heart and 'shake the superflux' to the impoverished (III.iv.33–6), and Gloucester's no less compassionate plea that 'distribution should undo excess,/ And each man have enough' (IV.i.66–71), mark decisive movements towards the play's transvaluation of accepted values. But the philanthropic injunctions of both these celebrated speeches are hobbled by their tacit toleration of the existing hierarchical system, whose amelioration is sought in the divine reproof and moral rearmament of those who possess and rule, not in their abolition. The play in its entirety goes much further. The point of breakthrough is reached in Lear's astonishing lines to Gloucester in Act IV, which Edgar's subsequent aside prompts us to hear as 'matter and impertinency mix'd,/ Reason in madness!' (IV.vi.174–5):

Lear.	What, art mad? A man may see how this world goes with no eyes. Look with thine ears; see how yond justice rails upon yond simple thief. Hark in thine ear: change places, and handy-dandy, which is the justice, which is the thief? Thou hast seen a farmer's dog bark at a beggar?
Gloucester.	Ay, sir.
Lear.	And the creature run from the cur? There thou mightst behold the great image of authority: a dog's obey'd in office.

> Thou rascal beadle, hold thy bloody hand!
> Why dost thou lash that whore? Strip thy own back.
> Thou hotly lusts to use her in that kind
> For which thou whip'st her. The usurer hangs
>   the cozener.
> Through tatter'd clothes small vices do appear;
> Robes and furr'd gowns hide all. Plate sin with gold,
> And the strong lance of justice hurtless breaks;
> Arm it in rags, a pigmy's straw does pierce it.
> None does offend, none, I say none. I'll able 'em.

                                                    (IV.vi.150–68)

That last line is charged with the tragedy's knowledge that its causes are housed beyond the conscious culpability of individuals, and should be sought in the iniquitous arrangements that ultimately undo exploiters and exploited alike. Much as many a critic would prefer it to, *King Lear* refuses to halt at what might safely be applauded as a summons to Christian charity. It leaves us no choice but to identify the problem as the indefensible subjection of men and women to the injustices of a stratified society, and to seek the implied solution in the egalitarian standpoint created and vindicated by the play as a whole.

For a diehard traditionalist like Arthur Kirsch, whose book *The Passions of Shakespeare's Tragic Heroes* (1990) is a last-ditch defence of a Bard purged of history, *King Lear* offers consummate proof of 'the timelessness of Shakespeare's genius', which resides in his ability to capture 'enduring truths of our emotional and spiritual lives'.[50] But radical historicists cannot claim to be much nearer the mark, when their efforts to contextualize *King Lear* leave them lamenting 'Shakespeare's inability to imagine any real alternative beyond the disintegrating traditional order and the utterly destructive individualism which emerges from it'.[51] In fact the play prises itself away from both the ideologies at war within its world through a relentless process of internal disruption and inversion. It aligns itself instead – 'handy-dandy' – with the mad, the blind, the beggared, the speechless, the powerless, the worthless: with those who, like Cordelia, are 'most rich being poor,/ Most choice forsaken, and most lov'd despis'd' (I.i.250–1); with all 'Who with best meaning have incurr'd the worst' (V.iii.4) through their heroic failure to be 'as the time is' (V.iii.31), to think, feel and act as history ordains. For figures such as these, the play knows, there can be no place in a regime of whose malevolence they are the living proof, and which must therefore exile or destroy them. For the tragic protagonists of *King Lear*, 'Freedom lives hence' indeed, 'and banishment is here' (I.i.181), in history.

The close of the tragedy addresses the cold fact of their obliteration with implacable honesty, making no soothing sense of it whatsoever. For those who die, and for those who are left alive, there is no consolation, no paradoxical redemption or subtle moral triumph in which to take comfort or find compensation. Broken and bewildered by unremitting pain, Lear ends the play, like his beloved daughter Cordelia, simply and irredeemably 'dead as earth' (V.iii.262). They die in a world where 'All's cheerless, dark, and deadly' (V.iii.291), and where the ring of Albany's reassurance that 'All friends shall taste/ The wages of their virtue, and all foes/ The cup of their deservings' (V.iii.303–5) is pathetically hollow. What survives, if we are ready to read the play this way, is the understanding of why such tragedies happen, and anger at the price still paid in needless suffering to keep society divided.

4

Shakespearean Comedy and Romance: The Utopian Imagination

'let wonder seem familiar'

If Shakespeare's tragedies give us the measure of what it means to sink beneath the burden of history, crushed by 'The weight of this sad time' (*King Lear*, V.iii.324), his comedies and romances create opportunities to explore the way the world might look and feel with the dead weight of prevalence and probability lifted from its shoulders. The tragedies are preoccupied with the destruction of the potential by the actual, of the more desirable forms living might take by the forces currently conspiring to obstruct their realization. But in his Elizabethan romantic comedies, and in the haunting last plays of his Jacobean period, Shakespeare's gaze is levelled at the remote horizon of what could be, rather than absorbed in the immediate tyranny of what is. The primary concern of these plays is to dramatize the surrender of the prevailing to the possible, the triumph of benevolent human desires over the harsh constraints of historical actuality. The wishful projection of this metamorphosis is always qualified, however, by a realistic registration of the fact that humanity remains in thrall so far to the callous sway of the here and now. Reassessed from this point of view, Shakespearean comedy and romance could be argued to be no less powerful and valuable than the tragedies. For they can be seen as pursuing an equally uncompromising assault on the existing terms of life, through their overt education of our imagination in utopian norms and expectations.

Needless to say, this is not how plays such as *As You Like It* or *The Winter's Tale* are regarded in the standard accounts. Consider, for example, C. L. Barber's immensely influential study, *Shakespeare's Festive Comedy*, which we encountered in Chapter 2 in connection with *Henry IV.*[1] The many virtues of this book are ultimately yoked to a reading of the comedies as cathartic parables of orthodoxy preserved. In these plays, Barber contends, the usual order of things is suspended for a licensed period of therapeutic inversion and release, in order to discharge the subversive steam built up by the repression of unruly appetites. Having given vent to these dangerous drives and turbulent desires, society is able to reinstall its normal form all the more securely, once the midsummer madness, the unbridled misrule of Twelfth Night, or the levelling liberty of Arden is over. If Shakespearean comedy exploits the special freedom of carnival to turn the Elizabethan world upside down, it does so only to reinforce the reasons for keeping it the right way up: 'Just as a saturnalian reversal of social roles need not threaten the social structure, but can serve instead to consolidate it, so a temporary, playful reversal of sexual roles can renew the meaning of the normal relation.'[2]

Still dominating the reading-lists alongside Barber is Northrop Frye's study of Shakespearean comedy and romance, *A Natural Perspective*. At first glance, Frye appears to offer a more promising view of these plays as enacting a desirable transformation rather than a purified restoration of the status quo. At the start of them, he suggests at one point, 'the irrational society represents social reality, the obstacles to our desires that we recognize in the world around us, whereas the society of the conclusion is the realizing of what we want but seldom expect to see'. But on closer inspection it becomes evident that the longed-for new society forged at the conclusion is nothing more than 'the old reformed'. For, according to Frye, 'The mythical backbone of all literature is the cycle of nature, which rolls from birth to death and back again to rebirth'; and the structure of comedy and romance 'is based on the second half of the great cycle, moving from death to rebirth, decadence to renewal, winter to spring, darkness to a new dawn'. The 'new reality' in which *Cymbeline* or *Much Ado* culminates is a rejuvenated, idealized instance of a society whose rank-ridden constitution Frye endows with the ever-green authority of natural law. Frye's observation that at the close of these plays 'Kings remain kings, and clowns clowns,'[3] that the structure of society is left unchanged by the comic action, can scarcely be faulted as far as it goes. But it fails to see that what *is* dramatically altered by Shakespearean comedy is our perception of that stratified structure. Far from boosting their power to point us beyond the established order, Frye's 'natural perspective' reduces these plays to a servile means of conserving that order, as surely as Barber's conception of them as 'a civilized equivalent for exorcism'.[4]

Elliot Krieger's *A Marxist Study of Shakespeare's Comedies* proceeds on the same basic assumption as the orthodox critics it might otherwise seem to contest. For Krieger, too, the comedies seek to idealize and stabilize Elizabethan society, but they do so by disguising the hegemony of the aristocracy and blurring the actual class-divisions. This is achieved mainly through the creation of a parallel 'second world' within the plays, such as the forest of Arden in *As You Like It*:

> The clarified image that the second world reveals serves the interests of the ruling class protagonists . . . by creating the illusion that ruling class interests do not exist – more specifically, that the protagonists seek only harmony and concord, universal good. Harmony and concord, however, originate not as universal truths but as aspects of aristocratic needs and fantasies. When seen in terms of aristocratic needs, the abstractions harmony and concord become rephrased and translated into social policy: hierarchy and stability.[5]

In a new-historicist variation on this manoeuvre, Leonard Tennenhouse argues that Shakespeare's comedies exercise 'the power of theatre to create the illusion of a totalizing community out of the contradictory bodies of power':

> The multiple marriages at a comedy's conclusion make it seem as if desire had brought about a politically homogeneous community. At the same time, desire also preserves the sexual hierarchy, for the

subordination of wife to husband invariably invokes that of subject to king.

For all their revelling in inversion and disguising, 'the romantic comedies demonstrate that festival breaks down the hierarchical distinctions organizing Elizabethan society only – in the end – to be taken within the social order where it authorizes a new form of political authority'. The argument transparently recycles Barber's contention that the comedies introduce disorder as a means of fixing the established order more firmly in place. And for Tennenhouse 'the strategy at work in all the romances' is an equally 'perfect collaboration of art and ideology', accomplished this time through the disruption and reunification of the family: 'the unfolding of disorder within the domestic unit operates to reinscribe this unit within a hierarchy governed by the metaphysics of blood'. *Pericles*, *Cymbeline*, *The Winter's Tale* and *The Tempest* are exposed as reactionary fables, whose distinction is 'their use of the family to dramatize the need for a patriarchal figure who can reform corrupt social practices, supervise the exchange of women and insure the proper distribution of power'.[6] In the name of progressive criticism the comedies and romances are consigned to a cynical misconstruction of their past significance, which renders them impotent to assume the militant new meanings they are disposed to deliver to the present.[7]

Too many conventional and radical readings are crippled by their supposition that the imaginative energy of these plays must be invested in perpetuating the current social formation.[8] An excellent point from which to launch a refutation of this tenacious misconception is supplied, somewhat surprisingly, by a passage in H. B. Charlton's *Shakespearian Comedy*, which does much to redeem the same author's ploddingly predictable ideas on Shakespearean tragedy:

> Classical comedy is conservative. It implies a world which has reached stability sufficient for itself. Its members are assumed to be fully aware of the habits and the morals which preserve an already attained state of general well being. The main interest is the exposure of offenders against common practice and against unquestioned propriety in the

established fitness of things. Hence its manner is satire, and its standpoint is public common sense. But Shakespearian comedy is a more venturesome and a more imaginative undertaking. It does not assume that the conditions and the requisites of man's welfare have been certainly established, and are therefore a sanctity only to be safeguarded. It speculates imaginatively on modes, not of preserving a good already reached, but of enlarging and extending the possibilities of this and other kinds of good. Its heroes (or heroines, to give them the dues of their sex) are voyagers in pursuit of a happiness not yet attained, a brave new world wherein man's life may be fuller, his sensations more exquisite and his joys more widespread, more lasting, and so more humane.[9]

This seems to me a fundamentally accurate formulation of the nature and objectives of Shakespearean comedy. These plays are indeed not concerned with 'preserving a good already reached' under existing social conditions. They are committed to envisaging forms of life liberated from whatever forbids the free play and shared satisfaction of justified desires.

Walter Cohen is equally helpful in steering our perception of Shakespeare's last plays in the same direction. As he rightly observes, although tragedy has seemed until now to speak more compellingly than romance to audiences and critics alike,

> this difference has nothing to do with any timeless, intrinsically greater truth content of tragedy. Indeed, Marxism has always wagered that in the long run human history would have, or at least could have, the structure of romance. Precisely in its utopianism, then, romance may offer a legitimate vision not of the prehistory lived in class society, but of that authentic history that may someday succeed it.[10]

The radical possibilities of romance possess another persuasive advocate in Tom Moylan, who defines this form of literature at its most effective as 'a process of wish-fulfilment or utopian fantasy, that aims at *a displacement and transfiguration* of the given historical world in such a way as to revive the conditions of a lost paradise or to anticipate a future kingdom in which suffering and limitations have been effaced'. The utopian romance dislocates and reshapes the present moment of history, and so 'serves to stimulate in its readers a desire for a better life and to motivate that desire toward action by conveying a sense that the world is not fixed once and for all'.[11] Romances invite us to recognize and play experimentally with imaginable alternatives, which strengthen our conviction that a different kind of world could actually be realized.[12]

Both the major romantic comedies and the late romances of Shakespeare are engaged, I would suggest, in the dramatization of just such a vision. These plays exploit the powers of compression conserved in their fairy-tale formula to encapsulate the benign course of collective development that they anticipate. The coded projection of this speculative evolution demands a far higher level of abstraction from social reality than that on which the English or Roman history plays, or even the great tragedies, are obliged to operate. It is worth recalling in this connection Northrop Frye's shrewd observation that 'princes and princesses may be wish-fulfilment dreams as well as social facts'.[13] These plays have no intention of satisfying our appetite for convincing characterization and narrative. So much may be inferred at once from their notorious generic clichés: the groundless, incredible predicaments; the outrageous coincidences; the oversimplified extremes of innocence and malevolence; the abrupt, psychologically unaccountable transfigurations of character and plot; and the shamelessly contrived conclusions, especially those effected by the arbitrary intervention of fairies or gods. Such features signal from the start that literal-minded attempts to square a play like *Twelfth Night* or *Pericles* with the verifiable routines of familiar experience are doomed to founder and should be abandoned as irrelevant. This undisguised surrender of the laws of likelihood to the rule of the miraculous, to eventualities 'monstrous to our human reason' (*The Winter's Tale*, V.i.41), frees Shakespeare's imagination to forsake the plausible logic of past or probable events, and follow instead the implausible logic of the *as yet* improbable wherever it may lead.

That this perspective is more distanced, and thus wider and longer, than that to be found in *Richard II* or *Julius Caesar* or *Macbeth* is often implicit in the titles of the romantic comedies. Whereas the histories and tragedies single out an individual, or pair of individuals, to occupy the foreground of our attention, the comedies tend to announce in their titles a concern with a mode or category of experience, with a condition, process or situation viewed as a matter of common rather than special application. The preoccupation is less with the life of individuals at odds with what surrounds or seizes them, and more with a general pattern of development to whose laws individuals are subject: 'O time, thou must untangle this, not I' (*Twelfth Night*, II.ii.40). The comedies and romances evince little or no interest in plumbing the inward subjectivity of psychologically complex protagonists. Nothing could be more foreign to characters such as Benedick or Imogen than the sustained soliloquizing on the quandaries of selfhood into which Hamlet and Macbeth move in-stinctively. The standpoint of Shakespearean comedy and romance is altogether more external and detached, more fascinated with the destiny of the constellation than with the fate of a single star.

There is a further point to be made about the titles of the major comedies, which draws attention to qualities less blatantly apparent in the romances as well. *A Midsummer Night's Dream*, *Much Ado About Nothing*, *As You Like It*, *Twelfth Night, or What You Will*: these titles alert us to the fact that the plays which they describe occupy a privileged realm beyond the reach of the attitudes that ordinarily programme people's lives. With these comedies, as the title of *Twelfth Night* explicitly declares, we are entering a licensed temporal period, a liminal dream-time, during which we may expect the reverse of what officially passes for normal to prevail. Hierarchies of social and sexual power may be turned upside down or levelled, sexual identities transformed and confused, and all fixed positions and settled assumptions destabilized and laid open to dispute. To qualify this, moreover, as much ado about nothing or a mere fit of midsummer madness, is not simply a defensive ruse. It is also an ironic strategy, playfully employed to tip us off to a general inversion of meanings and values. It announces that what we usually regard as serious may now be treated lightly or irreverently, while matters conventionally discounted as fantasy, folly or insanity can here be taken seriously as vital to the achievement of what we will, of a world shaped as we would like it, where 'Nought shall go ill' (*A Midsummer Night's Dream*, III.ii.462).

The comedies and the romances project, through symbolically condensed dramatic parables, foreshortened accounts of our voyage to the land where 'wishes fall out as they're will'd' (*Pericles*, V.ii.16). They provide us with a means of grasping the future concretely in the guise of the present, of experiencing the possible as if it were already actual. Or, as *A Midsummer Night's Dream* puts it:

> The poet's eye, in a fine frenzy rolling,
> Doth glance from heaven to earth, from earth to heaven;
> And as imagination bodies forth
> The forms of things unknown, the poet's pen
> Turns them to shapes, and gives to aery nothing
> A local habitation and a name.
> Such tricks hath strong imagination
> That if it would but apprehend some joy,
> It comprehends some bringer of that joy;
>
> (V.i.12–20)

The 'strong imagination' of Shakespearean comedy and romance telescopes the process by which the bitter reality of being 'to the world and awkward casualties/ Bound...in servitude' (*Pericles*, V.i.94–5) might be surmounted and converted into cooperative harmony and mutual delight.

The otherwise inconceivable means and tracts of time required to effect this transition – the 'circumstantial branches, which/ Distinction should be rich in' (*Cymbeline*, V.v.383–4) – are imaginatively contracted and accelerated by the plays. They are subjected to a 'fierce abridgment' (*Cymbeline*, V.v.382), which advances the arrival of the utopian resolution summoned by the anguish of the present. In the comedies, the compression is achieved mainly by displacing the action from the customary reality depicted or posited by the play into an exceptional, permissive environment: the unpredictable pastoral world of Arden; the delirious nightwood invisibly ruled by Oberon and Puck; the festive post-war pause for courtship and regeneration in *Much Ado*; or the brief reign of absurdity and bewilderment in Illyria. Prospero's enchanted island serves a similar purpose in *The Tempest*: it speeds up history in order to bring within the compass of the present a premonition of the future's power to grant it absolution.

In *Pericles* the narratorial interventions of Gower achieve the abbreviated convergence of desire and reality by enlisting the audience's collaboration at every stage:

> Thus time we waste, and long leagues make short;
> Sail seas in cockles, have and wish but for't,
> Making, to take our imagination,
> From bourn to bourn, region to region.
>   (IV.iv.1–4)

> The interim, pray you, all confound.
> In feather'd briefness sails are fill'd,
> And wishes fall out as they're will'd.
> At Ephesus the temple see,
> The king and all his company.
> That he can hither come so soon
> Is by your fancies' thankful doom.
>   (V.ii.14–20)

The deliberately naive, archaic doggerel that distinguishes the choric couplets of 'ancient Gower' (I.Chorus.2) distances the brazenly concocted universe of *Pericles* still further. His outmoded idiom sharpens the audience's sense of the contrasting modernity, and hence the historicity, of the world in which they themselves, 'born in these latter times' (I.Chorus.11), watch the play. All these effects are explicitly advertised in the amazing speech by Time in *The Winter's Tale*. As he steps onto the threshold of Act IV to conjure a bridge across the void dividing 'things dying' from 'things new born' (III.iii.114), he accosts the audience directly with this plea:

> I, that please some, try all, both joy and terror
> Of good and bad, that makes and unfolds error,
> Now take upon me, in the name of Time,
> To use my wings. Impute it not a crime
> To me, or my swift passage, that I slide
> O'er sixteen years and leave the growth untried
> Of that wide gap, since it is in my pow'r

To o'erthrow law, and in one self-born hour
To plant and o'erwhelm custom. Let me pass
The same I am, ere ancient'st order was,
Or what is now receiv'd. I witness to
The times that brought them in; so shall I do
To th' freshest things now reigning, and make stale
The glistering of this present, as my tale
Now seems to it. Your patience this allowing,
I turn my glass, and give my scene such growing
As you had slept between.

(IV.i.1–17)

Time's speech lays bare the creative methods at work throughout
the romantic comedies and the last plays. In the first place, it
interrupts the evolution of a hitherto tragic spectacle, putting the
baleful course of events on hold and creating a hiatus designed to
derail and redirect the trajectory of the plot. Secondly, its flaunting
of the play's omnipotent artifice at once detaches and conscripts the
audience: it detaches them in so far as it heightens their sense of the
play *as* a play by objectifying it; and it conscripts them in as much as
it solicits their collusion in the play's contraction of protracted time.
'Imagine me,/ Gentle spectators, that I now may be/ In fair Bohemia'
(IV.i.19–21), the speech continues, insisting on the manipulative
nature of the performance before us, on its status as a theatrical
fabrication of reality. Thirdly, to punctuate the script by inserting
such a bold parenthesis and 'baring the device' is to frame the time
and space within which the characters move. And by framing the
continuum they inhabit, the play projects itself and us beyond it,
quickening the script's consciousness of its obsolescence and
awakening our awareness of the transience of the world in which
we watch it acted. As 'th' argument of Time' (IV.i.29) fast-forwards
us to the virtual reality of the encroaching future, what might have
seemed immutable laws are unmasked as arbitrary inventions, conquered by the calendar, and what might have seemed the human
condition itself is exposed as ephemeral 'custom', the fleeting con-
trivance of a particular culture. As surely as the order of things in
antique times strikes the modern world as obsolete, so 'what is now
receiv'd' as normal and natural, not only by Shakespeare's contem-

poraries and by ourselves, but also by audiences as yet unborn, will one day be surpassed, become forever previous.

These techniques of relativization and estrangement radicalize our perception of the conventional categories with which the plays undeniably operate. Their impact is amplified by the intrinsic polyphony of Shakespeare's drama. *A Midsummer Night's Dream* embraces not only the views and values of the Athenian ruling class (Theseus, Hippolyta, the lovers), but those of the fairies (Oberon, Titania, Puck) and those of the 'Hard-handed men that work in Athens here' (V.i.72) – Bottom, Flute, Snout and the rest of the 'hempen homespuns' (III.i.77); and divergent attitudes to love and life thrive within these groups as well, especially between the sexes. *Twelfth Night* juxtaposes and confuses the romantic 'upstairs' agonizing of Orsino, Olivia and Viola with the intoxicated 'downstairs' misrule of Sir Toby, Feste, Sir Andrew and Maria, and these in turn with the puritanical authoritarianism of Malvolio. And *The Tempest* intertwines the incongruous outlooks expressed or embodied by the world-weary wizard Prospero, the wide-eyed innocent Miranda, the drunken buffoons Stephano and Trinculo, the mercurial, lyrical spirit Ariel and the sullen, vengeful slave Caliban, the 'freckled whelp, hag born' (I.ii.283).

By extending our sympathies, and diverting our attention, across a range of conflicting selves and standpoints, the plays strive to free us from the reductive grip of a single attitude or interest. Their mission is to release all the positions they dramatize into dialogic solution, and thus divest them of the authority each might exercise alone over our conception of the world. The experience of assimilating a plurality of theatrical voices fosters a levelling mode of perception. Shakespeare's multivocal comedy cuts across the lived divisions of class and gender, breaking down the barriers of language and opinion that protract their dominion. This submerged vision sometimes surfaces as an explicit formulation, as when the disguised Imogen replies to Arviragus's question, 'Are we not brothers?':

> So man and man should be,
> But clay and clay differs in dignity,
> Whose dust is both alike.
>
> (*Cymbeline*, IV.ii.3–5)

The same wish is memorably echoed in the Jailer's words towards the end of the same play: 'I would we were all of one mind, and one mind good' (V.iv.203–5). Such quotations afford only the most patent confirmation of the consistent pressure exerted by these plays to transport us to a realm liberated from the dictatorship of divisive ways of seeing.

The relativizing principle is perfectly illustrated by the exchange between Corin and Touchstone in *As You Like It*. 'And how like you this shepherd's life, Master Touchstone?' asks Corin, oblivious to the dialectical whirlwind about to hit him. 'Truly, shepherd,' answers Touchstone,

> in respect of itself, it is a good life; but in respect that it is a shepherd's life, it is naught. In respect that it is solitary, I like it very well; but in respect that it is private, it is a very vile life. Now in respect it is in the fields, it pleaseth me well; but in respect it is not in the court, it is tedious.... Hast any philosophy in thee, shepherd?
>
> (III.ii.11–22)

The phrase 'in respect that' encapsulates the restless dynamic of dramatic polyphony, whose aim is to situate and qualify everything it touches. The passage also exemplifies once more the fool's gift for foregrounding the vision of the play that happens to be housing him. Certainly, the fool as personified by Touchstone and Feste is a curiously amphibious creature, dwelling in a borderland at once within the world of the play and yet outside it, watching with the eyes of the audience. Touchstone and Feste are fettered to no fixed identity, social position, mode of language or point of view. They prefer to slip opportunistically from one provisional attitude to another, inventing themselves afresh in response to each new encounter – be it with Orlando or Audrey, Olivia or Malvolio – in order to deflate whatever mental or emotional pose confronts them at the moment. The value of the fool, as Bakhtin points out while discussing his role in early modern narrative, is that by his very presence in the text 'he makes strange the world of social conventionality'. For the fool is invested with 'the right to be "other" in this world, the right not to make common cause with any single one of the existing categories that life makes available'.[14]

The objective incarnate in the fool is furthered by Shakespeare's exploitation of the convention of male actors impersonating women and the added complications triggered by the themes of disguise and mistaken identity. *Twelfth Night* presupposes a male actor in the role of Viola, who is disguised as a boy and in love with a man (Orsino) while loved by another woman (Olivia), who ends up, by virtue of the identical twins device, 'betroth'd both to a maid and man' (V.i.263). Still more notoriously, *As You Like It* postulates at its most involuted a man playing the part of a woman (Rosalind), who is masquerading as a man (Ganymede), who is in turn pretending to be a woman on whom Orlando can practise his courtship of Rosalind; or 'in class terms, an artisan plays an aristocrat playing a farmer playing an aristocrat'.[15] A similar, if less dizzying, blurring of sexual and social identities takes place in *Cymbeline*, whose original conception entails a male actor playing the role of the princess Imogen, who, in disguising herself as the page Fidele,

> must forget to be a woman; change
> Command into obedience, fear and niceness
> (The handmaids of all women, or more truly
> Woman it pretty self) into a waggish courage,
> Ready in gibes, quick-answer'd, saucy, and
> As quarrelous as the weasel;
>
> (III.iv.154–9)

Such complex cross-dressing activates forms of mimicry and parody that dislocate sexual stereotypes and place them clearly within quotes as cultural constructions. Theatrical transvestism explodes the myth that masculinity and femininity are organic qualities inalienably inscribed in the individual's constitution. The escalating androgynous confusions of Shakespearean comedy suggest that sexual identity is more plural, discontinuous and volatile than the official definitions and approved models can afford to admit; although this is an insight which perhaps came easily to a poet prone to address his young male friend in the *Sonnets* as 'the master mistress of my passion' (Sonnet 20). By means of these theatrical tropes, as Catherine Belsey has shown, Shakespearean comedy 'disrupts the system of differences on which sexual stereotyping depends'. By 'calling in question that set of relations between terms which proposes as inevitable an antithesis between masculine and feminine, men and women',[16] it strikes at the very basis of patriarchy, unfixing the assumptions and categories which legitimate it, and holding out the possibility of sexualities unbridled by these reductive, disabling distinctions.[17]

A parallel point can be made about the guerrilla war Shakespeare wages on conventional uses and ideas of language. The comedies and romances are as intent as the rest of his repertoire on shaking our trust in the stability of familiar words and discourses by severing their correspondence to settled meanings and assured realities. Belsey is again instructive on what is at stake here: 'To fix meaning, to arrest its process and deny its plurality, is in effect to confine what is possible to what *is*. Conversely, to disrupt this fixity is to glimpse alternative possibilities.... New meanings release the possibility of new practices.'[18] The most effective verbal weapons mobilized by Shakespeare to widen the scope of the conceivable are the rapid-fire punning, wilful misprisions and compulsive riddling supremely deployed by those linguistic terrorists Touchstone, Feste and the Fool in *Lear*. They are also wielded to devastating effect by witty female protagonists such as Beatrice and Rosalind, and by naive and knowing clown-figures, ranging from Bottom and Dogberry to Autolycus and the shepherds in *The Winter's Tale* and Stephano and Trinculo in *The Tempest*. The plays' flights of verbal fancy and equivocation expose the unfixable nature of language, and hence the instability of the structures of meaning that perpetuate the conventions of contemporary life. As Feste, Olivia's self-confessed 'corrupter of words' (III.i.36), remarks in *Twelfth Night*, 'A sentence is but a chev'ril glove to a good wit. How quickly the wrong side may be turn'd outward!' 'Nay, that's certain,' replies Viola, 'They that dally nicely with words may quickly make them wanton' (III.i.11–15). The quip neatly captures the promiscuous, ungovernable disposition of both language and sexuality, of meaning and desire alike.

By turning themselves into minefields of quibbles and semantic quicksands, these scripts resist invasion by essentialist notions of language and meaning that plague us still. But that is not their only line of defence against these insidious preconceptions. Equally vital is the way the multiple voices of a play flourish their fabrication from a shifting spectrum of literary and theatrical discourses. *The Winter's Tale*, for example, shuffles together the formal and more idiomatic modes of blank verse and prose in the court scenes, the colloquial prose and naturalistic phrasing of the shepherds and the wily Autolycus, and the distinctive registers and styles of the pastoral lyric, the popular ballad and the masque. Indeed, lest the fact of their play's verbal artifice escape us, the characters themselves have a habit of tilting it towards our attention: 'Nay then God buy you,' exclaims a disgusted Jaques to Orlando, 'and you talk in blank verse' (*As You Like It*, IV.i.31–2); while an exasperated Posthumus upbraids an incredulous Lord with 'You have put me into rhyme' (*Cymbeline*, V.iii.63). Spectator and reader are repeatedly reminded of the linguistic loom on which the illusions and illuminations of the play have been woven. The language of works like *The Winter's Tale* or *Twelfth Night* forbids discursive unity and transparency, which would tend to imply a consistent experience and agreed perception of reality. It insists instead on the diversity of the text's discourses, whose conflicting values disclose the plural, contested character of the real society transfigured by the play.[19]

The verbal self-consciousness of the comedies and romances is reinforced by their penchant for citing their own status as a staged event, as a scripted and performed fiction reflecting, yet not to be conflated with, the realities lived beyond the charmed circumference of the Globe. This feature is most obvious in the mounting of an actual or virtual play, complete with audience, within the play proper, as in the masque of the Muscovites and the disastrous Pageant of the Nine Worthies in *Love's Labour's Lost*. The same comedy contrives a still more complex situation, in which the audience finds itself watching Berowne eavesdropping on the King spying on Longaville, who is covertly observing Dumaine: '"All hid, all hid", an old infant play' (IV.iii.76), as Berowne points out in one of the scene's many staggered asides to the audience. In *A Midsummer Night's Dream* we are treated to the mechanicals' unwittingly hilarious, parodic demolition of the tragic course the main plot might have followed; but that plot itself, including its happy resolution, is framed as a production stage-managed by its internal authors and audience, Oberon and Puck, who leaps through the layers of illusion at the very end to address us directly, as actor to audience, about the performance we have witnessed:

> If we shadows have offended,
> Think but this, and all is mended,
> That you have but slumb'red here
> While these visions did appear.
> And this weak and idle theme,
> No more yielding but a dream.
> Gentles, do not reprehend.
> If you pardon, we will mend.
> (V.i.423–30)

The characters periodically jolt us into consciousness of our relationship with the play through overtly self-mirroring remarks. 'I see the play so lies,' muses Perdita, 'That I must bear a part' (*The Winter's Tale*, IV.iv.655–6). And the same work's closing review of its fantastic events is admitted to be 'Like an old tale still, which will have matter to rehearse, though credit be asleep and not an ear open' (V.ii.63). In *Pericles*, as we have already noted, Gower persistently appeals to the spectators to collude in creating the necessary illusion:

> In your imagination hold
> This stage the ship, upon whose deck
> The seas-toss'd Pericles appears to speak.
> (III.Chorus.58–60)

The most glaring instance occurs, however, in *Twelfth Night* when, after watching a play within a play, into whose leading role Malvolio has unwittingly stepped, Fabian exclaims, 'If this were play'd upon a stage now, I could condemn it as an improbable fiction' (III.iv.127–8).

The effect of these elaborate strategies is not, however, to leave the mind lost in a maze of visual and verbal deception, in which the border between representation and reality has been abolished. They stimulate in the spectator an awareness that both the stage world and the lived world it transposes are provisional versions of experience which invite revision, not inviolable instances or definitive editions of what life is, or might be, like. The audience is obliged to assess the validity of the theatrical representation in the light of the actualities with which it begs comparison; but they must also reappraise the real production in which they have been cast by history in light of the play's fresh account of it. As with all the defamiliarizing devices embedded in Shakespeare's drama, the aim is to historicize the ways of life transformed upon the stage, and so sharpen our sense of their transience and susceptibility to change.

We can now turn to the decisive task of disputing the conservative reading to which the endings of the comedies and romances are tirelessly subjected. In the first place, these plays frankly confess that their resolutions cannot be achieved *within* the normal social framework they present or presuppose. The dire predicament confounding the characters can be surmounted and turned to delight only by removing them from their regular roles and familiar circumstances. The protagonists' problems are solved by releasing events to evolve in a privileged realm or parenthetical state in which the grim imperatives responsible for their plight have been suspended. This can be an imaginary location like Arden or Illyria, or it can be a more diffuse condition, like the phase of aimless exile and disguised wandering that Pericles and Imogen must endure before coming home at last to reunion. Those who would construe the ends of the plays as surrenders to conformity must face the fact that the adequacy of those endings is undermined by the richer definitions of identity and possibility adumbrated in the previous acts. In the wake of this widening of horizons and raising of expectations, the final return to the old regime, as kingdoms, ranks, families and gender roles are restored, exposes the poverty of what custom and habit decree.

But this is not the only reason why a diagnosis of the endings as ideologically enslaved cannot be sustained. The culminating moments of concord, 'When earthly things made even/ Atone together' (*As You Like It*, V.iv.109–10), also bristle with estrangement-effects. These demand that the denouement be grasped as a symbolic fiction, whose mood is subjunctive rather than indicative, and whose satisfactions therefore lie beyond the reach of contemporary society.

Hence the blatantly contrived resolution of *Twelfth Night*, centred on the ritual recognition-scene between the identical twins, Viola and Sebastian: 'One face, one voice, one habit, and two persons' (V.i.216). In the same way, *As You Like It* ruptures any surviving illusions of verisimilitude by introducing Hymen, the god of marriage, who materializes from nowhere to conduct a mass wedding of all the 'country copulatives' (V.iv.556). The romances proclaim their shameless resorts to the incredible no less boldly. The revelations and reunions of *Pericles* are triggered by a dream-vision, in which the hero receives the vital instructions direct from 'celestial Dian' (V.i.250). In a still more spectacular dream-sequence, it takes nothing less than the descent of Jupiter astride an eagle, in answer to the prayers of the ghosts of Posthumus's parents, to set the winding-up of *Cymbeline* in motion. And at the marvellous, moving close of *The Winter's Tale* we find ourselves being gently 'mock'd with art' (V.iii.68), when we are required by Paulina to 'awake [our] faith' (V.iii.95) that a statue of one thought dead might 'be stone no more' (V.iii.99) and breathe again; that the open wound of 'this wide gap of time, since first/ We were dissever'd' (V.iii.154–5) might be healed by a magical 'art/ Lawful as eating' (V.iii.110–11). As Paulina readily concedes:

> That she is living,
> Were it but told you, should be hooted at
> Like an old tale; but it appears she lives,
> Though yet she speak not.
>
> (V.iii.115–18)

That tentative 'appears' highlights the proliferation of circumspect verbs and conjunctions at the climactic moments of recognition and reconciliation. Consider, for example, the phrasing of Rosalind's formal, stylized pledge: 'I'll have no father, if you be not he;/ I'll have no husband, if you be not he' (*As You Like It*, V.iv.122–3). Or take the reservation attached to Hymen's summons to collective wedlock: 'Here's eight that must take hands/ To join in Hymen's bands,/ If truth holds true contents' (*As You Like It*, V.iv.128–30). The same formula inflects Orsino's response to the clarification of identities in *Twelfth Night*: 'If this be so, as yet the glass seems true,/ I shall have share in this most happy wrack' (V.i.265–6). 'If you have told Diana's altar true,' Pericles is informed in the temple, 'This is your wife' (V.iii.17–18). The close of *The Tempest*, too, is shot through with expressions of uncertainty, such as Alonso's 'This must crave/ (And if this be at all) a most strange story' (V.i.116–17), or Gonzalo's 'whether this be,/ Or be not, I'll not swear' (V.i.22–3). The presence and the object of this strategy are brought explicitly into focus by the fool: 'Your If is the only peacemaker; much virtue in If' (*As You Like It*, V.iv.102–3). The profusion of conditional locutions places the close of the play in brackets, suspends it between quotation marks. We are being urged to regard the denouement as a frankly imaginary resolution of conflicts that remain unresolved outside the theatre, and are not even contained by the devices of fiction within the pale of the play.

This implication is deepened in *As You Like It* by the malcontent Jaques's refusal of pleas to join the wedding celebrations, which seek to include everyone in the circle of satisfaction: 'I am for other than for dancing measures' (V.iv.193). A more aggressive note of discord is sounded in *Twelfth Night* by the 'most notoriously abus'd' (V.i.379) Malvolio, who not only cold-shoulders the romantic rejoicing, but taints it with the prospect of embittered retaliation: 'I'll be reveng'd on the whole pack of you' (V.i.378). The most drastic disruption among the earlier comedies occurs, of course, in *Love's Labour's Lost*, where the conventional marital conclusion is frustrated by a chilling announcement of unforeseen death, and postponed until a later date, subject to the men's fulfilment of the women's conditions:

Berowne.	Our wooing doth not end like an old play:
	Jack hath not Gill. These ladies' courtesy
	Might well have made our sport a comedy.
King.	Come, sir, it wants a twelvemonth an' a day,
	And then 'twill end.
Berowne.	That's too long for a play.

(V.ii.874–8)

Uncomfortable insinuations infect the ending of *The Winter's Tale*, too, as when Leontes observes of the supposed statue, 'But yet, Paulina,/ Hermione was not so much wrinkled, nothing/ So aged as this seems' (V.iii.27–9). The unwittingly cruel remark recalls the callous facts of time, loss and physical decay, which the enchantment of the scene strives to hold at bay. A different kind of sceptical unease is prompted at the end of *Cymbeline*. Whether 'The harmony of this peace' (V.v.467) has indeed been attained hangs on a soothsayer's strained reading of Jupiter's cryptic prophecy, which would seem to have been fulfilled by recent events. The echoes of unvoiced incredulity reverberate long after the proclamations of lasting concord and prosperity have died away.[20]

The utopian closure of Shakespearean comedy and romance is qualified by the intrusion of these harsher, unredeemed realities and disquieting intimations which it cannot repress, and which stress the fragile fictionality and incompleteness of its state of concord. By casting their comedic resolutions of the tragedy of history in contemporary terms, these plays reveal the text of the future stored inside the narrative of the present. Obstructive actualities are made to serve as the symbolic guarantee of their own ultimate transformation. Through their infiltration and subversion of conventional plots and conclusions the comedies and romances dramatize the utopian within the historical. They excite our hope that these dreams of release from the coercions of history might one day be realized, by giving us provisional images, lodged in recognizable and thus more persuasive forms, of what such a realization might look and feel like. But our sense of the real world's intransigence is never allowed to dissolve into an escapist delusion of fantasies vicariously fulfilled. On the contrary, as these plays take pains to caution us, the bridges between the lives we tolerate and a truly happy ending of historical struggle in genuine community are still a long way from completion. In the meantime, the precursive imagination of Shakespearean comedy and romance inspires us to dream ahead and 'let wonder seem familiar' (*Much Ado About Nothing*, V.iv.70). It accustoms us to the inconceivable and paves the way for the impossible, granting us a foretaste of the future through its estranged vision of our past.

Playing for Time: *The Comedy of Errors*

One of the most intriguing features of the comedies is the relentless
war they wage on conceptions of time that lock people into the
predictable scripts of their culture. They have no time for the
quantified time of mere succession mocked by the wise fool Touchstone in *As You Like It*, as he mirrors Jaques's myopic gloom in an
exquisite act of parody, which Jaques himself finds irresistible in his
account of their encounter:

> 'Good morrow, fool', quoth I. 'No, sir', quoth he,
> 'Call me not fool till heaven hath sent me fortune.'
> And then he drew a dial from his poke,
> And looking on it, with lack-lustre eye,
> Says very wisely, 'It is ten a'clock.
> Thus we may see,' quoth he, 'how the world wags.
> 'Tis but an hour ago since it was nine,
> And after one hour more 'twill be eleven,
> And so from hour to hour, we ripe and ripe,
> And then from hour to hour, we rot and rot;
> And thereby hangs a tale.'
> (II.vii.18–28)

– the 'tale' being precisely that melancholy narrative of acquiescence
in the inevitable which the fool and the comedic world he rules are
pledged to transfigure.

The next act of the same play furnishes another splendid instance
of Shakespeare's assault on this mortifying temporal teleology:

> *Rosalind.* I pray you, what is't a'clock?
> *Orlando.* You should ask me what time o' day; there's no clock in the
> forest.
> *Rosalind.* Then there is no true lover in the forest, else sighing every
> minute and groaning every hour would detect the lazy foot of
> Time as well as a clock.
> *Orlando.* And why not the swift foot of Time? Had not that been as
> proper?

Rosalind. By no means, sir. Time travels in divers paces with divers
persons. I'll tell you who Time ambles withal, who Time
trots withal, who Time gallops withal, and who he stands
still withal.

(III.ii.299–311)

And Rosalind proceeds, through a vivid sequence of satirical
examples, to do just that, demolishing the spurious objectivity of
the clock by demonstrating the relativity of our perception of time,
the way it gets warped by subjectivity and circumstance. All the
comedies conspire in this plot to release the plurality of time as the
precondition of scripting the different storylines we might live. That
is why Orlando's remark is so pregnant: there is indeed 'no clock in
the forest' of Shakespearean comedy, because the logic of these plays
is committed to liberating us from the tyranny of that temporal
regime. This aspiration is indivisible from making the space to
cultivate difference and setting language loose, but the exact nature
of the connections between time and place and words in these plays
is not immediately apparent and merits closer scrutiny.

The phrase 'there's no clock in the forest' takes us a long way by
itself, for it identifies the privileged space of exile beyond the
jurisdiction of the state with the condition in which conventional
time has been suspended, along with its attendant urgencies and
obligations. Whether they are lingering in some rustic *locus amoenus*
like Arden or banished to the spellbound enclave of Prospero's isle,
whether they are condemned to a life *en voyage* like Pericles or
insulated in the park of the King of Navarre in *Love's Labour's Lost*,
the protagonists of the comedies are intent on *killing time*. These
plays are full of figures whose dislocation from their habitat and
habitual routines has turned them into footloose wanderers like
Imogen in *Cymbeline*; urban strollers – prototypes of Walter Benjamin's *flâneur* – like Antipholus of Syracuse in the mad marketplace
of Ephesus; idlers in the interludes of romance between or after
battles, as in *Troilus* and *Much Ado*; or loafers and languishers like
most of the cast of *Twelfth Night* and *As You Like It*, whose task is to
spend their time filling in, hanging about, kicking their heels and

spinning things out, until the approach of the denouement breaks the spell and lets them off the hook.

One of the deepest pleasures of Shakespearean comedy comes from its disclosure of space and time we never knew we had. Small wonder that Celia concludes Act I of *As You Like It* with the couplet: 'Now go we in content/ To liberty, and not to banishment' (I.iii.137–8). Quibbling, riddling, punning and badinage have a crucial role to play in keeping this breathing space open and holding the thraldom of clock time at bay for both actors and audience. The verb that neatly links such abuse of language to the question of time and place is *to extemporize*. The word means to improvise, to skip the script and wing it, making it up as you go along. And its root Latin meaning is, of course, to speak *out of time*, which connotes talking out of turn, in contempt of sequence and decorum. At its most exuberant, Shakespearean comedy sometimes seems to be simply a pretext for inspired extemporaneous nonsense, a plot devised to furnish points of departure into pointless verbal virtuosity. And so it is, in so far as these impromptu digressions and compulsive pursuits of irrelevance are there to dilate the space of comedy and defer its surrender to the time that ticks outside the theatre. Procrastination is the thief of time indeed, and it is not hard to see why Hamlet's mastery of the art must proceed in the guise and idiom of a fool, a resurrected Yorick, whose antic disposition and manic equivocations allow him to stall the tragedy and postpone the catastrophe.

Shakespeare's obsession with these matters is evident from his very first comedy, *The Comedy of Errors*. In fact, the fundamental impulse of Shakespearean comedy is billed boldly up front in the title of the play: this, like all its successors in one way or another, will be a comedy not only of mistakes and confusions, but also of 'errors' in the word's seminal Latin sense of wandering, straying, transgressing. *The Comedy of Errors* is, of course, literally about straying into taboo territory. Egeon, the father of the Antipholus twins, in the course of his lifelong quest to reunite his sons, crosses the forbidden border of Ephesus and incurs the impending death penalty that triggers the plot and dictates its relentless tempo. The twin who hails like his father from Syracuse is obliged to disguise his provenance from the Ephesians, lest his wealth be confiscated by this hostile nation as the price of his liberty. Having just disembarked in the harbour, he finds himself with time on his hands before he is due to dine and turn in for the night, and he resolves to take an aimless stroll and do a little sightseeing:

> Within this hour it will be dinner-time;
> Till that, I'll view the manners of the town,
> Peruse the traders, gaze upon the buildings,
> And then return and sleep within mine inn,
> For with long travel I am stiff and weary.
>
> (I.ii.11–15)

Unfortunately for Antipholus, this is Shakespearean comedy, where to play the *flâneur* is to play with fire. A few moments later, his reiteration of his touristic intent takes an ominous turn: 'I will go lose myself', he says, 'And wander up and down to view the city' (I.ii.30–1). And losing himself in a more than geographical sense is just what he proceeds to do, as his parting words intimate:

> I to the world am like a drop of water,
> That in the ocean seeks another drop,
> Who, falling there to find his fellow forth,
> (Unseen, inquisitive), confounds himself.
>
> (I.ii.35–8)

Instantly the wrong twin servant Dromio appears, as if summoned by this speech, and the carnival of errors arrives in earnest, bringing a train of cruelty, injustice and treachery in its wake.

'This sympathized one day's error' (V.i.398), as the Abbess terms it at the end, takes place, aptly enough, in the marketplace, the fluid public space of traffic and exchange between the three private houses on its boundary to which the characters resort. In this anarchic arena the 'liberties of sin' (I.ii.102) run riot: identities fuse or dissolve, while secret, adulterous desires and sadistic appetites can be satisfied with the ultimate impunity vouchsafed by comedy, or rather by the confidence of resolution that our contract with comedy entails:

What, was I married to her in my dream?
Or sleep I now and think I hear all this?
What error drives our eyes and ears amiss? . . .
Am I in earth, in heaven, or in hell?
Sleeping or waking, mad or well-advis'd?
Known unto these, and to myself disguis'd?
I'll say as they say, and persever so,
And in this mist at all adventures go.
                        (II.ii.182–4, 212–16)

The swarms of unanswered questions that plague Antipholus of
Syracuse express perfectly the abject bewilderment provoked by his
predicament. But straying off the point and verbal diversions are as
vital to the ends of Shakespearean comedy as physical disorientation
and sanctioned transgression.

It is hard to think of a comedy by Shakespeare more tightly
gripped by clock time than *The Comedy of Errors*. The whole Plautine
intrigue proceeds within the brief stay of execution granted Egeon
by the Duke of Ephesus. The passing and lifting of the sentence
mark the start and close of the play, so that everything that occurs in
between is charged for the audience with a fatal urgency, to which
most of the characters are oblivious. In this play, which observes only
to violate the unities of time and place, every second counts, and we
can hear them being counted at intervals throughout the play as
time runs out and the confusions escalate:

By this I think the dial points at five.
Anon I'm sure, the Duke himself in person
Comes this way to the melancholy vale,
The place of death and sorry execution,
Behind the ditches of the abbey here.
                        (V.i.118–22)

Nor is Egeon's deadline the only one to inflict anxiety on the
persons of the play, which is packed with individuals bound to
appointments by debt or obligation: 'Your worship's wife, my mistress at the Phoenix;/ She that doth fast till you come home to
dinner;/ And prays that you will hie you home to dinner' (I.ii.88–

90); 'You know since Pentecost the sum is due,/ And since I have not much importun'd you...Therefore make present satisfaction,/ Or I'll attach you by this officer' (IV.i.1–2, 5–6). That last quotation shows how inextricably the bonds of time and the bonds of debt are entwined; it is Egeon's inability to discharge on time the fine he owes the Duke for trespassing on Ephesian soil that will determine his death at the appointed hour. *The Comedy of Errors* exposes this conspiracy of time and debt expressly in order to undo it by logical legerdemain and sleight of phrase:

S. Dromio.	No, no, the bell, 'tis time that I were gone:
	It was two ere I left him, and now the clock strikes one.
Adriana.	The hours come back! that did I never hear.
S. Dromio.	O yes, if any hour meet a sergeant, 'a turns back for very fear.
Adriana.	As if Time were in debt! How fondly dost thou reason!
S. Dromio.	Time is a very bankrout and owes more than he's worth to season.
	Nay, he's a thief, too: have you not heard men say,
	That Time comes stealing on by night and day?
	If 'a be in debt and theft, and a sergeant in the way,
	Hath he not reason to turn back an hour in a day?
	(IV.ii.53–62)

Here the sly contention of the witty servant as wise fool turns the tables on clock time, reversing the power relations between us and it. Commodified, calibrated, linear time is the spawn of early modern capitalist society at its most invasive and extortionate, colonizing human consciousness so completely as to redefine the landscape of the mind, transmuting the innermost contours of the self into the mentality demanded by the market, upon whose site the exchanges of *The Comedy of Errors* take place. The normal perception presupposed by the above quotation is that we mortals stand in constant debt to time, paying back the borrowed, finite hours of our existence to our merciless creditor until death comes to cancel the obligation and leave us all square. And, if we do manage to filch a few extra hours for ourselves by postponing and prevaricating, it is usually we who are indicted as the thieves of time. But, in this sublime piece of calculated nonsense, Dromio puts the plot on hold to reverse the roles and turn back the clock, creating the space to move us back to the future by throwing time into reverse.

Even though Dromio has the whole weight of the comedy behind him, he has his work cut out. For this is a world in which time appears to be omnipotent. Compared to women, as Luciana notes, it may well be that 'A man is master of his liberty'; but (she continues) 'Time is *their* master, and when they see time,/ They'll go or come' (II.i.7–9; my italics). So complete and pervasive does that mastery seem, that it penetrates the body to inscribe itself by violence in the flesh:

> The clock hath strucken twelve upon the bell:
> My mistress made it one upon my cheek . . .
> Methinks your maw, like mine, should be your clock,
> And strike you home without a messenger.
>
> (I.ii.45–6, 66–7)

> O! grief hath chang'd me since you saw me last,
> And careful hours with time's deformed hand
> Have written strange defeatures in my face:
>
> (V.i.298–300)

It takes all the ingenuity at comedy's command to undo this damage, but once again Dromio of Syracuse seems up to it in this extemporized exchange with his master:

S. Antipholus.	Well, sir, learn to jest in good time – there's a time for all things.
S. Dromio.	I durst have denied that before you were so choleric.
S. Antipholus.	By what rule, sir?
S. Dromio.	Marry, sir, by a rule as plain as the plain bald pate of Father Time himself.
S. Antipholus.	Let's hear it.
S. Dromio.	There's no time for a man to recover his hair that grows bald by nature.
S. Antipholus.	May he not do it by fine and recovery?

S. Dromio.	Yes, to pay for a fine periwig, and recover the lost hair of another man.
S. Antipholus.	Why is Time such a niggard of hair, being (as it is) so plentiful an excrement?
S. Dromio.	Because it is a blessing that he bestows on beasts, and what he hath scanted men in hair he hath given them in wit.
S. Antipholus.	Why, but there's many a man hath more hair than wit.
S. Dromio.	Not a man of those but he hath the wit to lose his hair.
S. Antipholus.	Why, thou didst conclude hairy men plain dealers, without wit.
S. Dromio.	The plainer dealer, the sooner lost; yet he loseth it in a kind of jollity.
S. Antipholus.	For what reason?
S. Dromio.	For two – and sound ones too.
S. Antipholus.	Nay, not sound, I pray you.
S. Dromio.	Sure ones then.
S. Antipholus.	Nay, not sure, in a thing falsing.
S. Dromio.	Certain ones then.
S. Antipholus.	Name them.
S. Dromio.	The one, to save the money that he spends in tiring; the other, that at dinner they should not drop in his porridge.
S. Antipholus.	You would all this time have prov'd there is no time for all things.
S. Dromio.	Marry, and did, sir: namely, e'en no time to recover hair lost by nature.
S. Antipholus.	But your reason was not substantial, why there is no time to recover.
S. Dromio.	Thus I mend it: Time himself is bald, and therefore, to the world's end, will have bald followers.
S. Antipholus.	I knew 'twould be a bald conclusion. But soft, who wafts us yonder?

(II.ii.65–109)

Dromio's cod logic – or rather, codpiece logic – wastes time wonderfully. In this absurd excursus, nominally devoted to proving that bald Father Time does indeed have us by the short and curlies, because 'there is no time for all things', servant and master swerve off into a double act that romps with reason and frolics with language, as if we had all the time in the world – and in the meantime the plot can go and hang itself, until they are ready to return to it with 'But soft, who wafts us yonder?' There is a nice touch of poetic justice, too, in Dromio's obliging Father Time to suffer the same physical sign of his own depradations that he inflicts on male mortals – with a little help from venereal disease, as the ribald equivocations suggest.

This loopy outbreak of syphilitic sophistry is a classic instance of the kind of frivolous badinage and quibbling innuendo that is the hallmark of Shakespearean comedy, the ridiculous discourse with which it feels most at home, and which Shakespeare will drop the plot for at the drop of a hat every chance he gets. Mining what Thomas Nashe calls the 'extemporall veine'[21] affords an intrinsically exuberant release from narrative consequence, an unbridled interlude in which words rebel against the tyranny of relevance and the clock's grim chronology, playing fast and loose with sound and sense for the sake of it. The pointlessness of such wordplay *is* the point. George Bernard Shaw was driven to distraction by Shakespeare's relentless verbal juggling, and long before him Johnson famously complained in his *Preface to Shakespeare* that the pun was the Bard's 'fatal Cleopatra', because he would cheerfully blow a whole play for the sake of a play on words: 'A quibble is to Shakespeare what luminous vapours are to the traveller; he follows it at all adventures, it is sure to lead him out of his way, and sure to engulf him in the mire.'[22] And few critics since Shaw have had enough patience with the Bard's compulsive bouts of quibbling to pause and ask what their global role might be in the crazy economy of comedy.

Successfully duped by their brazen incongruity, most commentators still slide over the comedies' *obiter dicta* to attend to the main business of the plays, which these narrative *non sequiturs* have wilfully interrupted and postponed. But to neglect these sequences is as misguided as it would be to neglect the frame of a picture, which defines it as a picture and shapes our perception of it; or to reduce the meaning of a complex sentence to its main clause alone, as if the subordinate clauses and parentheses were not as vital to the articulation of its import as every punctuation mark. By their own secret alchemy, these giddy departures from sense and purpose accelerate the metamorphosis on which the comedy is intent. By lifting the weight of necessity from the language, by investing the discourse of the drama with a buoyancy it would otherwise lack, they make the medium dance, however dark and painful the realities it must voice may be. It is due in no small part to the subtle ministries of such absurdities that the miraculous finale somehow seems as exquisitely inevitable as it is incredible. For the impromptu deviations of the comedies are a way of *spacing things out* that transforms theatrical time, transposing actors and audience from one temporal plane to another, from a retrospective to a prospective continuum.

The battles of wit and paroxysms of punning in which not just fools and clowns, but witty lovers like Beatrice and Benedick and Kate and Petruchio indulge, take on a new meaning when viewed from this angle. But there are other implications sparked off by such passages too. It is no accident that lovers slip so spontaneously into this discourse, because there is something innately sexy about it, something that goes deeper than the bawdy wisecracks with which such exchanges are riddled. Much of the delight created by these riffs of rampant banter comes, I have suggested, from the liberating thrust of their irrelevance, and the way that it changes our purchase on time. But there is also an obscure but profound erotic energy released when Shakespeare's language lights out on one of its sprees, an energy most flagrantly manifest in the obligatory epidemic of prurient puns. There is perhaps a clue to what is at issue here in a common synonym for speaking extempore or off the cuff: *ad-libbing*. *Ad lib* is the abbreviation for *ad libitum*, the New Latin phrase meaning *according to one's pleasure*. Talking out of time, out of turn, and the bliss of an unbridled tongue seem to be inseparable in Shakespearean comedy; giving time the slip through the slipperiness of language involves an elemental, if elusive, form of libidinal gratification.

As Stephen Greenblatt reminds us in his suggestive essay 'Fiction and Friction', puritan enemies of the Elizabethan theatre such as Philip Stubbes, author of *The Anatomie of Abuses* (1595), condemned it as 'Venus' Palace', a salacious site of erotic arousal. And Greenblatt surely has a point when he describes 'the erotically charged sparring that is the heart of the lovers' experience' as a euphemism for sexual congress, which invests Shakespearean comedy with 'a powerful sexual commotion, a collective excitation, an imaginative heat that the plots promise will be realized offstage, in the marriage beds toward which they gesture: "We'll begin these rites,/ As we do trust they'll end, in true delights".'[23] That quotation comes, of course, from *As You Like It* (V.iv.197–8), but the quote that really clinches the case for the reciprocity of the linguistic and the libidinal occurs, as has already been noted, in the course of the quip-fest between Viola and Feste that opens Act III of *Twelfth Night, or What You Will*, a play whose double title enshrines the comedies' twin drives to speak *ex tempore* and *ad libitum*, to splice together the temporal licence of carnival and the sovereignty of the pleasure principle:

Viola.   'Save thee, friend, and thy music! Dost thou live by thy tabor?
Clown.   No, sir, I live by the church.
Viola.   Art thou a churchman?
Clown.   No such matter, sir. I do live by the church, for I do live at my house, and my house doth stand by the church.
Viola.   So thou mayst say the king lies by a beggar, if a beggar dwells near him; or the church stands by thy tabor, if thy tabor stand by the church.
Clown.   You have said, sir. To see this age! A sentence is but a chev'ril glove to a good wit – how quickly the wrong side may be turn'd outward!
Viola.   Nay, that's certain. They that dally nicely with words may quickly make them wanton.
Clown.   I would therefore my sister had had no name, sir.
Viola.   Why, man?
Clown.   Why, sir, her name's a word, and to dally with that word might make my sister wanton. But indeed, words are very rascals since bonds disgrac'd them.
Viola.   Thy reason, man?
Clown.   Troth, sir, I can yield you none without words, and words are grown so false, I am loath to prove reason with them.
                                                        (III.i.1–25)

There is no need to labour the way this exchange highlights the affinity of sexual and semantic wantonness, the mutual refusal of eros

and logos to observe propriety in comedy. So let me conclude instead
by drawing attention to another point embedded in this passage, a
point which gets us a little closer to clarifying the connection
between ad-libbed equivocation and our displacement into the utopian dimension in which the resolutions of comedy take place.
Consider the levelling burden of the gags that preoccupy the first
ten lines of this unscheduled dialogue, impudently collapsing the
distinctions that divide sacred from secular, the king from the
beggar. The choice of subjects for wordplay is hardly fortuitous; it
testifies to the subliminal power of language unleashed to unhinge
hegemony, to translate the discourse of domination into the prefigurative rhetoric of consensus. In the same spirit, at the close of *The
Comedy of Errors*, the last words are rightly given to the reunited twin
servants, who have been beaten black and blue by everyone throughout the play, but who articulate in the comedy's final lines the
envisaged collapse of the hierarchy that still divides us:

E. Dromio.	Methinks you are my glass, and not my brother.
	I see by you I am a sweet-fac'd youth.
	Will you walk in to see their gossiping?
S. Dromio.	Not I, sir, you are my elder.
E. Dromio.	That's a question; How shall we try it?
S. Dromio.	We'll draw cuts for the senior, till then, lead thou first.
E. Dromio.	Nay then thus:
	We came into the world like brother and brother;
	And now let's go hand in hand, not one before another.

                                                    (V.i.417–25)

Measure for Measure: Double Trouble

To claim, however, that the same radical utopian vision is embodied
still more powerfully in *Measure for Measure*, that twisted, queasy
comedy in which, as Hazlitt noted, 'our sympathies are repulsed and
defeated in all directions',[24] would appear to be utopian indeed, in
the usual, contemptuous sense of futile and self-deluding.

The most cogent critiques of the play to date contend that *Measure for Measure* is a perfect dramatization of the grim tale told by Foucault's *Discipline and Punish*.[25] Nor is it hard to see why: *Measure for Measure* might have been written in order to vindicate Foucault's analysis of the origins of the carceral society. The play provides a textbook instance of the transition from a culture in which power asserts itself through spectacular, public displays of punitive violence, to one which secures subjection by subtler strategies of surveillance, concession and repressive tolerance. As a result, the play seems to finger itself as a pawn of power and its author as the secret agent of authority – as one of the 'King's Men' indeed, in the more sinister sense that lurks within that designation.

In Shakespeare's drama, according to Leonard Tennenhouse, 'The strategies of theater resembled those of the scaffold, as well as court performance . . . in observing a common logic of figuration that both sustained and testified to the monarch's power.' Thus in *Measure for Measure*, Tennenhouse maintains, the Duke's 'powers of disguise, of substitution, of staging scenes which transfer authority or reveal a crime, characterize the Jacobean theater as surely as they do the monarch's statecraft'.[26] As a figure of the dramatist himself, Duke Vincentio epitomizes the complicity of theatre and throne in deepening the mystique of the monarchy and sealing its supremacy against dissent. The play's plot contrives a situation of corruption, confusion and crisis, which can only be resolved by the omniscient intervention of the patriarchal principle incarnate, who reclaims mastery over the instruments of state by regulating the sexual behaviour of his subjects through marriage. The Duke contrives for his surrogate Angelo a trap which catches him in a treacherous act of lechery, and entangles the principal characters in a deadly web of culpability, from which the Duke's omnipotence alone can free them in a publicly staged spectacle of exposure and remission.

'My business in this state/ Made me a looker-on here in Vienna' (V.i.316–17), explains the man Lucio dubs 'the old fantastical Duke of dark corners' (IV.iii.156–7). The Duke vanishes, only to return in a form which allows him to police those dark corners of his realm unimpeded, and penetrate the hidden reaches of its citizens' hearts and minds. In the person of this invisible voyeur it is difficult not to see a prevision of the modern society in which power imposes itself not through force, but through the tyranny of transparency, by exposing everyone to the impersonal ubiquity of its remorseless gaze:

> *Angelo.* O my dread lord,
> I should be guiltier than my guiltiness,
> To think I can be undiscernible,
> When I perceive your Grace, like pow'r divine,
> Hath look'd upon my passes.
>
> (V.i.366–70)

In *Discipline and Punish*, Foucault finds the architectural epitome of this regime in the panopticon, whose principal objective is 'to induce in the inmate a state of conscious and permanent visibility that assures the automatic functioning of power'.[27] It would plainly be inaccurate to describe the Duke's Vienna as a fully-fledged panopticon, but it seems not unreasonable to suggest that it affords us a remarkable image of the culture of incarceration in embryo, as it evolves within a more primitive, but still potent, society of the spectacle. The Vienna of *Measure for Measure* revolves, after all, around the prison, to which most of the dramatis personae gravitate, blurring the normally blatant boundary between the world within and the world beyond its walls.

Consider also Angelo's eagerness to forfeit his life in retribution for his crime, once he apprehends the Duke's omniscience: 'I crave death more willingly than mercy:/ 'Tis my deserving, and I do entreat it' (V.i.476–7). If that is put together with the Duke's deliberate creation of anxiety in Isabella by withholding his knowledge of her brother's safety, consigning her to prison, and putting her through the pantomime of begging for her would-be rapist's life, it is impossible to deny that *Measure for Measure* has more than a glancing insight into the psychological manipulation that attends the culture of surveillance, turning subjects into willing agents of their own subjection. The problem is that the critics who espouse this angle on the play want to go much further: they want to insist on the culpable collusion of Shakespeare's play in this oppressive process of conditioning. Foucault remarks of the cells of the panopticon that 'They are like so many cages, so many small theatres, in which each actor is alone, perfectly individualized and constantly visible.'[28] Critics have not been slow to take such hints as their cue to arraign the theatre of the Bard, and *Measure for Measure* in particular, as powerful implements for expanding the visibility of contemporary conduct. By making every private nook and cranny of experience conspicuous, so the argument runs, Shakespeare's theatre actively adapts the spectating citizen to the nascent imperative of internalized surveillance. 'These are the measures of *Measure for Measure*,' concludes Jonathan Goldberg, 'the principle of representation that prescribes a single law for the state and the theater.'[29]

In *Will Power*, Richard Wilson sums up the charges levelled against the play by radical historicist criticism. *Measure for Measure* provides, in Wilson's view, 'a conspectus of the Damoclean methods of the disciplinary state' – 'Damoclean' because they work by breeding a constant state of trepidation from the prospect of punishment, from the suspension of penalties that may be exacted at any moment by an obscure authority. Nor is the activation of this state of mind confined to the characters. The sustained tension of the plot is generated for the audience by the impending doom of Claudio and our anxiety that his death be averted. Once it has been averted, the Duke concocts a fresh batch of anxieties (the prospect of Isabella's imprisonment, the death sentences on Angelo and Lucio) to keep us attentive by keeping us apprehensive. 'From the outset,' argues Wilson, 'this play presents a power that has learned the lesson of modernity, that subjection is obtained not by oppression, but by self-repression. The state over which Vincentio presides has long ago begun the experiment of abandoning its public violence in return for private discipline of its citizens, and it knows its legitimacy depends upon its incitement of transgression.'[30] Shakespeare is implicitly indicted for rationalizing the new disciplinary regime, for creating a play whose cultural function is to serve as midwife to a far more insidious form of oppression by making it plausible and admirable:

> *Measure for Measure* is a mirror for magistrates, then, in which Angelo, who begins his rule 'Hoping [to] find good cause to whip them all' (II.i.136), discovers that the quality of mercy is such as to subjugate

more completely than the axe or lash; that, in the words of the commonplace, 'the more power he hath to hurt, the more admirable is his praise, that he will not hurt' (Sidney, *The Countess of Pembroke's Arcadia*, II, 15). So, what the play dramatizes is the wisdom of the cryptic *Sonnet 94*, that 'They that have power to hurt and will do none', are those installed in regality: 'They rightly do inherit heaven's graces.' 'Mercy', Isabella assures the judge, 'will breathe within your lips,/ Like man new made' (II.ii.78–9); but the 'new man' so made is 'the demi-god, Authority' (I.ii.112), as omnipotent as 'Merciful Heaven' (115). Thus we glimpse in the text a strategy of power that will 'make mercy... play the tyrant' (III.ii.188) more effectively than any 'pelting petty officer' (II.ii.113).[31]

The Duke's resort to mercy is exposed, on closer inspection, as not the exemplary virtue of a wise, benevolent ruler, but yet another ruse of tyranny at its most devious. By placing his formidable dramatic skill and rhetorical ingenuity at the service of the Duke's charade of 'apt remission' (V.i.491), Shakespeare duplicates in the theatre, it is alleged, the Duke's duping of his subjects. The Bard blinds his audience to the face of domination behind the mask of mercy by contriving their relieved applause for the Duke's last-minute re-prieves. If there is indeed 'A single law for the state and the theater', as Goldberg contends, when it comes right down to it, there is no telling the Duke from the dramatist.

That, at least, is what the new-historicist and cultural-materialist consensus on *Measure for Measure* would have us believe, and up to a point this account of the play is convincing and illuminating. *Measure for Measure* does portray with extraordinary prescience the emergence of an unprecedented mode of hegemony, which is all the more effective for being obscure and diffuse, and whose latest manifestation in post-industrial Western cultures is arguably so successful as to have become truly impalpable. But to maintain that Shakespeare is the willing or unwitting prop of dominion's dark designs on his audience is to part company with credibility, for such a proposition can be sustained only by screening out the devices Shakespeare employs to demystify the ploys of power and subject them to a lethal critique. That critique is strengthened by the fact that *Measure for Measure* comes clean about its implication in the structures of subjection it depicts, warning us to be wary of art's incriminating compact with power, the devil's deals that even the most unbiddable authors must strike with authority. Even Shakespeare's breeziest, upbeat comedies are also comedies of coercion, which bend the intractable, tragic stuff of history to their festive will. In the figure of the manipulative Duke of Vienna, who inflicts comedic closure on a play which is, as Swinburne protested, 'in its very inmost essence a tragedy',[32] Shakespeare blows the whistle on the violence involved in representation, on the cost of capitulating to convention both in art and in life. *Measure for Measure* has the nerve to put itself and its author in the dock alongside the cast. It *displays* the liability incurred by the act of dramatic duplication, by this theatrical doubling of the real, even as it undoes the authority of what counts as reality in its time.

A less myopic view of *Measure for Measure* than that of the critics I have been quoting is supplied by Walter Pater's inspired essay on the play in *Appreciations*. Pater applauds the play hissed by Coleridge as 'a hateful work, although Shakspearian throughout':[33]

> Out of these insignificant sources Shakespeare's play rises, full of solemn expression, and with a profoundly designed beauty, the new body of a higher, though sometimes remote and difficult poetry, escaping from the imperfect relics of the old story, yet not wholly transformed, and even as it stands but the preparation only, we might think, of a still more imposing design. For once we have in it a real example of that sort of writing which is sometimes described as *suggestive*, and which by the help of certain subtly calculated hints only, brings into distinct shape the reader's own half-developed imaginings. Often the quality is attributed to writing merely vague and unrealised, but in *Measure for Measure*, quite certainly, Shakespeare has directed the attention of sympathetic readers along certain channels of meditation beyond the immediate scope of his work.[34]

What our attention is being directed towards is an intimation of what Pater terms 'poetical justice':

> The action of the play, like the action of life itself for the keener observer, develops in us the conception of this poetical justice, and the

yearning to realise it, the justice of which Angelo knows nothing, because it lies for the most part beyond the limits of any acknowledged law... It is for this finer justice, a justice based on a more delicate appreciation of the true conditions of men and things, a true respect of persons in our estimate of actions, that the people in *Measure for Measure* cry out as they pass before us; and as the poetry of this play is full of the peculiarities of Shakespeare's poetry, so in its ethics it is an epitome of Shakespeare's moral judgments.[35]

Pater never brings to satisfactory definition what he means by this ulterior 'poetical justice', allowing his intuition to evaporate into evocative rhetoric. But he seizes upon something absolutely central to *Measure for Measure* with his idea that the play points towards a moral perspective which cannot be encompassed or enacted, because it lies beyond the purview of the characters, because it is a perspective which only the sympathetic reader or spectator is placed to discern and develop. It is vital, however, that this prospective morality is distinguished from the established morality that it subverts. In this regard, Pater's view of the Bard chimes perfectly with that of Hazlitt, whose reflections on *Measure for Measure* in his *Characters of Shakespear's Plays* lead him to conclude that 'In one sense Shakespear was no moralist at all: in another, he was the greatest of all moralists.' Hazlitt rightly suspects, moreover, although he does not elaborate the point, that *Measure for Measure*'s assault on the moral dispensation of the day is spearheaded by Barnardine, whom he hails as 'a fine antithesis to the morality and the hypocrisy of the other characters of the play'.[36]

Barnardine is indeed the key to *Measure for Measure*, because he marks the boundary of the moral universe by which the denizens of Vienna are circumscribed. By his defiant insistence on dwelling beyond that boundary, he allows us to identify the dilemmas of Vienna as the consequences of its constitution, and, at the same time, he affords us a position uncontaminated by the codes that constrain the rest of the cast. In Barnardine we behold the embodiment of the point to which the play as a whole strives to transport us. For one brief, uncanny moment, a stance that spurns the assumptions upon which the Duke's plan depends becomes incarnate in the

shambling guise of Barnardine, who refuses point blank to comply
with Vincentio's version of the comedy. 'A man that apprehends
death no more dreadfully but as a drunken sleep, careless, reakless,
and fearless of what's past, present, or to come' (IV.ii.142–4), a man
who would not bother to escape even if he were invited to, Barnardine proves immune to punishment and pardon alike, confounding
the Duke's devices by his sublime indifference to his fate. In fact,
Barnardine's impassivity lends him a strange, mesmeric power over his
executioners, who are compelled to dance attendance on his disposition: 'I will not consent to die this day, that's certain. . . . I swear I will
not die today for any man's persuasion' (IV.iii.55–6, 59–60).

Barnardine is the outward sign of the play's inward drive to clear a
space in which a superior conception of justice can secretly flourish. I
say 'secretly', because the play's visionary displacement of the Vien-
nese regime is mainly achieved by subliminal means, by the structural manipulation of perspective and supposition rather than by
overt assertion. This is not to deny that overt assertion plays a crucial
role in complicating our assumptions and uncoupling us from the
imperative of subjection. The first arresting instance occurs when
Escalus seeks clemency for Claudio from Angelo by asking him to
search his own conscience:

> Had time coher'd with place, or place with wishing,
> Or that the resolute acting of your blood
> Could have attain'd th' effect of your own purpose,
> Whether you had not sometime in your life
> Err'd in this point which now you censure him,
> And pull'd the law upon you.
>
> (II.i.11–16)

Angelo is ready for that and meets it with icy objectivity: ''Tis one
thing to be tempted, Escalus,/ Another thing to fall' (II.i.17–18).
But, like the aspersions that Lucio casts on the Duke's moral character,
the argument Escalus initiates will not go away: it sticks like a burr.

Angelo has a much tougher time resisting it when it crops up
again one scene later in the mouth of Isabella, who puts the case far
more forcibly than Escalus:

Isabella.   If he had been as you, and you as he,
              You would have slipp'd like him, but he, like you,
              Would not have been so stern.
Angelo.   Pray you be gone.
Isabella.   I would to heaven I had your potency,
              And you were Isabel! Should it then be thus?
              No; I would tell what 'twere to be a judge,
              And what a prisoner.
                                             (II.ii.64–70)

The thrust of Isabella's speech is that Angelo should imagine himself
in Claudio's place and be merciful, on the grounds that there but for
the grace of God goes he. But the terms in which she puts the point,
and especially her astute reversal of roles and confusion of identities,
make it cut deeper than a mere summons to compassion. Within a
hundred lines, it becomes clear just how deep:

                                   Go to your bosom,
         Knock there, and ask your heart what it doth know
         That's like my brother's fault. If it confess
         A natural guiltiness such as is his,
         Let it not sound a thought upon your tongue
         Against my brother's life.
                                             (II.ii.136–41)

In case we still cannot see where this is heading, Angelo delivers the
irrefutable conclusion that spells it out for us:

                                   O, let her brother live!
         Thieves for their robbery have authority
         When judges steal themselves.
                                             (II.ii.174–6)

This catapults us to the core of the matter. As characters locked
inside their predicament, Isabella's conscious concern is to secure her
brother's reprieve by begging for mercy, while Angelo is intent on
agonizing over his right to judge Claudio for succumbing to the
appetites to which Angelo himself is about to capitulate. But the

arguments of both characters unbolt an inference which ends up undermining the validity of the plot and the rationale of mercy itself. We have already observed the same seditious reasoning at work in two stunning speeches in two other plays, in which Shakespeare turns an equally ruthless gaze on the legitimacy of the law and what masquerades as justice.

The first speech occurs in the trial scene of *The Merchant of Venice*, which was discussed in Chapter 1.[37] Excoriated by the Christians for remaining deaf to their pleas for compassion, Shylock points out that their own Venetian law has upheld his right to cut off a pound of Antonio's flesh. Not only is he committing no crime by insisting on his butcher's bond – as they themselves are compelled to admit – but he is doing no more than the Christians have taught him by their own example:

> You have among you many a purchas'd slave,
> Which like your asses, and your dogs and mules,
> You use in abject and in slavish parts,
> Because you bought them. Shall I say to you,
> 'Let them be free! Marry them to your heirs!
> Why sweat they under burthens? Let their beds
> Be made as soft as yours, and let their palates
> Be season'd with such viands'? You will answer,
> 'The slaves are ours.' So do I answer you:
> The pound of flesh which I demand of him
> Is dearly bought as mine, and I will have it.
> If you deny me, fie upon your law!
>
> (IV.i.90–101)

Here Shylock makes nonsense of the Christians' appeal for clemency by demonstrating that his 'strange apparent cruelty' (IV.i.21) is the unacknowledged mainstay and endemic ethos of Venice, whose routine barbarity is rubber-stamped by its courts.

Even more penetrating are the deranged King Lear's lines to Gloucester, lines which, as we noted in Chapter 3,[38] Edgar hails as 'matter and impertinency mix'd,/ Reason in madness!' (IV.vi. 174–5):

Lear.	What, art mad? A man may see how this world goes with no eyes. Look with thine ears; see how yond justice rails upon yond simple thief. Hark in thine ear: change places, and handy-dandy, which is the justice, which is the thief? Thou hast seen a farmer's dog bark at a beggar?
Gloucester.	Ay, sir.
Lear.	And the creature run from the cur? There thou mightst behold the great image of authority: a dog's obey'd in office.

> Thou rascal beadle, hold thy bloody hand!
> Why dost thou lash that whore? Strip thy own back.
> Thou hotly lusts to use her in that kind
> For which thou whip'st her. The usurer hangs the
>   cozener.
> Through tatter'd clothes small vices do appear;
> Robes and furr'd gowns hide all. Plate sin with gold,
> And the strong lance of justice hurtless breaks;
> Arm it in rags, a pigmy's straw does pierce it.
> None does offend, none, I say none. I'll able 'em.
>
>   (IV.vi.150–68)

This speech, which was probably written within a year or so of *Measure for Measure*, hammers home the point of that last quotation from Angelo, and throws more light on *Measure for Measure* than most modern critics of the play combined. Like Shylock's speech, it demands the understanding that there can be no justice in a constitutionally unjust society, which is programmed to preserve its unequal distribution of status, wealth and power. How can a structurally immoral social order indict anyone for transgressions of which it is the precondition, for the immorality which it does not merely foster but *requires* in order to ratify its authority, to sanction its sway? To Lucio's question, 'Whence comes this restraint?' Claudio replies, 'From too much liberty, my Lucio, liberty' (I.ii.124–5). The exchange neatly captures the reciprocity of licence and legality, virtue and depravity, the spurious moral poles between which the populace of Vienna is doomed to shuttle.

What counts as licit and illicit, however, as Pompey knows full well, is actually the arbitrary construction of a given culture at a given time. It is what those who rule decide to define and enforce until it becomes expedient to change it. 'Is it a lawful trade?' asks Escalus reproachfully of Madam Mitigation's right-hand man. 'If the law would allow it, sir,' retorts Pompey, deftly whipping the magistrate's assumptions from under his feet (II.i.225–7). The law and its administration in a divided world are not the source of the solution but part of the problem – and the same goes for mercy. In *The Merchant of Venice*, Portia's celebrated eulogy of mercy is revealed as the contemptible hypocrisy of those who can afford the luxury of that virtue, because they have the power to bestow it. In *Measure for Measure* likewise, the mercy that Isabella begs Angelo to show Claudio, and the Duke's climactic display of mercy to all those whom he has placed at his mercy, are revealed as the symptoms of the disease for which they are touted as the cure. To put it another way, the author of *Measure for Measure* would have found the opening stanza of Blake's poem 'The Human Abstract' instantly intelligible:

> Pity would be no more
> If we did not make somebody Poor;
> And Mercy no more could be
> If all were as happy as we.[39]

Measure for Measure demystifies mercy, which feeds off the oppressive hierarchy it secretly consolidates – the power-structure that produces the need for mercy in the first place. As a consequence, the critical view that the play endorses the Duke by staging his compassionate finale collapses. But it collapses not only because of the visible pressure exerted upon it by the speeches I have quoted, but also because its foundations are eroded by the implicit perspective that governs the play. The unjust justice and the immoral morality of Vienna depend for their authority and efficacy on hierarchy, on the stratified system of social differences to which they are keyed and which they serve to sustain. But *Measure for Measure* dramatizes the lives of individuals trapped within that system from a viewpoint that unhinges hierarchy, even as it records the crippling consequences of its dominion.

How the play does that is best explained by explaining its obsession with doubles and doubling, its compulsive multiplication of alter egos and substitutes. The Duke appoints Angelo his deputy, addressing him in the opening scene as 'one that can my part in him advertise' and commanding him 'In our remove be thou at full ourself' (I.i.41, 43). We are invited to read Angelo's subsequent career not only as a wilful departure from the Duke's design, but also as a manifestation of the Duke himself, a pursuit by his double of the course Vincentio might have taken, had he not had this stand-in to hand. The Duke is certainly happy to step into Angelo's shoes at the end, to hijack as his bride the woman whom Angelo has plagued in his name and placed within his power. The difference that divides the Duke from Angelo, and both of them from their supposed inferiors, those whom they have the power to consign to the dungeon or the gallows, is also blurred by the parallels between the couples Angelo and Mariana, Claudio and Juliet, Lucio and Kate Keepdown, and even poor Elbow and his wife, who (like her counterparts in this licentious list) 'was respected with him before he married with her' (II.i.170–1), if Pompey at least is to be believed. Substitution and analogy bind everyone in the play to each other, playing havoc with official social and moral distinctions. Escalus stands in for Angelo in the cod trial of Pompey and deputizes for the Duke at the denouement. Mariana takes the place of Isabella in the infamous bed-trick, of which the Duke observes: 'the doubleness of the benefit defends the deceit from reproof' (III.i.257–8). Mariana's maidenhead is exchanged for the unmuffled head of Claudio, which has itself been replaced by the head of Ragozine, which in turn had been swapped for the stubborn bonce of Barnardine. And Pompey Bum swaps his life as a pimp for the hangman's hood without batting an eyelid: all his former clients are now banged up in the slammer after all, making the difference between knocking-shop and nick purely academic.

Duplication and exchange swarm through the body politic of Vienna like a contagious disease, infecting high and low, the virtuous and the vicious alike, and thereby erasing the divisions upon which such discriminations rest. The phrasing of the script gets in on the act, too, tuning us to the play's impartial wavelength at every turn. From its self-mirroring title down to its final lines, *Measure for Measure* is littered with locutions framed to convey symmetry, equivalence, inversion or repetition. The Duke closes the play with a perfect instance of chiasmus, when he promises the astounded Isabella: 'What's mine is yours, and what is yours is mine' (V.i.537). It is a trick of speech that he shares, not surprisingly, with his surrogate: 'When I would pray and think, I think and pray,' says Angelo at II.iv.1. Likewise, the tic of repetition dubbed the 'doublet' in contemporary handbooks of rhetoric is equally at home on the tongue of Elbow: 'Thou art to continue now, thou varlet, thou art to continue' (II.i.191–2); Angelo: 'What's this? what's this?' (II.ii.162); Isabella: 'Seeming, seeming!' (II.iv.150); the Duke: 'Go mend, go mend' (III.ii.27); and the anonymous boy who serenades the melancholy Mariana with his echoing refrain: 'bring again, bring again . . . seal'd in vain, seal'd in vain' (IV.i.5–6).

The play's constant resort to cloning and transposition is equally apparent in the organization of its scenes. At first, the effect of swinging the spotlight back and forth between the rulers and the ruled, of switching our attention from the upholders to the violators of the law, from the corridors of power to the jail and the bordello and back again, is to sharpen our awareness of what sets these social spheres apart. But, as the play proceeds, that awareness gradually gives way to a recognition of what unites them, as the grounds of incongruity dissolve. Which indeed is the wiser (to echo Escalus), Justice or Iniquity (II.i.172)? By compounding the standpoints of the different classes and their distinct moral codes in this way, *Measure for Measure* transfigures the fact of degree and discord into the potential for union and consensus.

'Though you change your place,' Pompey assures Mistress Overdone, 'you need not change your trade' (I.ii.107–8). Or, as the hangman Abhorson prefers to put it: 'Every true man's apparel fits your thief' (IV.ii.43). Style and form collaborate in *Measure for Measure* to expose the fragility of the class distinctions and moral oppositions on which the action is built. By disclosing the repressed identity that mocks imposed disparities, *Measure for Measure* unravels the dispensation that the Duke's plot defends and that radical critics have accused it of endorsing. The persons of the play, the citizens of Vienna, have no option but to take their fictional world as they find it. But the perspective on *Measure for Measure* that the spectator or reader is encouraged to adopt is dramatically different from theirs. Shakespeare does indeed direct our sympathies, as Pater surmised, 'along certain channels of meditation beyond the immediate scope of his work', 'beyond the limits of any acknowledged law', in quest of the 'still more imposing design' of a 'finer justice', the as yet purely 'poetical', as yet merely imaginary, justice for which 'the people in *Measure for Measure* cry out as they pass before us'. Even as it seems to surrender to the ideology of subjection, and frankly admits its connivance in the comedy of coercion, *Measure for Measure* forges for us, from this bleak narrative of constraint, the prospect of an undivided community, on whose basis alone the true justice for which our world still hungers might one day prove attainable.

The Tempest: The Complicities of Art

The Tempest is remarkable for the tenacity and complexity with which it probes the darker implications of making the improbable plausible, of dramatizing the eventual as a dimension of the given. In his last masterpiece, Shakespeare stretches the powers of romance to breaking point, broaching a searching process of reflection on the aspirations and the limits of his dramatic art.

As one might expect, the available criticism on *The Tempest* proves largely unhelpful in guiding us towards a satisfactory account of the play. 'Historically,' as Stephen Orgel points out, 'there has been a consistent tendency to ignore its ambivalences, sweeten and sentimentalise it, render it altogether neater and more comfortable than the text that has come down to us.'[40] Thus Frank Kermode contends that in *The Tempest* 'Shakespeare offers an exposition of the themes of Fall and Redemption by means of analogous narrative.'[41] This allegorizing, idealist approach to *The Tempest* derives, unsurprisingly, from Wilson Knight's reading in *The Crown of Life*, which maintains that 'A reader sensitive to poetic atmosphere must necessarily feel the awakening light of some religious or metaphysical truth symbolized in the plot and attendant machinery.'[42] The continuing prevalence of this view of the play is reflected in the principal British casebook on *The Tempest*, where both the Arden introduction and Wilson Knight's account are still firmly ensconced, several decades after their first publication, as exemplary interpretations.[43]

It is a welcome contrast, therefore, to witness recent radical criticism sweeping this approach aside with illuminating reassessments of *The Tempest* as a play which cannot suppress 'a fundamental disquiet concerning its own functions within the projects of colonialist discourse',[44] and which can thus be repunctuated so that it may 'speak something of the ideological contradictions of its political unconscious'.[45] But the problem with this contribution to our grasp of the play's modern significance is that it excludes the utopian possibilities of *The Tempest* as completely as do the mystifications perpetrated by the work's conservative critics.[46]

The grounds for construing the play as a radical romance are established in the opening storm scene. They crystallize in the exchange between the boatswain, labouring desperately with his crew to save the ship and the lives of everyone it holds, and their noble passengers, who are good for nothing but impeding the sailors' work with pointless questions and reproofs:

> *Gonzalo.* Nay, good, be patient.
> *Boatswain.* When the sea is. Hence! What cares these roarers for the name of king? To cabin! silence! trouble us not.
> *Gonzalo.* Good, yet remember whom thou hast aboard.
> *Boatswain.* None that I more love than myself. You are a councillor; if you can command these elements to silence, and work the peace of the present, we will not hand a rope more. Use your authority.
>
> (I.i.15–22)

The raging elements display a scandalous indifference to 'the name of king' and the 'authority' of his lords. The boatswain's riposte betrays in this moment of crisis the secret that everyone knows: the system that segregates people into masters and servants, and normally keeps the latter in subjection to the former, is a transparent charade, which has no natural foundation or inherent validity. The prospect of the imminent demise of rulers and ruled incites an assertion of equality confirmed by their common mortality, which makes nonsense of rank and the distribution of power and prestige that attends it. The opening scene questions the basis of the roles and relationships of everyone in *The Tempest* from the levelling standpoint of the play's utopian logic.

Looked at from this standpoint, the plot may be summarized thus: Prospero abducts three treacherous voyagers from the heartland of contemporary history in order to bring them to trial at the court of their victim; there he forgoes the exaction of an eye for an eye, treating his prisoners instead to a humane, enlightened judgement, authorized by the island's freedom from the culture that bred the original crime. The confrontation of the all-powerful Prospero with his enemies from the past brings the Machiavellian facts of corruption, duplicity and violence face to face with the means of their transfiguration. Prospero personifies the force required to translate such sordid, demeaning realities into a world stirred by other objectives: the renouncing of dominion and aggression in favour of empathy and concession in a civilized community of peace and plenty.

These priorities become increasingly overt as the play proceeds. They plainly govern the love that binds together Miranda and Ferdinand, the children of the two hostile fathers, and lights the way to a future free not only of the guilt and anger that have scarred the older generation, but also from all deprivation and distress. The play's ideals are expansively celebrated in the masque of the spirits, who bless the 'contract of true love' (IV.i.4) with 'a most majestic vision' (IV.i.118) of joyful, unending plenitude:

> *Ceres.* Earth's increase, foison plenty,
> Barns and garners never empty;
> Vines with clust'ring bunches growing,
> Plants with goodly burthen bowing;
> Spring come to you at the farthest
> In the very end of harvest!
> Scarcity and want shall shun you,
> Ceres' blessing so is on you.
>
> (IV.i.110–17)

The climax of this version of the plot is reached when, with his foes of old at his mercy at last, Prospero swallows his urge to retaliate, founding his preference for compassion and appeasement on his ultimate identity with these 'three men of sin . . .'mongst men/ Being most unfit to live' (III.iii.53, 57–8):

Ariel.	. . . Your charm so strongly works 'em
	That if you now beheld them, your affections
	Would become tender.
Prospero.	Dost thou think so, spirit?
Ariel.	Mine would, sir, were I human.
Prospero.	And mine shall.
	Hast thou, which art but air, a touch, a feeling,
	Of their afflictions, and shall not myself,
	One of their kind, that relish all as sharply
	Passion as they, be kindlier mov'd than thou art?
	Though with their high wrongs I am strook
	to th' quick,
	Yet, with my nobler reason, 'gainst my fury
	Do I take part. The rarer action is
	In virtue than in vengeance. They being penitent,
	The sole drift of my purpose doth extend
	Not a frown further.

(V.i.17–30)

Thereupon he commands the release of, and absolves, not only Alonso, Antonio and Sebastian, but also 'the beast Caliban and his confederates' (IV.i.140), despite their 'foul conspiracy' (IV.i.139) to assassinate him and take over the island. Having given Ariel his last orders before he too becomes free, it only remains for Prospero to keep his promise to renounce the sorcerer's arts ('this rough magic/ I here abjure' (V.i.50–1)), and quit his enchanted empire to return to his home in history, there to end his days in the dukedom now restored to him. The play's fulfilment of its aims as a dramatic fable, in which the art of the possible triumphs over the intransigence of the actual, causing it to undergo 'a sea change/ Into something rich and strange' (I.ii.401–2), is summed up and sealed by Gonzalo:

Was Milan thrust from Milan, that his issue
Should become kings of Naples? O, rejoice
Beyond a common joy, and set it down
With gold on lasting pillars: in one voyage
Did Claribel her husband find at Tunis,
And Ferdinand, her brother, found a wife
Where he himself was lost; Prospero, his dukedom
In a poor isle; and all of us, ourselves,
When no man was his own.

(V.i.205–13)

But to leave *The Tempest* there would be to withhold the fact that throughout the play, inextricably entwined with its telescoped utopian vision, there is ample evidence of its thraldom to the very forms of oppression it is striving to escape. The creative loyalties of *The Tempest* are divided between a poetic conversion of history to comedy and a sober admission of how tightly our hearts and minds are clutched by inherited perceptions. The utopian impulse gets a rougher ride in *The Tempest* than in the other romances, because the plausibility of that impulse is more severely contested from the start by a less sanguine assessment of its viability.

The double-bind staged and explored by the play is ironically framed in the opening scene of Act II, when Gonzalo's brief flight of utopian fantasy is abruptly grounded by his companions. 'Had I plantation of this isle, my lord,' declares Gonzalo, 'And were the king on't',

I' th' commonwealth I would, by contraries,
Execute all things; for no kind of traffic
Would I admit; no name of magistrate;
Letters should not be known; riches, poverty,
And use of service, none; contract, succession,
Bourn, bound of land, tilth, vineyard, none;
No use of metal, corn, or wine, or oil;
No occupation, all men idle, all;
And women too, but innocent and pure;
No sovereignty —

Sebastian.   Yet he would be king on't.
Antonio.   The latter end of his commonwealth forgets the beginning.

(II.i.144, 146, 148–59)

This blank contradiction between hierarchy and community, between authority and liberty, which Sebastian and Antonio expose with such withering sarcasm, is focused throughout *The Tempest* in the figure of Prospero himself. Prospero appears both as the agent of benign transformation, the fount and exemplar of cultivated values, and as the epitome of the principle obstructing such transformation. He is at once the harbinger of the flourishing state his name invokes and the brooding embodiment of absolute power, who dominates everyone in the play and determines everything that happens to them.

His claim on our sympathy and respect is compromised from the beginning by the irascible, authoritarian attitude he displays towards Miranda: 'here/ Have I, thy schoolmaster, made thee more profit/ Than other princes can' (I.ii.171–3). He constantly interrupts his long, expository harangue with bullying commands that she fix her attention on him: 'Obey, and be attentive' (I.ii.38). Prospero contrives and controls his daughter's first encounter with Ferdinand, their courtship and their subsequent betrothal. He supervises their most intimate exchanges like some invisible voyeur, ensuring that every step proceeds according to his plan: '[*Aside*] It goes on, I see,/ As my soul prompts it' (I.ii.420–1). Above all, he polices their desire for each other with obsessive, vicious threats:

> If thou dost break her virgin-knot before
> All sanctimonious ceremonies may
> With full and holy rite be minist'red,
> No sweet aspersion shall the heavens let fall
> To make this contract grow; but barren hate,
> Sour-ey'd disdain, and discord shall bestrew
> The union of your bed with weeds so loathly
> That you shall hate it both.
>
> (IV.i.13–22)

In this respect Prospero answers Ferdinand's judgement of him earlier, when, having been forced to undergo a pointless trial period of menial drudgery, he complains: 'her father's crabbed;/ And he's compos'd of harshness' (III.i.8–9).[47] But the external subjection inflicted on the lovers by Prospero is mirrored by their own psychological imprisonment in the language of subjugation. 'The very

instant that I saw you,' swears Ferdinand, 'did/ My heart fly to your
service, there resides,/ To make me slave to it' (III.i.64–6). And
Miranda protests in turn, 'I'll be your servant,/ Whether you will or
no' (III.i.84–6). The discourse of conquest, treachery and collusion
even stains the brief, showcased exchange between the two, when
Prospero reveals them playfully quarrelling over a game of chess:

Miranda.	Sweet lord, you play me false.
Ferdinand.	No, my dearest love,
	I would not for the world.
Miranda.	Yes, for a score of kingdoms you should wrangle,
	And I would call it fair play.

(V.i.172–5)

Prospero is the principal link in a chain of domination and subservience, which shackles every figure in his programmed universe to
him and to each other. The entire cast of Prospero's prescripted play
are trapped in narratives of sovereignty and submission, of tyranny
and usurpation, which define their actual or imaginary relationships
and the way they see themselves. The action of *The Tempest* is dictated
from first to last by the original violent seizure of Prospero's dukedom
in Milan. Uprooted from history by the storm and tossed onto 'this
most desolate isle' (III.iii.80), the perpetrators of that crime import
the mentality of their formative milieu intact. Prospero's prompting
of Antonio's and Sebastian's conspiracy to assassinate Alonso – an
action replay of his own former fate – is designed to prove just that.
The point is reinforced by the farcical duplication of the conspiracy in
the plot of Trinculo, Stephano and Caliban against Prospero himself.
Their drunken fantasies and protestations – 'His daughter and I will
be king and queen' (III.i.166–7); 'and I, thy Caliban,/ For aye thy foot
licker' (IV.i.218–19) – parody the fictions of subordination ensnaring
the minds of their avowed superiors.

It is in Prospero's relationship with Ariel and Caliban that the
brutality of his power becomes most graphic. Only if Ariel agrees to
endure 'more toil' and 'pains' (I.ii.242) in order to accomplish the plan
Prospero could not complete without him, will he be granted the
'liberty' (I.ii.245) he aches for. If he persists in protesting, however:

> I will rend an oak
> And peg thee in his knotty entrails till
> Thou has howl'd away twelve winters.
>
> (I.ii.294–6)

The cruelty is even more pronounced in the case of the exploited and tormented creature whom Prospero describes as 'Caliban my slave' (I.ii.308), who 'does make our fire,/ Fetch in our wood, and serves in offices/ That profit us' (I.ii.311–13). Caliban defiantly refuses to feel grateful or contrite for the consequences of Prospero's attempts to civilize him, which he knows are a cloak for the naked theft of his land and liberty:

> This island's mine by Sycorax my mother,
> Which thou tak'st from me...
> For I am all the subjects that you have,
> Which first was mine own king; and here you sty me
> In this hard rock, whiles you do keep from me
> The rest o' th' island.
>
> (I.ii.331–2, 341–4)

Dominion demands and creates servitude in order to define and legitimate itself. The injustice of Caliban's being made 'subject to a tyrant' (III.ii.42), who 'hath cheated [him] of this island' (III.ii.44) and who plagues him with excruciating pains, is never brought home more movingly than when we glimpse the sad, elusive longings concealed in his heart:

> Be not afeard, the isle is full of noises,
> Sounds, and sweet airs, that give delight and hurt not.
> Sometimes a thousand twangling instruments
> Will hum about mine ears; and sometimes voices,
> That if I then had wak'd after long sleep,
> Will make me sleep again, and then in dreaming,
> The clouds methought would open, and show riches
> Ready to drop upon me, that when I wak'd
> I cried to dream again.
>
> (III.ii.135–43)

This speech, as much as any in the play, gives us the measure of Prospero's despotism, the price paid in mental and physical suffering for his omnipotence. It counts the cost of the transfiguring magic that bends the action towards its closure in forgiveness, restitution and renewal.[48]

As the incarnation of the problem and the source of its solution, Prospero contains the play's discovery that the potential for equality and community cannot be divorced from the structures of domination in which it is rooted. *The Tempest* obliges us to wrestle with the fact that the means of emancipation from our narratives of oppression are contaminated by the forms of power and perception which they are meant to dismantle. In this play Shakespeare acknowledges that the art of the possible is indivisible from the nightmare of history, which both provokes and frustrates its endeavours.

Thus *The Tempest* problematizes the nature of its own art and the power of the dramatist himself. It opens up, in poetic and theatrical terms, issues which had to wait until the twentieth century to be explicitly addressed in this celebrated passage from Walter Benjamin's 'Theses on the Philosophy of History':

> Whoever has emerged victorious participates to this day in the triumphal procession in which the present rulers step over those who are lying prostrate. According to traditional practice, the spoils are carried along in the procession. They are called cultural treasures, and a historical materialist views them with cautious detachment. For without exception the cultural treasures he surveys have an origin which he cannot contemplate without horror. They owe their existence not only to the efforts of the great minds and talents who have created them, but also to the anonymous toil of their contemporaries. There is no document of civilization which is not at the same time a document of barbarism.[49]

The character of Prospero includes, as is generally accepted, a portrait of the artist as dramatist within the play. Prospero is the omniscient creator of the drama in which he participates, contriving and controlling everything, from the tempest of the title to the audience's final response. His most famous speech openly solicits this identification:

Our revels now are ended. These our actors
(As I foretold you) were all spirits, and
Are melted into air, into thin air,
And like the baseless fabric of this vision,
The cloud-capp'd tow'rs, the gorgeous palaces,
The solemn temples, the great globe itself,
Yea, all which it inherit, shall dissolve,
And like this insubstantial pageant faded
Leave not a rack behind.

                                    (IV.i.148–56)

At the same time, it coaxes the audience yet again to tease out the parallels and contradictions between 'this insubstantial pageant faded' and the actualities it mirrors and transmutes. In his meta-dramatic role as a medium through which the play reflects upon itself, Prospero objectifies the intrinsic complicities of *The Tempest*. He enshrines the play's collusion with the factual oppression that it presupposes, and the authoritarian mentality that it exemplifies. For, however complex, self-aware and open-ended the play's vision seeks to be, it cannot avoid imposing this construction on reality at the expense of all the other versions it excludes.

The Tempest owns up to its involuntary entanglement in barbarity and repression. It knows that every act of representation is also, inescapably, an act of complicity and an act of violence. And, with its closing words, the play springs on us the awkward question of our own incriminating share in Prospero's creation. In the Epilogue, the deviser of the play we have just seen deliberately casts the audience in the role he has relinquished. He bequeaths to us the ambivalent authority and magical imaginative power to judge and complete *The Tempest* ourselves:

            Let me not,
    Since I have my dukedom got,
    And pardon'd the deceiver, dwell
    In this bare island by your spell,
    But release me from my bands
    With the help of your good hands.
    Gentle breath of yours my sails

Must fill, or else my project fails,
Which was to please. Now I want
Spirits to enforce, art to enchant,
And my ending is despair,
Unless I be reliev'd by prayer,
Which pierces so, that it assaults
Mercy itself, and frees all faults.
As you from crimes would pardon'd be,
Let your indulgence set me free.   [*Exit.*]
                              (Epil. 5–20)

Shakespeare's last masterpiece is designed to ensure that we keep the representation and the reality, and the relations between them, under constant surveillance. It urges us to question not only the authority of the author, but also the assumptions that shape our response to his work. *The Tempest* cautions us not to lose sight of the parts played by Shakespeare and ourselves in cultures wedded to violence and exploitation, even as we strive to restore and activate the progressive potential of his drama in our time. It reminds us that the hierarchical principle of social organization, whose validity Shakespeare's drama so forcefully disputes, remains arrogantly entrenched in our daily lives, and that the task of delivering our kind into an as yet utopian world, undisfigured by class-divisions or by racial and sexual injustice, remains formidable.

5

'Dreaming on things to come': Shakespeare and the Future of Criticism

The principal ambition of this book is to open up a fresh perspective on the study of Shakespeare. But that ambition is inseparable from the broader objective that underpins it, which is to help unlock the impasse in which most modern criticism, it seems to me, has languished for too long. As I argued in Chapter 2,[1] when we set out to study a novel, play or poem from the past, and especially from the distant past, we are basically obliged to opt for one of two equally unsatisfactory alternatives. We can either adopt an historical approach, and try to work out what the work once meant by situating it in the world and time from which it sprang; or we can play down the demands of history, and treat the work in effect as if it had been written today, raiding it for reflections of our current preoccupations. One route leads to an archaeological dig, an act of excavation and restoration, which at its best brings the strangeness and remoteness of the work vividly to life, but at its worst turns the text into yet another casualty of the stultifying antiquarianism that still flourishes in modish guises. The other route ends in a blatant act of appropriation, which can indeed capture the work's relevance to our most pressing modern concerns, but at the cost of repressing or distorting those features of the work that pull it back into the past, that insist on the text's resistance to our assaults upon its original import. Even the most sophisticated kind of historical criticism, well aware of the way its own modernity warps its view of authors of a bygone age, remains incorrigibly retrospective, the critical equivalent of a driver whose eyes are glued to the rear-view mirror, and who neglects to look out through the windscreen at the unwinding road ahead.

There are few features of modern criticism more dismaying than the smug diagnostic attitude that seems to have infected almost every reach of the discipline. I mean the sort of approach that reduces the literary work to a mere symptom of something else – be it history, the unconscious, power, sexuality or language – and then passes sentence on it from the supposedly superior vantage point of hindsight. For what this diagnostic approach denies the work is the power not only to throw into question the world in which it was first forged and the world in which we now encounter it, but also to foreshadow futures that would otherwise remain impalpable. It is an approach to literature that usually goes hand in hand with a scorn for form and close reading, a contempt for the belief that there is something special about the creative use of language and form in imaginative literature that sets it apart from other kinds of discourse and provides us with ways of seeing the world which no other kind of writing can deliver. Nor is this any wonder, since it is precisely in the unpredictable detail of diction and design that the work's impatience with the past and its intolerance of the present find their most potent expression.

In an admirable essay called 'The Third World of Criticism', Jerome McGann writes:

> When we think of poems 'in their historical contexts', our historicist biases – even in their New Historicist modes – take those 'contexts' to be located primarily in the past, or – if we have read our Nietzsche and Foucault with care – in the present and the past. And when we think even more deeply about such matters we also understand that these historical contexts are multiple and conflicting: heteroglossial, as Bakhtin would say. But if it is true that all futures are functions of the past (and the present), then we must expect to find those futures being carried out in the works that seem to be speaking and acting only from the past.

Poems imagine more than they know. The *Oresteia* is a far greater work, in those future contexts of reality it had not discussed and did not desire, than it is when we read it merely in the context of its own grandiose – and mistaken – self-conceptions.[2]

The point is that what holds true for Aeschylus holds even truer for Shakespeare, the cornerstone of the canon and the gold standard of literary value, whose plays and poetry reveal more plainly than the work of any other author the truth of Bloch's contention that every great work of literature is created 'in the light of a future which has not yet come into being, and indeed of some ultimate resolution as yet unknown'.[3]

It was only after completing the second edition of this book, however, that I realized what I should have suspected all along: that these fundamental problems faced by modern criticism as it contemplates the literature of the past had been foreseen a century ago by three wily Irishmen as they struggled to lay the ghost of the Bard whom one of them dubbed 'Great Shapesphere'. I refer, of course, to the unholy trinity of Oscar Wilde, George Bernard Shaw and James Joyce, all of whom strove to allay their anxiety about the influence of their mighty precursor by remaking him in their own inimitable images.

Consider, to begin with, *The Portrait of Mr W. H.* (1889), Oscar Wilde's wonderful tale about the true identity of the mysterious individual to whom Shakespeare dedicated his 'sugared *Sonnets*' – the tale so cruelly obliged to bear witness against its author at his notorious trial six years later.[4] The story concerns the obsessive quest of three men to prove that the beautiful youth whom Shakespeare called 'the master mistress of my passion' (Sonnet 20) was neither the Earl of Pembroke nor the Earl of Southampton, but an exquisite boy actor who shared the playwright's Christian name, the irresistible Willie Hughes. The narrator recounts how he first heard the theory from his friend Erskine, who had in turn contracted the hypothesis years before from *his* friend, Cyril Graham. Erskine relates to the narrator the rise and demise of his passion for the theory for which his friend Cyril had been prepared to lie and die. Pressed by Erskine for tangible proof of Willie Hughes's historical existence, Cyril had paid a painter to forge an Elizabethan portrait of 'Master Will Hews', posed with one hand resting on the dedicatory page of the *Sonnets*. Erskine's detection of the fraud had put paid to his own conviction, but had served only to intensify that of his fixated friend, Cyril. To prove the inviolability of his faith in his theory, Cyril had shot himself and bequeathed to the appalled Erskine the task of revealing Shakespeare's secret to the world.

Erskine reveals the secret, however, to the narrator alone, and is alarmed to observe that he has infected the latter with Cyril's fatal conjecture. Erskine explains in vain the glaring flaw at the heart of the Willie Hughes hypothesis: 'You start by assuming the existence of the very person whose existence is the thing to be proved.' But it is too late. The narrator is hooked, and he spends most of the story marshalling the textual and circumstantial evidence he needs to clinch Cyril Graham's contention. He begins with a close analysis of the *Sonnets*, to show how the theory makes lines hitherto obscure intelligible and transforms the meaning of lines previously deemed to be transparent. He then proceeds to place the intense relationship of Will Shakespeare and Willie Hughes in its intellectual and cultural context, invoking the analogous male intimacies of Michelangelo and Montaigne to establish the normality of Shakespeare's liaison and deflect the attacks of those 'who had regretted that the Sonnets had ever been written, who had seen in them something dangerous, something unlawful even'. Then he narrows the focus still further on Master Hughes by reconstructing the social origins and theatrical fate of the androgynous boy actors of the Elizabethan stage. More plundering of the archives yields to the narrator the identity, if not the name, of the Dark Lady of the *Sonnets*; the surmise that Marlowe was Shakespeare's poetic rival for the lad's allegiance; and the certainty that he has managed 'to place the new interpretation of the Sonnets on something like a secure historic basis'.[5]

But no sooner has the narrator grasped that satisfaction than it slips through his fingers. He realizes that what his search for the objective historical truth of these texts has actually unearthed is his own buried life, the subjective truth of 'a life that had once been mine': 'A book of Sonnets, published nearly three hundred years ago, written by a dead hand and in honour of a dead youth, had suddenly explained to me the whole story of my soul's romance.' In the portrait of Mr W.H. he finally perceives the image of himself. Meanwhile, in one last ironic twist of the tale, the narrator's fresh proofs have reconverted Erskine to the cause, and nothing the narrator says can disabuse him. So consumed is Erskine that he pretends, in a deathbed letter to the narrator, that he too has taken his life to testify to the truth of the thesis to which his beloved Cyril sacrificed himself, and to whose vindication he vainly begs the narrator to consecrate himself anew. As the narrator reflects: 'To die for one's theological opinions is the worst use a man can make of his life; but to die for a literary theory! It seemed impossible.' The narrator ends his tale dismayed by Erskine's attempt to deceive him by 'the pathetic fallacy of martyrdom', which 'was to me merely a tragic form of scepticism, an attempt to realise by fire what one had failed to do by faith'. Nevertheless, he admits in his final sentence, every time he looks at the forged portrait of Mr W.H., he cannot help feeling that 'there is really a great deal to be said for the Willie Hughes theory of Shakespeare's Sonnets'.[6]

Unless I am much mistaken, what we find depicted in *The Portrait of Mr W. H.* is precisely the plight of historicist critics of our own day a century before the fact. If that claim seems as strained as Cyril Graham's readings of the *Sonnets*, perhaps it is worth recalling that Wilde was the author of a learned treatise called 'The Rise of Historical Criticism' and a trailblazing scholarly study of stage costume and theatrical transvestism in Shakespeare entitled 'The Truth of Masks'; while in his essay 'The Critic as Artist', which he was writing about the same time as *The Portrait of Mr W. H.*, we can find Wilde wrestling explicitly with the theoretical problems posed by his story.

The key dictum of 'The Critic as Artist' is: 'The one duty we owe to history is to rewrite it.' Inspired by Erskine's anecdote, the narrator of *The Portrait of Mr W. H.* begins by developing the dialogue with the dead – the dialogue between past and present – initiated by Cyril Graham: the creative reinterpretation of the *Sonnets*, to which modern readers bring as much as they borrow from the text. He then seeks to buttress his reading by scouring the archives for the contextual corroboration that will set it on 'a secure historic basis'. But, budding postmodernist that he is, the narrator realizes that his pursuit of an ultimate, objective point of origin in which to anchor his argument is doomed, and that his dialogue with the shade of Shakespeare was a delusion. The harder the critic struggles to recover the strangeness of the past from the printed voice of its poets and playwrights, the more completely he discloses the desires of the present and his own personality. Criticism of the highest kind, declares Wilde in 'The Critic as Artist', 'is in its essence purely subjective, and seeks to reveal its own secret and not the secret of another'. It may seem that 'the meaning of any beautiful created thing is, at least, as much in the soul of him who looks at it as it was in his soul who wrought it'. But 'it is rather the beholder who lends to the beautiful thing its myriad meanings, and makes it marvellous for us, and sets it in some new relation to the age, so that it becomes a vital portion of our lives, and a symbol of what we pray for, or perhaps of what, having prayed for, we fear that we may receive'.[7]

The search for the Holy Grail of historical validation continues to obsess Wilde nonetheless. A few pages after that last quotation, in the second part of 'The Critic as Artist', he insists that 'he who desires to understand Shakespeare truly must understand the relations in which Shakespeare stood to the Renaissance and the Reformation, to the age of Elizabeth and the age of James'.[8] Or, as the narrator of *The Portrait of Mr W. H.* puts it, perhaps there is something to be said for the Willie Hughes theory of the *Sonnets* after all. At the close of the nineteenth century the story predicts and explores the dilemma of historicist critics at the dawn of the twenty-first: driven by the desire to respect and preserve the difference of the past, yet dogged by an ironic awareness that the constructions they place upon the textual traces of that past may well turn out to be inscriptions of their own imperatives.

No such qualms, needless to say, vexed the conscience of George Bernard Shaw, as he laboured at his lifelong task of demolishing what he called 'The Idol of the Bardolaters'[9] and erecting in its place a Shakespeare who was more suited to the political needs of the present, and who consequently bore an uncanny resemblance to Shaw himself. In GBS we surely behold the great granddaddy of those critics of our time who hold that to hunt for the primal historical meaning of *Macbeth* or *Much Ado* is to chase a will o' the wisp, because, to quote once again the words of Gary Taylor, 'We find in Shakespeare only what we bring to him or what others have left behind; he gives us back our own values.'[10] For such critics, as we observed in Chapter 1, the pursuit of the plays' pristine import is pointless, since what really matters is what they can be induced to mean now. Thus for Terence Hawkes, we may recall, 'The point of Shakespeare and his plays' lies not in the light they shed on the lives led by Shakespeare and his contemporaries, but 'in their capacity to serve as instruments by which we make cultural meaning for ourselves'.[11]

Unconstrained by the obligation Wilde's narrator felt to ground his version of Shakespeare in historical facts, Shaw set about shouldering aside all rivals to his view of Stratford's sole claim to fame. Shakespeare, he wrote to Ellen Terry, 'is to me one of the towers of the Bastille, and down he must come'.[12] Shakespeare's ideas he dismissed as 'platitudinous fudge' when compared with Ibsen's.[13] Indeed, 'With the single exception of Homer,' wrote Shaw at one point, 'there is no eminent writer, not even Sir Walter Scott, whom I can despise so entirely as I despise Shakespear when I measure my mind against his.'[14] The creator of Hamlet and Lear, Shaw liked to proclaim in this iconoclastic vein, was 'for an afternoon, but not for all time'.[15]

Shaw's struggle to give the long shadow of the Bard the slip in both his critical and his creative writing lasted well over sixty years. In fact, he was still at it the year before he died, when he wrote a self-mocking puppet show called *Shakes versus Shav*, which was performed at the inauguration of the Malvern Festival in 1949. 'This,' declared Shaw in a preface, 'in all actuarial probability is my last play and the climax of my eminence, such as it is.' The show starts with the puppet Shakes explaining to the audience:

> Hither I raging come
> An infamous impostor to chastize,
> Who in an ecstasy of self-conceit
> Shortens my name to Shav, and dares pretend
> Here to reincarnate my very self.

When Shav, the Shaw puppet, enters, unfazed by Shakes's indictment of him as 'this fiend of Ireland' and a 'shameless fraud', the two puppets resort to fisticuffs to settle the question of supremacy and Shaw's puppet persona (unsurprisingly) knocks Shakespeare's out. Shakes, however, is generously granted the last word. After a vigorous exchange of gibes Shav cries: 'Peace, jealous Bard:/ We both are mortal. For a moment suffer/ My glimmering light to shine.' Then, according to the stage direction, '*A light appears between them*' and, with the immortal words 'Out, out, brief candle!', the Shakespeare puppet '*puffs it out*' and ends the play.[16]

Shaw had not been quite so magnanimous fifty years earlier in *Caesar and Cleopatra* (1898), which endeavours to cut both of these mighty Shakespearean protagonists down to size, along with the heroic and romantic ideals they respectively embody, within the compass of a single play. Shaw's preface to the play in *Three Plays for Puritans* (published two years later) bears as its title the impudent question 'Better than Shakespeare?' To which Shaw's answer turns out to be yes, in so far as Shaw's *ideas* are more advanced than his precursor's; but no, in as much as Shakespeare's verbal power and theatrical craft cannot be surpassed, even by GBS:

> It is the philosophy, the outlook on life, that changes, not the craft of the playwright. . . . [T]he humblest author, and much more a rather arrogant one like myself, may profess to have something to say by this time that neither Homer nor Shakespear said. And the playgoer may reasonably ask to have historical events and persons presented to him in the light of his own time, even though Homer and Shakespear have already shewn them in the light of their time.[17]

Of course, that does not mean that Shaw can countenance Oscar Wilde's attempt to show Shakespeare in the light of *his* time too. In his preface to *The Dark Lady of the Sonnets* a decade later, Shaw alludes repeatedly, and sympathetically, to Wilde's fall from grace, while conspicuously omitting all mention of the infamous Willie Hughes. But he concedes the force of Wilde's homoerotic hermeneutics by his emphatic endorsement of Frank Harris's contention 'that Shakespear was a man of normal constitution sexually, and was not the victim of that most cruel and pitiable of all the freaks of nature: the freak which transposes the normal aim of the affections'. As far as the more effusive verses addressed to Mr W.H. are concerned, Shaw writes: 'No reader who had not been tampered with by the psychopathic monomaniacs could ever put any construction but the obvious and innocent one on these passages.'[18] How Shaw would have reacted to the current vogue for queer readings of Shakespeare is not difficult to imagine.

What is admirable about this preface, however, is that it is equally intolerant of the assumption that still thrives today amongst radical and conservative historicists alike: the assumption that Shakespeare was the mouthpiece of the monarchy, that his drama was wittingly or unwittingly in cahoots with the Crown. By this stage in his career, Shaw is relaxed enough for a rapprochement with his gargantuan antagonist, if only because now 'I am convinced that he was very like myself: in fact, if I had been born in 1556 instead of 1856, I should have taken to blank verse and given Shakespear a harder run for his money than all the other Elizabethans put together.' Shakespeare, Shaw continues, 'had of course no prevision of democratic Collectivism'. But he judged the different social classes impartially, weighing rich and poor, the rulers and the ruled, in the same balance. And, as Shaw concludes superbly,

> whoever will read Lear and Measure for Measure will find stamped on his mind such an appalled sense of the danger of dressing man in a little brief authority, such a merciless stripping of the purple from the 'poor, bare, forked animal' that calls itself a king and fancies itself a god, that one wonders what was the real nature of the mysterious restraint that kept 'Eliza and our James' from teaching Shakespear to be civil to crowned heads . . .

In fact, Shaw goes further than this, hinting that the secret of Shakespeare's art lies in its prematurity, in its author's being, like Shaw himself, ahead of his time: 'it was not possible for a man of his powers to observe the political and moral conduct of his contemporaries without perceiving that they were incapable of dealing with the problems raised by their own civilisation'. And, quoting (or rather, slightly misquoting) that resonant phrase from the second line of Sonnet 107, Shaw gives us a glimpse of a playwright who, far from being complicit with the Crown or the helpless dupe of the dominant ideology of his day, 'proclaimed his place and his power in "the wide world dreaming of things to come"'.[19]

That quotation builds a neat bridge to Joyce, who openly salutes in *Ulysses* the blows struck by Shaw and Wilde in the Irish battle for the Bard. 'Shakespeare?' muses Buck Mulligan in mock puzzlement:

> – To be sure, he said, remembering brightly. The chap that writes like Synge...
>
> – The bard's fellowcountrymen, John Eglinton answered, are rather tired perhaps of our brilliancies of theorising.... Has no-one made him out to be an Irishman?...
>
> – The most brilliant of all is that story of Wilde's, Mr Best said, lifting his brilliant notebook. That *Portrait of Mr W.H.* where he proves that the sonnets were written by a Willie Hughes, a man all hues.
>
> – For Willie Hughes, is it not? The quaker librarian asked.
>
> Or Hughie Wills. Mr William Himself. W.H.: who am I?

Not surprisingly, the notion that the *Sonnets* are suffused with the 'Love that dare not speak its name' is entertained far more hospitably by Joyce than it was by Shaw. 'O, I must tell you what Dowden said!' cries Mulligan (Dowden being, of course, the eminent Shakespeare scholar at Trinity College, Dublin). 'I asked him what he thought of the charge of pederasty brought against the bard. He lifted his hands and said: *All we can say is that life ran very high in those days.* Lovely!' sighs Mulligan.[20]

The core of the 'Scylla and Charybdis' episode of *Ulysses* from which these quotations come consists of Stephen's ingenious elucidation of Shakespeare's complete works – and of *Hamlet* in particular – in terms of the Bard's biography, the dark family romance in which Stephen Dedalus beholds the spitting image of his own. I want to single out one startling passage, which pushes the argument about the appropriation of Shakespeare beyond anything Wilde or even Shaw foresaw, and which compels us to rethink what is at stake in our engagement with any great literature of another age. Wilde, Shaw and Joyce all wage war in their different ways on those who would doom Shakespeare to fester in the prison-house of the past, confined within the scope of what is taken to be his time. And no work of Shakespeare's attests more forcefully than *Hamlet* to the poverty of such approaches, whether they are wholly engrossed in the otherness of the past or frankly yoked to the dictates of the present.

Criticism which is oblivious to art's powers of precognition is incapable of grasping the quality of *Hamlet* that distinguishes Shakespeare's drama and the most valuable imaginative literature of any era: its *untimeliness*, its obstinate refusal to be fully intelligible in terms of its age, because the unvoiced assumptions that govern it are indeed far ahead of its time. What Dowden in his study of Shakespeare called 'the mystery, the baffling, vital obscurity of the play'[21] is the effect of its struggle to articulate through its language and form a vision for which no vocabulary is yet available. In an interview with Djuna Barnes published in the same year as *Ulysses* (1922), Joyce observed that '*Hamlet* is a great play, written from the standpoint of the ghost,'[22] whose part, according to legend, was taken by Shakespeare himself. I must confess that I never took Joyce's eccentric theory seriously – notwithstanding the virtuosity with which Stephen expounds its perplexing paradoxes – until I happened upon the following sentence in Derrida's *Specters of Marx*, a book much preoccupied with *Hamlet*: 'The future can only be for ghosts.'[23] That sent me back to Stephen's expository tour de force in the National Library in *Ulysses*. And there we find, prompted by Stephen's reflections on the grim apparition of the great Dane, this intimation of what happens to time as the creative imagination transfigures its material:

> so through the ghost of the unquiet father the image of the unliving son looks forth. In the intense instant of imagination, when the mind, Shelley says, is a fading coal, that which I was is that which I am and that which in possibility I may come to be. So in the future, the sister of the past, I may see myself as I sit here now but by reflection from that which then I shall be.[24]

Stephen understands, in other words, that *Hamlet*, like all great literature, is written in the future perfect tense.

Stephen cites Shelley, and I would like to quote another passage from the latter's *Defence of Poetry* which Joyce may have had in mind. Shelley describes the poet as someone who 'not only beholds intensely the present as it is, and discovers those laws according to which present things ought to be ordered, but he beholds the future in the present, and his thoughts are the germs of the flower and the fruit of latest time'. Poets are, Shelley continues, in an astonishing image, 'the mirrors of the gigantic shadows which futurity casts upon the present'.[25] My contention is that it is in the work's creative violations of conventional form and phrasing that we find these shadows of the future most clearly reflected. As Bakhtin puts it: 'Form serves as a necessary bridge to new, still unknown content.'[26] So that when we find *Hamlet* scuppering its own plot and deranging its own discourse to baffle and confound generations of critics, what we are feeling is nothing less than the tidal pull of the possible, of the as-yet-unrealized, twisting the script into this unique convolution of language and form that continues to hold us spellbound.

In the disrupted structure and dislocated idiom of *Hamlet* can be traced the tragedy's estrangement from its age, its resistance to what Dominick La Capra calls the 'rhetoric of contextualization', whose 'narrowly documentary readings' turn the text into 'little more than a sign of the times'.[27] For today's academic adepts of that rhetoric, the idea that (to adapt McGann) *Hamlet* might imagine more than it knows, that it might imply more than it states, that its true home might be somewhere in the future rather than the place from which it set forth in the past, is precluded from the start as historically untenable. Fortunately, not everyone has found such an idea so implausible. Hazlitt declared: 'This play has a prophetic truth, which is above that of history.'[28] And Coleridge, after remarking with his customary modesty, 'I have a smack of Hamlet myself, if I may say so,' goes on to make this instructive distinction: 'A Maxim is a conclusion upon observation of matters of fact, and is merely retrospective: an Idea, or, if you like, a Principle, carries knowledge within itself, and is prospective. Polonius is a man of maxims.' Which is why, Coleridge explains, 'Hamlet, as the man of ideas, despises him. A man of maxims only is like a Cyclops with one eye, and that eye placed in the back of his head.'[29] Historicist critics of Shakespeare, in short, are just like Polonius: men and women of maxims, one-eyed Cyclopses cursed with incorrigible hindsight, doomed like Lot's wife to gaze forever backwards.

I think that T. S. Eliot, too, was hot on the trail of the play's prospective impulse in his celebrated essay of 1919, when he wrote:

> Hamlet (the man) is dominated by an emotion which is inexpressible, because it is in *excess* of the facts as they appear. And the supposed identity of Hamlet with his author is genuine to this point: that Hamlet's bafflement at the absence of objective equivalent to his feelings is a prolongation of the bafflement of his creator in the face of his artistic problem.... None of the possible actions can satisfy [Hamlet's feelings]; and nothing that Shakespeare can do with the plot can express Hamlet for him.

Eliot's reductive contention that the bafflement stems from Shakespeare's failure to find an 'objective correlative' for Hamlet's disgust for his mother fails to convince Eliot himself, who is forced to concede that the source of the play's mystery must be sought elsewhere: '*Hamlet*, like the sonnets, is full of some stuff that the writer could not drag to light, contemplate, or manipulate into art. And when we search for this feeling, we find it, as in the sonnets, very difficult to localise'; so difficult, indeed, that in order to apprehend it 'We should have to understand things which Shakespeare did not understand himself.'[30] What Eliot is groping towards is the realization that came readily to Shakespeare's modern fellow dramatist Heiner Müller, author of the electrifying *Hamletmachine*: the realization that *Hamlet* is nothing less than 'the attempt to describe an experience that has no reality at the time of its description. An endgame at dawn, the red dawn of an unknown day.'[31]

What makes *Hamlet* such a vexing play is that its prefigurative vision is expressed principally by negation and distortion. The play's commitment to values which are the reverse of those that rule the rotten state of Denmark is dramatized *as* Hamlet's persistent postponement and evasion of revenge, which subvert the logic and fracture the framework of the tragedy. But it is also voiced through the violence done to dramatic discourse by the riddling equivocation not only of Hamlet himself, but also of the gravedigger, and by a host of verbal devices designed to stall the play's plot and cloud the clarity of its language.

The most striking of these devices is a figure of speech, which is employed so frequently that it becomes the signature trope of the tragedy, the tell-tale epitome of its creator's frame of mind as he composed it. In *Forms of Attention*, Frank Kermode has shown how the play's self-division is revealed by its obsessive resort to 'the strangest and most figurative of doublings, hendiadys'. In hendiadys two distinct words combine to express a single idea, as in 'the sensible and true avouch/ Of mine own eyes' (I.i.57–8), 'By this encompassment and drift of question' (II.i.10), or 'But in our circumstance and course of thought' (III.iii.83). *Hamlet* contains far more instances of this trope (well over sixty) than any other play by Shakespeare, and it is apt that a play so anxious to divorce itself from its own avowed enterprise should be so riddled with what Kermode calls 'the incestuous doublet of hendiadys', a trope which instils a sense of semantic unease 'by doing something other than we expect from words joined by "and", by a sort of violation of the promise of simple parataxis' or sequential coupling.[32] In this way the play mirrors, in the very fibre of its phrasing, the frustration of its tragic teleology by the barrage of revisions, diversions and dilations that Terence Hawkes has dubbed *Telmah* (*Hamlet* reversed). The aim of *Telmah*, the plot's disruptive siamese twin, is 'to undermine our inherited notion of *Hamlet* as a structure that runs a satisfactorily linear, sequential course from a firmly established and well-defined beginning through a clearly placed and signalled middle to a causally related and logically determined end which, planted in the beginning, develops, or grows out of it'.[33]

The play, in other words, is one long *Verfremdungseffekt*: a continuous undercutting of the assumptions inscribed in the characters, ideas and events with which it is obliged to work. It is by twisting, unhinging, interrupting and framing the script that *Hamlet* defines the gulf dividing its *implicit* utopian vision from the *explicit* values that imprison the divisive world in which it was written. In so

doing, it confirms with a vengeance Marcuse's view of the fundamental task of art: 'Inasmuch as man and nature are constituted by
an unfree society, their repressed and distorted potentialities can be
represented only in an *estranging* form. . . . The encounter with the
truth of art happens in the estranging language and images which
make perceptible, visible and audible that which is no longer, or not
yet, perceived, said and heard in everyday life.'[34]

In the *Sonnets*, of course, which Eliot instinctively and shrewdly
couples with *Hamlet*, the proleptic cast of Shakespeare's imagination
is immediately manifest from the outset. Here, in a sequence celebrated for its obsession with braving the ravages of time, we encounter poem after poem projecting itself into the future, anticipating
some eventual scenario or boldly predicting what shall come to pass,
as in the opening lines of Sonnet 55: 'Not marble nor the gilded
monuments/ Of princes shall outlive this pow'rful rhyme'; or the
closing lines of Sonnet 107: 'And thou in this shalt find thy
monument,/ When tyrants' crests and tombs of brass are spent.'
But Shakespeare's conviction that his poetry will live on the lips of
citizens of centuries to come surely receives its most haunting
expression in Sonnet 81:

> Or I shall live your epitaph to make,
> Or you survive when I in earth am rotten;
> From hence your memory death cannot take,
> Although in me each part will be forgotten.
> Your name from hence immortal life shall have,
> Though I (once gone) to all the world must die;
> The earth can yield me but a common grave,
> When you entombed in men's eyes shall lie;
> Your monument shall be my gentle verse,
> Which eyes not yet created shall o'er-read,
> And tongues to be your being shall rehearse
> When all the breathers of this world are dead;
>   You still shall live (such virtue hath my pen)
>   Where breath most breathes, even in the mouths of men.

To read these lines now is to testify to their uncanny prescience, to
fulfil Shakespeare's prophecy of their fate by ourselves becoming

those 'eyes not yet created', those 'tongues to be' that he foretold. As we read the *Sonnets*, it is hard to escape the eery realization that Shakespeare *knew* that we would be reading them now, in a world and time beyond even his imagination.

In Sonnet 106, moreover, we find Shakespeare adopting the role of the reader of the poetry of long ago – adopting the equivalent of our role, in other words, as we read him now – in order to stress not only the prophetic power of past literature, but also the vital part to be played by later readers in discerning the precocious modernity of its bequest:

> When in the chronicle of wasted time
> I see descriptions of the fairest wights,
> And beauty making beautiful old rhyme
> In praise of ladies dead and lovely knights,
> Then in the blazon of sweet beauty's best,
> Of hand, of foot, of lip, of eye, of brow,
> I see their antique pen would have express'd
> Even such a beauty as you master now.
> So all their praises are but prophecies
> Of this our time, all you prefiguring,
> And for they look'd but with divining eyes,
> They had not still enough your worth to sing:
>> For we which now behold those present days
>> Have eyes to wonder, but lack tongues to praise.

What Coleridge astutely identified as Shakespeare's 'fondness for presentiment'[35] is not simply a fascination for 'divining' the shape of things to come, for the phenomenon of prediction as such. It is, more precisely, a gift for catching glimpses of the present and the potential in the past, and a recognition of the prefigurative power of his own anachronistic art.

A strange moment in the final scene of *Cymbeline*, written in the twilight of its author's theatrical career, brings us closer to understanding the kind of reception Shakespeare's art trusts that it will secure from posterity, once it has passed in turn into 'the chronicle of wasted time'. After the avalanche of revelations and reconciliations has subsided, Lucius summons forth his soothsayer, Philharmonus, to 'declare the meaning' (V.v.434) of the cryptic prophecy inscribed

on the tablet that was placed on Posthumus's breast in a dream by
the ghosts of his parents and siblings. An exorbitant amount of space
and time is devoted to Philharmonus's painstaking elucidation of the
tablet, which concludes thus:

> The lofty cedar, royal Cymbeline,
> Personates thee; and thy lopp'd branches point
> Thy two sons forth; who, by Belarius stol'n,
> For many years thought dead, are now reviv'd,
> To the majestic cedar join'd, whose issue
> Promises Britain peace and plenty.
>
> (V.v.453–8)

But, en route to the gratifying punchline of the prophecy, the
soothsayer's reasoning reveals itself as strained, almost desperate, at
key points, most notably when he struggles to decipher the prediction that 'a lion's whelp shall . . . be embrac'd by a piece of tender air'
(V.v.435–7). The 'lion's whelp' he convincingly construes as signifying Posthumus Leonatus, but his credibility begins to crumble when
he tries to turn 'tender air' into Imogen:

> [*To Cymbeline*] The piece of tender air, thy virtuous daughter,
> Which we call *mollis aer*, and *mollis aer*
> We term it *mulier*; [*to Posthumus*] which *mulier* I divine
> Is this most constant wife, who, even now,
> Answering the letter of the oracle,
> Unknown to you, unsought, were clipt about
> With this most tender air.
>
> (V.v.446–52)

Even Cymbeline cannot stifle his scepticism: 'This hath some
seeming' (V.v.453) is the most enthusiastic response he can muster
to the soothsayer's attempt to place a 'fit and apt construction'
(V.v.444) on the prophecy.

This curious incident is instructive, because it provides a para-
digm of what is at stake in the modern critical interpretation of
Shakespeare's plays. The coded forecast on the tablet requires the
hermeneutic art of the soothsayer to unearth its buried meaning, and

up to a point the interpreter, armed with the advantage of hindsight, does a plausible job of squaring the semantic potential of the text with the ensuing events that it purports to foreshadow. But only up to a point, because the fit between the forecast and the facts can be seen to be imperfect, and the limits of the interpretation are exposed. However satisfactory the construction placed upon some parts of the text may be, other parts remain intractable and refuse to be converted into the terms of current understanding. The tablet secretes meanings that are still to be mined, and thus it harbours the possibility of evolving a significance more complex than, or quite different from, that which Philharmonus has laboured to extract from it.

In much the same way, the poetically encoded texts bequeathed to posterity by Shakespeare offer themselves to be construed today as memories of the future, as parables not only of the present time, but also of times to come. No matter how complete or cogent our interpretations may appear, and however faithfully they comply with the constraints of the texts, their blinkered standpoint in the present inevitably blinds them to all the other implications stored in the texts, waiting to be unpacked by critics, directors and actors of the future, with other matters on their minds. To grasp a Shakespeare play as fully as possible at any point in time is to recognize that its gaze is bent upon a vanishing point at which no reader or spectator can hope to arrive. Like the hat that the circus clown kicks out of reach every time he steps forward to pick it up, final comprehension of the play is indefinitely postponed by each act of interpretation. Built into Shakespeare's plays, as into his poems, is the expectation that whatever eyes are viewing them at a given moment, other 'eyes not yet created' will one day view them in another light. The soothsayer scene in *Cymbeline* is a salutary reminder that the plays and the poetry, just like cryptic prophecies, will never stop saying one thing and meaning another. Their imaginative reach exceeds our critical grasp, but by how much, and in what ways, only readers and spectators yet to be born will be able to tell.

The crucial question Shakespeare poses for criticism today is this: what if historicizing and modernizing critics alike have been peddling a view of literature which is the reverse of what is really the case, which has got things entirely the wrong way round? What if the changing meaning of the most valuable works is not held in the gravitational grip of the past or the present, but is printed into their form and texture by the pressure of futurity, by their secret contract with a dispensation that might do justice to our dreams? At the moment, as I suggested at the start of this chapter, most criticism seems to be trapped between equally unenticing alternatives. If you fail to see the appeal of a literature fated to speak only of what was, there seems little choice but to settle for a literature that must speak of what is, faithfully reflecting the present priorities of whoever gazes into it. But what if Henry James struck the heart of the matter when, in his splendid essay on *The Tempest*, he concluded that Shakespeare's drama 'renders the poverties and obscurities of our world...in the dazzling terms of a richer and better'?[36] In that case, it might become possible to grasp our greatest literature as shaped by the future in ways that include and transmute our understanding of the past and the present. To discover that Shakespeare's drama had all along been 'dreaming on things to come' would be to reclaim a rich legacy: the prospect of a critical practice through which the world as it was and the world as it is could engage in a dialogue – a genuine, unpredictable dialogue – about the world as it might one day be.

Notes

Chapter 1

1. See Peter Widdowson, 'The Crisis in English Studies', in *Re-reading English*, ed. Peter Widdowson (London and New York: Methuen, 1982), pp. 1–14; 'Professing Literature: A Symposium on the Study of English', *Times Literary Supplement*, 10 December 1982, pp. 1355–63; William E. Cain, *The Crisis in Criticism: Theory, Literature, and Reform in English Studies* (Baltimore: Johns Hopkins University Press, 1984); Terry Eagleton, 'The End of English', *Textual Practice*, 1:1 (Spring, 1987), 1–9; Colin MacCabe, 'Broken English', in *Futures for English*, ed. Colin MacCabe (Manchester: Manchester University Press, 1988), pp. 3–14; Peter Washington, *Fraud: Literary Theory and the End of English* (London: Fontana, 1989); Peter Brooker and Peter Humm (eds), *Dialogue and Difference: English into the Nineties* (London and New York: Routledge, 1989); Evan Watkins, *Work Time: English Departments and the Circulation of Cultural Value* (Stanford: Stanford University Press, 1989); Bernard Bergonzi, *Exploding English: Criticism, Theory, Culture* (Oxford: Clarendon Press, 1990); Alvin Kernan, *The Death of Literature* (New Haven and London: Yale University Press, 1990); Anthony Easthope, *Literary into Cultural Studies* (London and New York: Routledge, 1991); Robert Crawford, *Devolving English Literature* (Oxford: Clarendon Press, 1992); Stephen Greenblatt and Giles Gunn (eds), *Redrawing the Boundaries: The Transformation of English and American Literary Studies* (New York: Modern Language Association of America, 1992); Susan Gubar and Jonathan Kamholtz (eds), *English Inside and Out: The Places of Literary Criticism* (New York and London: Routledge, 1993); Josephine M. Guy and Ian Small, *Politics and Value in English Studies: A Discipline in Crisis?* (Cambridge: Cambridge University Press, 1994); William E. Cain (ed.), *Reconceptualizing American Literary/Cultural Studies: Rhetoric, History, and Politics in the Humanities* (New York and London: Garland, 1996); Michael Berube, *The Employment of English: Theory, Jobs, and the Future of Literary Studies* (New York: New York University Press, 1998); David Scott, *Refashioning Futures: Criticism After*

Postcoloniality (Princeton: Princeton University Press, 1999); Martin Schiralli, *Constructive Postmodernism: Toward Renewal in Cultural and Literary Studies* (Westport, CT and London: Bergin and Garvey, 1999).

2. See John Fekete, *The Critical Twilight: Explorations in the Ideology of Anglo-American Literary Theory from Eliot to McLuhan* (London, Henley and Boston: Routledge and Kegan Paul, 1978); Francis Mulhern, *The Moment of 'Scrutiny'* (London: New Left Books, 1979); Brian Doyle, 'The Hidden History of English Studies', in *Re-reading English*, ed. Widdowson, pp. 17–31, and *English and Englishness* (London and New York: Routledge, 1989); Chris Baldick, *The Social Mission of English Criticism, 1848–1932* (Oxford: Clarendon Press, 1983); Terry Eagleton, *Literary Theory: An Introduction* (Oxford: Blackwell, 1983; 2nd edn, 1996), Ch. 1, and *The Function of Criticism* (London: Verso, 1984); Stephen Ball, 'English for the English Since 1906', in *Social Histories of the Secondary Curriculum: Subjects for Study*, ed. I. F. Goodson (London: Falmer, 1985); I. F. Goodson and Peter Medway (eds), *Bringing English to Order: The History and Politics of a School Subject* (London: Falmer, 1990); Patrick Colm Hogan, *The Politics of Interpretation: Ideology, Professionalism and the Study of Literature* (New York and Oxford: Oxford University Press, 1990), Ch. 5; Franklin E. Court, *Institutionalizing English Literature: The Culture and Politics of Literary Study, 1750–1900* (Stanford: Stanford University Press, 1992); Isaiah Smithson and Nancy Ruff (eds), *English Studies/Cultural Studies: Institutionalizing Dissent* (Urbana: University of Illinois Press, 1994); Tom Steele, *The Emergence of Cultural Studies: Adult Education, Cultural Politics and the English Question* (London: Lawrence and Wishart, 1997); Anthony Easthope, *Englishness and National Culture* (London: Routledge, 1999).

3. See Derek Longhurst, 'Reproducing a National Culture: Shakespeare in Education', *Red Letters*, 11 (1981), 3–14, and '"Not for all time, but for an age": An Approach to Shakespeare Studies', in *Re-reading English*, ed. Widdowson, pp. 150–63; John Drakakis (ed.), *Alternative Shakespeares* (London and New York: Routledge, 1985), Chs 1, 2, 3, 10; Terence Hawkes, *That Shakespeherian Rag: Essays on a Critical Process* (London and New York: Methuen, 1986); Jean E. Howard and Marion F. O'Connor (eds), *Shakespeare Reproduced: The Text in History and Ideology* (New York and London: Methuen, 1987), Chs 1–3; Graham Holderness (ed.), *The Shakespeare Myth* (Manchester: Manchester University Press, 1988); Jonathan Dollimore, *Radical Tragedy: Religion, Ideology and Power in the Drama of Shakespeare and His*

Contemporaries, 2nd edn (Hemel Hempstead: Harvester Wheatsheaf, 1989), Ch. 16; Gary Taylor, *Reinventing Shakespeare: A Cultural History from the Restoration to the Present* (London: Hogarth Press, 1990); Howard Felperin, *The Uses of the Canon: Elizabethan Literature and Contemporary Theory* (Oxford: Clarendon Press, 1990), Ch. 1: 'Historicizing Bardolatry: Or, Where Could Coleridge Have Been Coming From?'; Michael D. Bristol, *Shakespeare's America, America's Shakespeare* (New York and London: Routledge, 1990); Jean I. Marsden (ed.), *The Appropriation of Shakespeare: Post Renaissance Reconstructions of the Works and the Myth* (Hemel Hempstead: Harvester Wheatsheaf, 1991); Hugh Grady, *The Modernist Shakespeare: Critical Texts in a Material World* (Oxford: Oxford University Press, 1991); Stephen Foley, 'Nostalgia and the "Rise of English": Rhetorical Questions', in *The Matter of Difference: Materialist Feminist Criticism of Shakespeare*, ed. Valerie Wayne (Hemel Hempstead: Harvester Wheatsheaf, 1991), pp. 237–55; Margreta de Grazia, *Shakespeare Verbatim: The Reproduction of Authenticity and the 1790 Apparatus* (Oxford: Clarendon Press, 1991); Terence Hawkes, *Meaning by Shakespeare* (London and New York: Routledge, 1992); Michael Dobson, *The Making of the National Poet: Shakespeare, Adaptation and Authorship, 1660–1769* (Oxford: Clarendon Press, 1992); Jonathan Dollimore and Alan Sinfield (eds), *Political Shakespeare: Essays in Cultural Materialism*, 2nd edn (Manchester: Manchester University Press, 1994), Chs 8 and 13; Richard Halpern, *Shakespeare Among the Moderns* (Ithaca, NY and London: Cornell University Press, 1997); John Joughin (ed.), *Shakespeare and National Culture* (Manchester and New York: Manchester University Press, 1997); Christy Desmet and Robert Sawyer (eds), *Shakespeare and Appropriation* (London and New York: Routledge, 1999); Hugh Grady (ed.), *Shakespeare and Modernity: Early Modern to Millennium* (London and New York: Routledge, 2000).

4. *Political Shakespeare*, ed. Dollimore and Sinfield, 2nd edn, pp. 155, 156. Traditional and radical versions of Shakespeare lock horns in Ivo Kamps (ed.), *Shakespeare Left and Right* (New York and London: Routledge, 1991), Chs 1–10, and Brian Vickers, *Appropriating Shakespeare: Contemporary Critical Quarrels* (New Haven and London: Yale University Press, 1993). For a recent survey of the critical battlefield, see Ivo Kamps, 'Alas, Poor Shakespeare! I Knew Him Well', in *Shakespeare and Appropriation*, ed. Desmet and Sawyer, pp. 15–32.

5. Longhurst, '"Not for all time, but for an age"', p. 151.

6. Christopher Norris, 'Post-structuralist Shakespeare: Text and Ideology', in *Alternative Shakespeares*, ed. Drakakis, p. 66. The latest avatar of this tradition is, of course, Harold Bloom, whose mammoth tome *Shakespeare: The Invention of the Human* (London: Fourth Estate, 1998) strives in vain to turn the clock back to the halcyon days before the 'gender-and-power freaks' (p. 10) rode roughshod through the sleepy hollow of Shakespeare studies.

7. Jonathan Dollimore, 'Introduction: Shakespeare, Cultural Materialism and the New Historicism', in *Political Shakespeare*, ed. Dollimore and Sinfield, 2nd edn, p. 4.

8. Francis Barker and Peter Hulme, '"Nymphs and reapers heavily vanish": The Discursive Con-texts of *The Tempest*', in *Alternative Shakespeares*, ed. Drakakis, p. 191.

9. Drakakis, 'Introduction', *ibid.*, pp. 22–3.

10. Alan Sinfield, 'Give an Account of Shakespeare and Education, Showing Why You Think They Are Effective and What You Have Appreciated about Them. Support Your Comments with Precise References', in *Political Shakespeare*, ed. Dollimore and Sinfield, 2nd edn, p. 159. See also Lesley Aers, 'Shakespeare in the National Curriculum', in *Shakespeare in the Changing Curriculum*, ed. Lesley Aers and Nigel Wheale (London and New York: Routledge, 1991), pp. 30–9; Bob Allen, 'A School Perspective on Shakespeare Teaching', *ibid.*, pp. 40–57; Simon Barker, 'Re-loading the Canon: Shakespeare and the Study Guides', in *Shakespeare and National Culture*, ed. Joughin, pp. 42–57; and Richard Wilson, 'NATO's Pharmacy: Shakespeare by Prescription', *ibid.*, pp. 58–80.

11. One of the more notable successes of this pedagogic enterprise is the former Chancellor of the Exchequer, Nigel Lawson, who in 1983 published his conviction that 'Shakespeare was a Tory, without any doubt', whose drama powerfully endorsed the philosophy of Mrs Thatcher's government: see Margot Heinemann, 'How Brecht read Shakespeare', in *Political Shakespeare*, ed. Dollimore and Sinfield, 2nd edn, pp. 226–7, and Isobel Armstrong, 'Thatcher's Shakespeare?', *Textual Practice*, 3:1 (Spring, 1989), 1–14.

12. Sinfield, 'Give an Account of Shakespeare and Education...', p. 177 (Sinfield's emphasis).

13. Sinfield, 'Introduction: Reproductions, Interventions', in *Political Shakespeare*, ed. Dollimore and Sinfield, 2nd edn, p. 155. See also Dollimore and Sinfield, 'History and Ideology: The Instance of *Henry V*', in *Alternative Shakespeares*, ed. Drakakis, pp. 206–8. For extended

critiques of Shakespeare on the modern British stage, see Robert Shaughnessy, *Representing Shakespeare: England, History and the RSC* (Hemel Hempstead: Harvester Wheatsheaf, 1994), and Susan Bennett, *Performing Nostalgia: Shifting Shakespeare and the Contemporary Past* (London and New York: Routledge, 1996).

14. Graham Holderness, 'Radical Potentiality and Institutional Closure: Shakespeare in Film and Television', in *Political Shakespeare*, ed. Dollimore and Sinfield, 2nd edn, p. 223. See also Holderness, 'Boxing the Bard: Shakespeare and Television', in *The Shakespeare Myth*, ed. Holderness, pp. 173–89; Peter Reynolds, 'Unlocking the Box: Shakespeare on Film and Video', in *Shakespeare in the Changing Curriculum*, ed. Aers and Wheale, pp. 189–203; Susan Willis, *The BBC Shakespeare Plays: Making the Televised Canon* (Chapel Hill: University of North Carolina Press, 1991); Lynda E. Boose and Richard Burt, 'Totally Clueless: Shakespeare Goes Hollywood in the 1990s', in *Shakespeare, The Movie: Popularizing the Plays on Film, TV, and Video*, ed. Lynda E. Boose and Richard Burt (London and New York: Routledge, 1997), pp. 8–22; Barbara Hodgdon, *The Shakespeare Trade: Performance and Appropriations* (Philadelphia: University of Philadelphia Press, 1998); Deborah Cartmell, *Interpreting Shakespeare on Screen* (London: Macmillan, 2000); and Denise Albanese, 'The Shakespeare Film and the Americanization of Culture', in *Marxist Shakespeares*, ed. Jean E. Howard and Scott Shershow (London and New York: Routledge, 2001), pp. 206–26.

15. Sinfield, 'Give an Account of Shakespeare and Education . . . ', p. 161.

16. Dollimore, 'Introduction: Shakespeare, Cultural Materialism and the New Historicism', p. 15.

17. Dollimore, 'Transgression and Surveillance in *Measure for Measure*', in *Political Shakespeare*, ed. Dollimore and Sinfield, 2nd edn, p. 84.

18. Dollimore, 'Introduction: Shakespeare, Cultural Materialism and the New Historicism', p. 15.

19. Terry Eagleton, *William Shakespeare* (Oxford: Blackwell, 1986), pp. ix–x.

20. Elizabeth Freund, '"Ariachne's broken woof": The Rhetoric of Citation in *Troilus and Cressida*', in *Shakespeare and the Question of Theory*, ed. Patricia Parker and Geoffrey Hartman (New York and London: Methuen, 1985), p. 22.

21. Howard Felperin, '"Tongue-tied, our queen?": The Deconstruction of Presence in *The Winter's Tale*', *ibid.*, p. 8.

22. Malcolm Evans, 'Deconstructing Shakespeare's Comedies', in *Alternative Shakespeares*, ed. Drakakis, p. 93.

23. The following review of recent perspectives on *Lear* is imported, with minor revisions, from my essay '*King Lear*: The Battle for the Bard', in *Critical Dialogues: Current Issues in English Studies in Germany and Great Britain*, ed. Isobel Armstrong and Hans-Werner Ludwig (Tübingen: Gunter Narr, 1995), pp. 28–40. For an invaluable history of the reception of *King Lear* and the tragedy's rise to preeminence among Shakespeare's plays, see R. A. Foakes, *Hamlet Versus Lear: Cultural Politics and Shakespeare's Art* (Cambridge: Cambridge University Press, 1993).

24. Gary Waller, 'Decentring the Bard: The Dissemination of the Shakespearean Text', in *Shakespeare and Deconstruction*, ed. G. Douglas Atkins and David M. Bergeron (New York, Bern, Frankfurt and Paris: Peter Lang, 1988), p. 23.

25. Malcolm Evans, *Signifying Nothing: Truth's True Contents in Shakespeare's Text*, 2nd edn (Hemel Hempstead: Harvester Wheatsheaf, 1989), p. 224.

26. Jonathan Goldberg, 'Perspectives: Dover Cliff and the Conditions of Representation', in *Shakespeare and Deconstruction*, ed. Atkins and Bergeron, p. 254. See also Jackson I. Cope, 'Shakespeare, Derrida and the End of Language in *Lear*', *ibid.*, pp. 267–83.

27. Taylor, *Reinventing Shakespeare: A Cultural History from the Restoration to the Present*, pp. 410–11.

28. *Ibid.*, p. 230.

29. *Ibid.*, pp. 356–62.

30. The review is reprinted in Hawkes, *Meaning by Shakespeare*, pp. 141–53.

31. *Ibid.*, p. 150.

32. *Ibid.*, p. 146.

33. *Ibid.*, p. 147.

34. For an illuminating exercise in this vein of criticism, see Nancy Klein Maguire, 'Nahum Tate's *King Lear*: "the king's blest restoration"', in *The Appropriation of Shakespeare*, ed. Marsden, pp. 29–42. See also Caroline Cakebread, 'Remembering *King Lear* in Jane Smiley's *A Thousand Acres*', in *Shakespeare and Appropriation*, ed. Desmet and Sawyer, pp. 85–102.

35. Stephen Greenblatt, 'Shakespeare and the Exorcists', in *Shakespeare and the Question of Theory*, ed. Parker and Hartman, p. 164.

36. Leonard Tennenhouse, *Power on Display: The Politics of Shakespeare's Genres* (London and New York: Methuen, 1986), p. 15.

37. Kathleen McLuskie, 'The Patriarchal Bard: Feminist Criticism and Shakespeare: *King Lear* and *Measure for Measure*', in *Political Shakespeare*, ed. Dollimore and Sinfield, 2nd edn, p. 105.

38. For a survey of recent feminist criticism of the play, see Ann Thompson, 'Are There Any Women in *King Lear?*', in *The Matter of Difference*, ed. Wayne, pp. 117–28.

39. Leah Marcus, *Puzzling Shakespeare: Local Reading and Its Discontents* (Berkeley, Los Angeles and London: University of California Press, 1988), pp. 148–59.

40. Annabel Patterson, *Shakespeare and the Popular Voice* (Oxford: Blackwell, 1989), pp. 106–16.

41. Evans, 'Deconstructing Shakespeare's Comedies', p. 89.

42. *Ibid.*, p. 90.

43. Francis Barker, *The Culture of Violence: Essays on Tragedy and History* (Manchester: Manchester University Press, 1993), p. 124.

44. *Ibid.*, pp. 124, 123. Barker's critique of new historicism is more fully developed in the chapter 'A wilderness of tigers', *ibid.*, pp. 143–206. For further discussion of the vexed issues raised by new-historicist, cultural-materialist and deconstructive approaches to Shakespeare and Renaissance literature, see: Louis A. Montrose, 'Professing the Renaissance: The Poetics and Politics of Culture', in *The New Historicism*, ed. H. Aram Veeser (London: Routledge, 1989), pp. 15–36; Stephen Greenblatt, *Learning to Curse: Essays in Early Modern Culture* (New York and London: Routledge, 1990), Ch. 9: 'Resonance and Wonder'; Felperin, *The Uses of the Canon*, Ch. 8: '"Cultural Poetics" versus "Cultural Materialism": The Two New Historicisms in Renaissance Studies'; Graham Holderness, 'Production, Reproduction, Performance: Marxism, History, Theatre', in *Uses of History: Marxism, Postmodernism and the Renaissance*, ed. Francis Barker, Peter Hulme and Margaret Iversen (Manchester: Manchester University Press, 1991), pp. 153–78; Alan Sinfield, *Faultlines: Cultural Materialism and the Politics of Dissident Reading* (Oxford: Clarendon Press, 1992), Ch. 2: 'Cultural Materialism, *Othello*, and the Politics of Plausibility'; Vickers, *Appropriating Shakespeare*, Ch. 4: 'New Historicism: Disaffected Subjects', and Ch. 3: 'Deconstruction: Undermining, Overreaching'; Graham Bradshaw, *Misrepresentations: Shakespeare and the Materialists* (Ithaca, NY and London: Cornell University Press, 1993); Steven Mullaney, 'After the New Historicism', in *Alternative Shakespeares 2*, ed. Terence Hawkes (London and New York: Routledge, 1996), pp.

17–37; and Halpern, *Shakespeare Among the Moderns*, Ch. 1: 'Shakespeare in the Tropics: From High Modernism to New Historicism'. For a concise history and critique of new historicism and cultural materialism, see Kiernan Ryan (ed.), *New Historicism and Cultural Materialism: A Reader* (London: Edward Arnold, 1996), 'Introduction', pp. ix–xviii. For a full-length discussion, see Jeremy Hawthorn, *Cunning Passages: New Historicism, Cultural Materialism and Marxism in the Contemporary Literary Debate* (London: Edward Arnold, 1996).

45. See Terry Eagleton, *Walter Benjamin, or Towards a Revolutionary Criticism* (London: Verso, 1981), pp. 41, 116, 121.

46. What follows is a revised and expanded version of my essay '*The Merchant of Venice*: Past Significance and Present Meaning', *Shakespeare Jahrbuch*, 117 (1981), 49–54. A subsequent attempt to address similar theoretical issues in relation to the same text, with quite different results, can be found in Walter Cohen's '*The Merchant of Venice* and the Possibilities of Historical Criticism', *English Literary History*, 49 (1982), 765–89. Compare also Thomas Moisan, ' "Which is the merchant here? and which the Jew?" Subversion and Recuperation in *The Merchant of Venice*', in *Shakespeare Reproduced*, ed. Howard and O'Connor, pp. 188–206; Steven Mullaney, 'Brothers and Others, or The Art of Alienation', in *Cannibals, Witches, and Divorce: Estranging the Renaissance*, ed. Marjorie Garber (Baltimore and London: Johns Hopkins University Press, 1987), pp. 67–89; Lisa Freinkel, '*The Merchant of Venice*: "Modern" Anti-Semitism and the Veil of Allegory', in *Shakespeare and Modernity*, ed. Grady, pp. 122–41; and Eric S. Mallin, 'Jewish Invader and the Soul of State: *The Merchant of Venice* and Science Fiction Movies', *ibid.*, pp. 142–67. A valuable anthology of recent criticism can be found in Martin Coyle (ed.), *The Merchant of Venice: Contemporary Critical Essays* (London: Macmillan, 1998).

47. The unconsidered assumption that the play is anti-semitic has even led to its being banned from the classroom by school administrations in the United States, a fact which highlights how acutely *The Merchant* poses the problem of adequate reception. See Samuel Schoenbaum, 'Alternative Shakespeare', *Times Literary Supplement*, 27 October 1978, p. 1262. The Shylock controversy is amply documented in John Gross, *Shylock: Four Hundred Years in the Life of a Legend* (London: Chatto and Windus, 1992), and Harold Bloom (ed.), *Major Literary Characters: Shylock* (New York: Chelsea House, 1991). For a comprehensive study of the question of anti-semitism in Shakespeare, see James Shapiro, *Shakespeare and the Jews* (New York:

Columbia University Press, 1996), and Halpern, *Shakespeare Among the Moderns*, Ch. 4: 'The Jewish Question: Shakespeare and Anti-Semitism'.

48. For a concise survey and critique of these readings see A. D. Moody, *Shakespeare: The Merchant of Venice* (London: Edward Arnold, 1964), pp. 15–21.

49. John Russell Brown, 'Love's Wealth and *The Merchant of Venice*', in *Shakespeare: The Merchant of Venice: A Collection of Critical Essays*, ed. John Wilders (London: Macmillan, 1969), p. 173.

50. Schoenbaum, 'Alternative Shakespeare', pp. 1262–3.

51. Elliot Krieger, *A Marxist Study of Shakespeare's Comedies* (London: Macmillan, 1979), pp. 8–36. See also Frank Whigham, 'Ideology and Class Conduct in *The Merchant of Venice*', in *Shakespeare's Comedies*, ed. Gary Waller (London and New York: Longman, 1991), pp. 108–28.

52. Christian Enzensberger, *Literatur und Interesse: eine politische Ästhetik*, 2 vols (Frankfurt am Main: Suhrkamp, 1981), II, pp. 15–89.

53. See John Gillies, *Shakespeare and the Geography of Difference* (Cambridge: Cambridge University Press, 1994), pp. 122–37, for further reflections on how 'the confrontation between Antonio and Shylock amounts to a struggle over the political and economic heart of Venice' (p. 129).

54. Complementary and contrasting feminist views of the play can be found in Marianne Novy, *Love's Argument: Gender Relations in Shakespeare* (Chapel Hill and London: University of North Carolina Press, 1984), Ch. 4: 'Giving and Taking in *The Merchant of Venice*'; Coppélia Kahn, 'The Cuckoo's Note: Male Friendship and Cuckoldry in *The Merchant of Venice*', in *Shakespeare's 'Rough Magic': Renaissance Essays in Honor of C. L. Barber*, ed. Peter Erickson and Coppélia Kahn (Newark: University of Delaware Press, 1985), pp. 104–12; and Carol Leventen, 'Patrimony and Patriarchy in *The Merchant of Venice*', in *The Matter of Difference*, ed. Wayne, pp. 59–79. For a reading that opens to question the assumptions on which such accounts rest, see Alan Sinfield, 'How to Read *The Merchant of Venice* Without Being Heterosexist', in *Alternative Shakespeares 2*, ed. Hawkes, pp. 122–39.

55. The term is lifted from Thomas Metscher, 'Literature and Art as Ideological Form', *New Literary History*, XI (1979), pp. 36ff.

56. For a concise introduction to the bold conjectures that have recently transformed Shakespearean textual scholarship, see John Kerrigan, 'Shakespeare as Reviser', in *English Drama to 1710*, ed. Christopher

Ricks, 2nd edn (London: Sphere Books, 1987), pp. 255–75, and David Scott Kastan, *Shakespeare After Theory* (New York and London: Routledge, 1999), Ch. 3: 'The Mechanics of Culture: Editing Shakespeare Today'. A fuller historical account is furnished by Grace Ioppolo, *Revising Shakespeare* (Cambridge, MA: Harvard University Press, 1991). On the editorial and interpretive consequences of the new procedures, see Leah S. Marcus, *Unediting the Renaissance: Shakespeare, Marlowe, Milton* (London and New York: Routledge, 1996).

57.   Greenblatt, 'Invisible Bullets: Renaissance Authority and its Subversion, *Henry IV* and *Henry V*', in *Political Shakespeare*, ed. Dollimore and Sinfield, 2nd edn, p. 33.

58.   At the end of his 'Afterword' to *Political Shakespeare*, ed. Dollimore and Sinfield, Raymond Williams asserts that the form of Shakespearean drama is 'inherently multivocal' and its composition 'inherently interactive', and he concludes by expressing his belief that 'the most practical and effective new direction will be in analysis of the historically based conventions of language and representation: the plays themselves as socially and materially produced, within discoverable conditions; indeed the texts themselves as history' (2nd edn, pp. 288–9). One aim of the present book is to help turn the study of Shakespeare in this direction.

59.   The following sketch of the main factors shaping the deep structure and dynamics of Renaissance literature draws on my essay 'The Extemporal Vein: Thomas Nashe and the Invention of Modern Narrative', in *Narrative: From Malory to Motion Pictures*, ed. Jeremy Hawthorn, Stratford-upon-Avon Studies, second series (London: Edward Arnold, 1985), pp. 44–5. It owes much to Robert Weimann, *Realismus in der Renaissance* (Berlin and Weimar: Aufbau Verlag, 1977), pp. 5–110, and to Agnes Heller, *Renaissance Man* (London: Routledge and Kegan Paul, 1978), pp. 2–5, 8–10.

60.   See Karl Marx, *Grundrisse: Foundations of the Critique of Political Economy* (Harmondsworth: Penguin, 1973), especially pp. 485–8, 540–2.

61.   Karl Marx, *The Revolutions of 1848: Political Writings I* (Harmondsworth: Penguin, 1973), I, p. 70.

62.   Marx, *Grundrisse*, p. 158.

63.   See Heller, *Renaissance Man*, pp. 428, 437, 452, 373.

64.   John Donne, *Devotions upon Emergent Occasions*, ed. Anthony Raspa (Montreal and London: McGill-Queen's University Press, 1975), p. 87.

65. Michel de Montaigne, *Essais*, ed. Maurice Rat, 2 vols (Paris: Garnier, 1962), II, p. 222. Florio's translation (1603) runs: 'Every man beareth the whole stampe of humane condition' (*The Essayes of Michael Lord of Montaigne*, 3 vols (London: Dent, 1928), III, pp. 23–4).

66. What follows is indebted to the groundbreaking studies of Robert Weimann, *Shakespeare and the Popular Tradition in the Theater* (Baltimore and London: Johns Hopkins University Press, 1978), pp. 161–252; Walter Cohen, *Drama of a Nation: Public Theater in Renaissance England and Spain* (Ithaca, NY and London: Cornell University Press, 1985), pp. 136–85; and Michael D. Bristol, *Carnival and Theater: Plebeian Culture and the Structure of Authority in Renaissance England* (New York and London: Methuen, 1985), pp. 107–24. More recent support for the main points made here can be found in Steven Mullaney, *The Place of the Stage: License, Play and Power in Renaissance England* (Chicago and London: University of Chicago Press, 1988), and Jean E. Howard, *The Stage and Social Struggle in Early Modern England* (New York and London: Routledge, 1994).

67. Weimann, *Shakespeare and the Popular Tradition*, p. 167.

68. J. B. Black, quoted *ibid.*, p. 162.

69. Cohen, *Drama of a Nation*, p. 149.

70. *Ibid.*, pp. 177, 151.

71. Weimann, *Shakespeare and the Popular Tradition*, p. 171.

72. Cohen, *Drama of a Nation*, pp. 180, 151.

73. *Ibid.*, pp. 19, 176.

74. Bristol, *Carnival and Theater*, p. 112.

75. Cohen, *Drama of a Nation*, p. 19.

76. Weimann, *Shakespeare and the Popular Tradition*, p. 174.

77. Bristol, *Carnival and Theater*, p. 108.

78. *Ibid.*, pp. 111–12.

79. *Ibid.*, pp. 107, 113.

80. *Ibid.*, Ch. 7: 'Authority and the Author Function'.

81. Weimann, *Shakespeare and the Popular Tradition*, p. 173.

82. *Ibid.*, p. 169.

83. Erich Auerbach, *Mimesis: The Representation of Reality in Western Literature*, trans. Willard R. Trask (Princeton: Princeton University Press, 1953), p. 322.

84. Jonathan Goldberg, 'Shakespearean Inscriptions: The Voicing of Power', in *Shakespeare and the Question of Theory*, ed. Parker and Hartman, p. 116.

85. Bristol, *Carnival and Theater*, pp. 122, 123.

86. *Ibid.*, p. 123.
87. Montaigne, *Essais*, II, p. 328. Florio translates: 'both male and female, are cast in one same moulde; instruction and custom excepted, there is no great difference between them' (Montaigne, *Essayes*, III, p. 128).
88. Shakespeare's variations on these themes are explored in Anne Righter [Anne Barton], *Shakespeare and the Idea of the Play* (Harmondsworth: Penguin, 1967), and James L. Calderwood, *Shakespearean Metadrama* (Minneapolis: University of Minnesota Press, 1971).
89. Weimann, *Shakespeare and the Popular Tradition*, p. 216.
90. *Ibid.*, p. 214.
91. See Bertolt Brecht, 'A Short Organum for the Theatre', in *Brecht on Theatre*, trans. and ed. John Willett (London: Methuen, 1964), pp. 179–205.

Chapter 2

1. For fuller expositions and further commentary, see William C. Dowling, *Jameson, Althusser, Marx: An Introduction to 'The Political Unconscious'* (London: Methuen, 1984); J. A. Berthoud, 'Narrative and Ideology: A Critique of Fredric Jameson's *The Political Unconscious*', in *Narrative: From Malory to Motion Pictures*, ed. Jeremy Hawthorn (London: Edward Arnold, 1985), pp. 101–16; Philip Goldstein, *The Politics of Literary Theory: An Introduction to Marxist Criticism* (Tallahassee: Florida State University Press, 1990), pp. 146–61; K. M. Newton, *Interpreting the Text* (Hemel Hempstead: Harvester Wheatsheaf, 1990), pp. 111–19; and Adam Roberts, *Fredric Jameson* (London and New York: Routledge, 2000), Ch. 4.
2. Fredric Jameson, *The Political Unconscious: Narrative as a Socially Symbolic Act* (Ithaca, NY: Cornell University Press, 1981), p. 18.
3. Fredric Jameson, 'Marxism and Historicism', in his *The Ideologies of Theory: Essays, 1971–1986*, Volume 2: *The Syntax of History* (London: Routledge, 1988), p. 175.
4. *Ibid.*, pp. 175, 176, 177.
5. Jameson, *The Political Unconscious*, p. 81.
6. See above, pp. 24–5.
7. Jameson, *The Political Unconscious*, p. 81.
8. *Ibid.*, p. 79.
9. *Ibid.*, p. 287.

10. *Ibid.*, p. 291.

11. On the issue of theatrical and verbal self-consciousness in *1* and *2 Henry IV*, see Sigurd Burckhardt, *Shakespeare's Meanings* (Princeton: Princeton University Press, 1968), pp. 144–205; James L. Calderwood, *Metadrama in Shakespeare's Henriad: Richard II to Henry V* (Berkeley: University of California Press, 1979); Graham Bradshaw, *Shakespeare's Scepticism* (Brighton: Harvester Wheatsheaf, 1987), pp. 50–65; and Ronald R. Macdonald, 'Uneasy Lies: Language and History in Shakespeare's Lancastrian Tetralogy', *Shakespeare Quarterly*, 35 (1984), 22–39.

12. John Kerrigan, '*Henry IV* and the Death of Old Double', *Essays in Criticism*, XXXX (1990), 24–53.

13. On the plays as dramatic historiography, see Phyllis Rackin, *Stages of History: Shakespeare's English Chronicles* (Ithaca, NY: Cornell University Press, 1990), pp. 137–48; Catherine Belsey, 'Making Histories Then and Now: Shakespeare from *Richard II* to *Henry V*', in *Uses of History: Marxism, Postmodernism and the Renaissance*, ed. Francis Barker, Peter Hulme and Margaret Iverson (Manchester: Manchester University Press, 1991), pp. 24–46; Jean E. Howard and Phyllis Rackin, *Engendering a Nation: A Feminist Account of Shakespeare's English Histories* (London and New York: Routledge, 1997), Chs 2 and 11; and Graham Holderness, *Shakespeare Recycled: The Making of Historical Drama* (Hemel Hempstead: Harvester Wheatsheaf, 1992), Ch. 4, and *Shakespeare: The Histories* (London: Macmillan, 2000), Chs 2 and 7.

14. *Elizabethan Critical Essays*, ed. G. Gregory Smith, 2 vols (Oxford, 1904), II, p. 370; quoted by Rackin, *Stages of History*, p. 143.

15. Scott McMillin, *Shakespeare in Performance: Henry IV, Part One* (Manchester and New York: Manchester University Press, 1991), pp. 11–12.

16. Quoted *ibid.*, p. 57.

17. Quoted *ibid.*, p. 83.

18. *Ibid.*, p. 87.

19. *Ibid.*, p. 85.

20. *Ibid.*, p. 86.

21. E. M. W. Tillyard, *Shakespeare's History Plays* (London: Chatto and Windus, 1944), pp. 320–1.

22. *Ibid.*, p. 269.

23. *Ibid.*, p. 277.

24. Holderness, *Shakespeare Recycled*, p. 27.

25. John Dover Wilson, *The Fortunes of Falstaff* (Cambridge: Cambridge University Press, 1943); G. Wilson Knight, *The Olive and the Sword* (Oxford: Oxford University Press, 1944); Lily B. Campbell, *Shakespeare's Histories: Mirrors of Elizabethan Policy* (San Marino, CA: Huntington Library, 1947).

26. C. L. Barber, *Shakespeare's Festive Comedy* (Princeton: Princeton University Press, 1959), p. 226.

27. Leonard Tennenhouse, *Power on Display: The Politics of Shakespeare's Genres* (London: Methuen, 1986), pp. 83–4.

28. Stephen Greenblatt, *Shakespearean Negotiations: The Circulation of Social Energy in Renaissance England* (Oxford: Clarendon Press, 1988), p. 40.

29. *Ibid.*, p. 65.

30. For an intriguing variation on this line of argument, see Steven Mullaney, *The Place of the Stage: License, Play, and Power in Renaissance England* (Chicago and London: University of Chicago Press, 1988), pp. 76–87.

31. Holderness, *Shakespeare Recycled*, p. 138.

32. Quoted in Fredric Jameson, *Marxism and Form* (Princeton: Princeton University Press, 1971), p. 149; translated by Jameson from Bloch, *Das Prinzip Hoffnung* (Frankfurt am Main: Suhrkamp, 1959), p. 110.

33. Theodor Adorno, *Minima Moralia*, trans. E. F. N. Jephcott (London: Verso, 1974), p. 247.

Chapter 3

1. See, for example, Leonard Tennenhouse, *Power on Display: The Politics of Shakespeare's Genres* (London: Methuen, 1986), Ch. 3: 'The Theater of Punishment: Jacobean Tragedy and the Politics of Misogyny'.

2. Francis Barker, *The Culture of Violence: Essays on Tragedy and History* (Manchester: Manchester University Press, 1993), p. 49.

3. G. Wilson Knight, '*King Lear* and the Comedy of the Grotesque', in *The Wheel of Fire: Essays in the Interpretation of Shakespearian Tragedy*, 4th rev. edn (London: Methuen, 1949), p. 176. The essay is anthologized in at least three standard critical casebooks: Laurence Lerner (ed.), *Shakespeare's Tragedies: An Anthology of Modern Criticism* (Harmondsworth: Penguin, 1963); Alfred Harbage (ed.), *Shakespeare: The Tragedies* (Englewood Cliffs, NJ: Prentice Hall, 1964); and Frank Kermode (ed.), *King Lear: A Selection of Critical Essays*, 2nd rev. edn (London: Macmillan, 1992).

4. H. B. Charlton, 'Humanism and Mystery', in *Shakespeare: The Traged-ies*, ed. Harbage, p. 10; reprinted from Charlton, *Shakespearian Tra-gedy* (Cambridge: Cambridge University Press, 1948).

5. Michael Long, *The Unnatural Scene: A Study in Shakespearean Tragedy* (London: Methuen, 1976), p. 35.

6. Quoted in Harold Jenkins (ed.), *Hamlet*, New Arden Shakespeare (London: Methuen, 1982), p. 122.

7. Maynard Mack, 'The World of Hamlet', in *Hamlet: A Selection of Critical Essays*, ed. John Jump (London: Macmillan, 1968); also anthologized in *Twentieth Century Interpretations of Hamlet*, ed. David Bevington (Englewood Cliffs, NJ: Prentice Hall, 1968), and in *Shakespeare: The Tragedies*, ed. Harbage.

8. *Hamlet*, ed. Jenkins, p. 159.

9. Willard Farnham, 'The Tragic Qualm', in *Shakespeare: The Tragedies*, ed. Harbage, pp. 20, 21; reprinted from Farnham, *The Medieval Heritage of Elizabethan Tragedy* (Berkeley: University of California Press, 1936).

10. A. C. Bradley, *Shakespearean Tragedy*, 3rd edn (London: Macmillan, 1992), p. 27.

11. Farnham, 'The Tragic Qualm', p. 22.

12. The phrase adopted by Northrop Frye for the title of *Fools of Time: Studies in Shakespearean Tragedy* (Toronto: University of Toronto Press, 1967).

13. J. W. Draper, *Stratford to Dogberry* (Pittsburgh: University of Penn-sylvania Press, 1961), p. 88.

14. John Lawlor, '*Romeo and Juliet*', in *Early Shakespeare*, ed. John Russell Brown and Bernard Harris, Stratford-upon-Avon Studies 3 (London: Edward Arnold, 1961), p. 132.

15. Frank Kermode, '*Romeo and Juliet*', in *The Riverside Shakespeare*, ed. G. B. Evans, 2nd edn (Boston, MA: Houghton Mifflin, 1997), p. 1103.

16. Norman Rabkin, *Shakespeare and the Common Understanding* (New York: Free Press, 1967), p. 151.

17. T. J. B. Spencer (ed), *Romeo and Juliet* (Harmondsworth: Penguin, 1967), pp. 21, 22.

18. Franklin M. Dickey, *Not Wisely But Too Well: Shakespeare's Love Tragedies* (San Marino, CA: Huntington Library, 1957), p. 63.

19. D. A. Stauffer, 'The School of Love: *Romeo and Juliet*', in *Shakespeare: The Tragedies*, ed. Harbage, p. 30.

20. Virgil K. Whitaker, *The Mirror up to Nature* (San Marino, CA: Huntington Library, 1965), p. 115.

21. Larry S. Champion, *Shakespeare's Tragic Perspective* (Athens, GA: University of Georgia Press, 1976), p. 84.

22. Julia Kristeva, 'Romeo and Juliet: Love-hatred in the Couple', in *Tales of Love*, trans. Leon S. Roudiez (New York: Columbia University Press, 1987), p. 222.

23. Irene G. Dash, *Wooing, Wedding and Power: Women in Shakespeare's Plays* (New York: Columbia University Press, 1981), p. 71.

24. Edward Snow, 'Language and Sexual Difference in *Romeo and Juliet*', in *Shakespeare's 'Rough Magic': Renaissance Essays in Honor of C. L. Barber*, ed. Peter Erickson and Coppélia Kahn (Newark: University of Delaware Press, 1985), pp. 168–92. See also Catherine Belsey, 'The Name of the Rose in *Romeo and Juliet*', in *Shakespeare's Tragedies: Contemporary Critical Essays*, ed. Susan Zimmerman (London: Macmillan, 1998), pp. 46–63.

25. Coppélia Kahn, 'Coming of Age in Verona', in *The Woman's Part: Feminist Criticism of Shakespeare*, ed. Carolyn Ruth Swift Lenz, Gayle Greene and Carol Thomas Neely (Urbana and London: University of Illinois Press, 1980), p. 185.

26. Dympna Callaghan, 'The Ideology of Romantic Love: The Case of *Romeo and Juliet*', in Dympna Callaghan, Lorraine Helms and Jyotsna Singh, *The Weyward Sisters: Shakespeare and Feminist Politics* (Oxford: Blackwell, 1994), pp. 61, 59–60. A complementary gay perspective on the play can be found in Jonathan Goldberg's essay '*Romeo and Juliet*'s Open Rs', in *Queering the Renaissance*, ed. Jonathan Goldberg (Durham, NC and London: Duke University Press, 1994), pp. 218–35.

27. *Marx: Surveys from Exile*, ed. David Fernbach (Harmondsworth: Penguin, 1973), p. 146.

28. Further reflections on the mutations of the lovers' language can be found in Harry Levin, 'Form and Formality in *Romeo and Juliet*', in *Twentieth Century Interpretations of Romeo and Juliet*, ed. Douglas Cole (Englewood Cliffs, NJ: Prentice Hall, 1970), pp. 85–95.

29. See also the striking instances Snow cites of verbal echoes whose 'effect is of two imaginations working in the same idiom', and which 'imply the existence of a single world of desire encompassing the two lovers' separate longings' ('Language and Sexual Difference in *Romeo and Juliet*', p. 169).

30. Callaghan, 'The Ideology of Romantic Love', p. 71.

31. *Othello*, ed. Alvin Kernan, Signet Classic Shakespeare (New York: New American Library, 1963), pp. xxxiv–xxxv.

32. *The Riverside Shakespeare*, ed. Evans, 2nd edn, p. 1250.

33. See in particular Ruth Cowhig, 'Blacks in English Renaissance Drama and the Role of Shakespeare's *Othello*', in *The Black Presence in English Literature*, ed. David Dabydeen (Manchester: Manchester University Press, 1985); pp. 1–25; Karen Newman, ' "And wash the Ethiop white": Femininity and the Monstrous in *Othello*', in her *Fashioning Femininity and English Renaissance Drama* (Chicago and London: Chicago University Press, 1991), pp. 71–93; Ben Okri, 'Meditations on *Othello*', *West Africa* (23 and 30 March 1987), pp. 562–4, 618–19; Martin Orkin, '*Othello* and the "plain face" of Racism', *Shakespeare Quarterly*, 38:2 (Summer, 1987), 166–88; John Salway, 'Veritable Negroes and Circumcised Dogs: Racial Disturbances in Shakespeare', in *Shakespeare in the Changing Curriculum*, ed. Lesley Aers and Nigel Wheale (London and New York: Routledge, 1991), pp. 108–24; Sudipto Chatterjee and Jyotsna G. Singh, 'Moor or Less? The Surveillance of *Othello*, Calcutta 1848', in *Shakespeare and Appropriation*, ed. Christy Desmet and Robert Sawyer (London and New York: Routledge, 1999), pp. 65–82; and Dympna Callaghan, *Shakespeare Without Women: Representing Gender and Race on the Renaissance Stage* (London and New York: Routledge, 2000), Ch. 3: ' "Othello was a white man": Properties of Race on Shakespeare's Stage'.

34. G. M. Matthews, '*Othello* and the Dignity of Man', in *Shakespeare in a Changing World*, ed. Arnold Kettle (London: Lawrence and Wishart, 1964), p. 126.

35. Arthur Kirsch, *Shakespeare and the Experience of Love* (Cambridge: Cambridge University Press, 1981), p. 39.

36. See, for example, John Bayley, 'The Fragile Structure of *Othello*', *Times Literary Supplement*, 20 June 1980, pp. 707–9. Professor Bayley betrays his assumptions most conspicuously when he finds it a 'paradox' that Shakespeare 'should invest the black man with the power of love, as he had invested Shylock with the voice of humanity, while Iago, the friend and trusted officer of the military and social establishment, is the spokesman of sex in its crudest and most acquisitive form' (p. 709). Professor Kirsch, on the other hand, needs no more than a 'but' to blow the gaff on his preconceptions: 'It is no wonder that Othello . . . should in such a world find it tragically impossible to hold to the scriptural belief, which is also Desdemona's, that he is "black, but beautiful" ' (*Shakespeare and the Experience of Love*, p. 37).

37. See also Carol Thomas Neely, 'Women and Men in *Othello*: "What should such a fool/ Do with so good a woman?"', in *The Woman's Part*, ed. Lenz, Greene and Neely, pp. 211–39; Dash, *Wooing, Wedding and Power*, Ch. 5: 'A Woman Tamed: *Othello*'; Marianne Novy, *Love's Argument: Gender Relations in Shakespeare* (Chapel Hill: University of North Carolina Press, 1984), Ch. 7: 'Marriage and Mutuality in *Othello*'; Valerie Wayne, 'Historical Differences: Misogyny and *Othello*', in *The Matter of Difference: Materialist Criticism of Shakespeare*, ed. Valerie Wayne (Hemel Hempstead: Harvester Wheatsheaf, 1991), pp. 153–79; Janet Adelman, *Suffocating Mothers: Fantasies of Maternal Origin in Shakespeare's Plays, Hamlet to The Tempest* (New York and London: Routledge, 1992), Ch. 3: '"Is thy union here?": Union and its Discontents in *Troilus and Cressida* and *Othello*'; Patricia Parker, 'Fantasies of "Race" and "Gender": Africa, *Othello*, and Bringing to Light', in *Shakespeare's Tragedies*, ed. Zimmerman, pp. 167–93; and Dympna Callaghan, 'Looking Well to Linens: Women and Cultural Production in *Othello* and Shakespeare's England', in *Marxist Shakespeares*, ed. Jean E. Howard and Scott Shershow (London and New York: Routledge, 2001), pp. 53–81.

38. Kenneth Muir (ed.), *Macbeth*, 10th rev. edn, New Arden Shakespeare (London: Methuen, 1972), p. xlv.

39. The most stimulating recent challenges to this consensus can be found in Alan Sinfield (ed.), *Macbeth: Contemporary Critical Essays* (London: Macmillan, 1992).

40. Terry Eagleton, *William Shakespeare* (Oxford: Blackwell, 1986), pp. 2, 3.

41. There is now a rich critical literature on masculinity in *Macbeth*. See in particular Coppélia Kahn, 'The Milking Babe and the Bloody Man in *Coriolanus* and *Macbeth*', in her *Man's Estate: Masculine Identity in Shakespeare* (Berkeley, Los Angeles and London: University of California Press, 1981), pp. 172–92; Marjorie Garber, 'Macbeth: The Male Medusa', in her *Shakespeare's Ghost Writers: Literature as Uncanny Causality* (New York and London: Methuen, 1987), pp. 87–123; Marilyn Williamson, 'Violence and Gender Ideology in *Coriolanus* and *Macbeth*', in *Shakespeare Left and Right*, ed. Ivo Kamps (New York and London: Routledge, 1991), pp. 147–66; and Adelman, *Suffocating Mothers*, Ch. 6: 'Escaping the Matrix: The Construction of Masculinity in *Macbeth* and *Coriolanus*', pp. 130–46.

42. J. K. Walton, '*Macbeth*', in *Shakespeare in a Changing World*, ed. Kettle, pp. 104–5.

43. See above, pp. 7–13. For a selection of representative modern views of the tragedy, see Kiernan Ryan (ed.), *King Lear: Contemporary Critical Essays* (London: Macmillan, 1993).

44. *The Riverside Shakespeare*, ed. Evans, 2nd edn, p. 1299.

45. Bradley, *Shakespearean Tragedy*, 3rd edn, p. 246.

46. Kenneth Muir (ed.), *King Lear*, New Arden Shakespeare (London: Methuen, 1972), pp. lii, l, lv.

47. Jan Kott, 'King Lear, or Endgame', in his *Shakespeare Our Contemporary*, 2nd rev. edn (London: Methuen, 1967); reprinted in *Shakespeare: King Lear*, ed. Kermode.

48. George Orwell, 'Lear, Tolstoy and the Fool', in *Shooting an Elephant* (London: Secker and Warburg, 1950); reprinted in *Shakespeare: King Lear*, ed. Kermode.

49. For a fuller exploration of the play as patriarchal tragedy, see Novy, *Love's Argument*, Ch. 8: 'Patriarchy, Mutuality, and Forgiveness in *King Lear*'; Coppélia Kahn, 'The Absent Mother in *King Lear*', in *Rewriting the Renaissance*, ed. Margaret Ferguson, Maureen Quilligan and Nancy Vickers (Chicago and London: University of Chicago Press, 1986), pp. 33–49; and Adelman, *Suffocating Mothers*, Ch. 5: 'Suffocating Mothers in *King Lear*'.

50. Arthur Kirsch, *The Passions of Shakespeare's Tragic Heroes* (Charlottesville and London: University of Virginia Press, 1990), p. 127.

51. David Aers and Gunther Kress, 'The Language of Social Order: Individual, Society and Historical Process in *King Lear*', in David Aers, Bob Hodge and Gunther Kress, *Literature, Language and Society in England 1580–1680* (Dublin: Gill and Macmillan, 1981), pp. 98–9.

Chapter 4

1. See above, p. 62.

2. C. L. Barber, *Shakespeare's Festive Comedy* (Princeton: Princeton University Press, 1959), p. 245.

3. Northrop Frye, *A Natural Perspective: The Development of Shakespearean Comedy and Romance* (New York: Columbia University Press, 1965), pp. 75, 130, 119, 121, 75, 104.

4. Barber, *Shakespeare's Festive Comedy*, p. 139. Annabel Patterson supplies a salutary antidote to Barber and Frye in her *Shakespeare and the Popular Voice* (Oxford: Blackwell, 1989), Ch. 3: 'Bottom's Up: Festive

Theory'. See also François Laroque, *Shakespeare's Festive World: Eliza-bethan Entertainment and the Professional Stage* (Cambridge: Cambridge University Press, 1991).

5. Elliot Krieger, *A Marxist Study of Shakespeare's Comedies* (London: Macmillan, 1979), pp. 5–6. *A Midsummer Night's Dream* receives similar treatment from James H. Kavanagh's essay 'Shakespeare in Ideology', in *Alternative Shakespeares*, ed. John Drakakis (London and New York: Routledge, 1985), pp. 152–6. For a recent compendium of more fruitful approaches to the play, see Richard Dutton (ed.), *A Midsummer Night's Dream: Contemporary Critical Essays* (London: Mac-millan, 1996).

6. Leonard Tennenhouse, *Power on Display: The Politics of Shakespeare's Genres* (New York and London: Methuen, 1986), pp. 44, 62, 74, 185, 183, 171.

7. Richard Wilson ploughs the same Foucauldian furrow as Tennen-house, though with far more elegance and wit, in *Will Power: Essays on Shakespearean Authority* (Hemel Hempstead: Harvester Wheatsheaf, 1993), Ch. 5: 'The Quality of Mercy: Discipline and Punishment in Shakespearean Comedy', and Ch. 6: 'Observations on English Bodies: Licensing Maternity in Shakespeare's Late Plays'.

8. For a useful selection of representative recent criticism on the com-edies, see Gary Waller (ed.), *Shakespeare's Comedies* (London and New York: Longman, 1991).

9. H. B. Charlton, *Shakespearian Comedy*, 2nd edn (London: Methuen, 1938), pp. 277–8.

10. Walter Cohen, *Drama of a Nation: Public Theater in Renaissance Eng-land and Spain* (Ithaca, NY: Cornell University Press, 1985), p. 391.

11. Tom Moylan, *Demand the Impossible: Science Fiction and the Utopian Imagination* (New York and London: Methuen, 1986), pp. 31, 35 (Moylan's italics).

12. The contrast between this conception of romance and the religiose assumptions governing more traditional studies of Shakespeare's last plays could scarcely be more pronounced. See especially E. M. W. Tillyard, *Shakespeare's Last Plays* (London: Chatto and Windus, 1938); G. Wilson Knight, *The Crown of Life: Essays in Interpretation of Shakespeare's Final Plays* (Oxford: Oxford University Press, 1947); and Derek A. Traversi, *Shakespeare: The Last Phase* (London: Hollis and Carter, 1954). The range of conventional criticism on the roman-ces can also be sampled in three collections of essays: John Russell Brown and Bernard Harris (eds), *Later Shakespeare* (London: Edward

Arnold, 1966); Richard Tobias and Paul G. Zolbrod (eds), *Shakespeare's Late Plays* (Athens: University of Ohio Press, 1974); and C. M. Kay and H. E. Jacobs (eds), *Shakespeare's Romances Reconsidered* (Lincoln: University of Nebraska Press, 1978). Useful surveys of previous criticism on the romances are furnished by Philip Edwards, 'Shakespeare's Romances: 1900–1957', *Shakespeare Survey*, 11 (1958), 1–18; F. D. Hoeniger, 'Shakespeare's Romances Since 1958: A Retrospect', *Shakespeare Survey*, 29 (1976), 1–10; and Norman Sanders, 'An Overview of Critical Approaches to the Romances', in *Shakespeare's Romances Reconsidered*, ed. Kay and Jacobs, pp. 1–10. For a comprehensive survey of twentieth-century criticism on the romances and a selection of the most significant recent essays on these plays, see Kiernan Ryan (ed.), *Shakespeare: The Last Plays* (London: Longman, 1999).

13. Frye, *A Natural Perspective*, p. 146.

14. Mikhail Bakhtin, *The Dialogic Imagination* (Austin and London: University of Texas Press, 1981), pp. 404, 162.

15. Cohen, *Drama of a Nation*, p. 191.

16. Catherine Belsey, 'Disrupting Sexual Difference: Meaning and Gender in the Comedies', in *Alternative Shakespeares*, ed. Drakakis, pp. 190, 167.

17. For extended engagements with the issues broached in this paragraph, see Marianne Novy, *Love's Argument: Gender Relations in Shakespeare* (Chapel Hill: University of North Carolina Press, 1984), Ch. 10: 'Shakespeare's Imagery of Gender and Gender Crossing'; Jean E. Howard, 'Renaissance Antitheatricality and the Politics of Gender and Rank in *Much Ado About Nothing*', in *Shakespeare Reproduced: The Text in History and Ideology*, ed. Jean E. Howard and Marion F. O'Connor (New York and London: Methuen, 1987), pp. 163–87; Stephen Greenblatt, *Shakespearean Negotiations: The Circulation of Social Energy in Renaissance England* (Oxford: Clarendon Press, 1988), Ch. 3: 'Fiction and Friction'; Cristina Malcolmson, '"What You Will": Social Mobility and Gender in *Twelfth Night*', in *The Matter of Difference: Materialist Feminist Criticism of Shakespeare*, ed. Valerie Wayne (Hemel Hempstead: Harvester Wheatsheaf, 1991), pp. 29–57; Valerie Traub, 'Desire and the Differences It Makes', *ibid.*, pp. 81–114; Marjorie Garber, *Vested Interests: Cross-Dressing and Cultural Anxiety* (London and New York: Routledge, 1992); Peter Stallybrass, 'Transvestism and the "Body Beneath": Speculating on the Boy Actor', in *Erotic Politics: Desire on the Renaissance Stage*, ed. Susan Zimmerman (New York and London: Routledge, 1992), pp. 64–83;

Lesley Ferris (ed.), *Crossing the Stage: Controversies on Cross-Dressing* (London: Routledge, 1993); Carol Cook, '"The sign and semblance of her honour": Reading Gender Difference in *Much Ado About Nothing*', in *Shakespeare and Gender: A History*, ed. Deborah E. Barker and Ivo Kamps (London and New York: Verso), pp. 75–103; Lisa Jardine, *Reading Shakespeare Historically* (New York and London: Routledge, 1996), Ch. 4: 'Twins and Travesties: Gender, Dependency and Sexual Availability in *Twelfth Night*'; Stephen Cohen, '(Post)modern Elizabeth: Gender, Politics, and the Emergence of Modern Subjectivity', in *Shakespeare and Modernity: Early Modern to Millennium*, ed. Hugh Grady (New York and London: Routledge, 2000); and Dympna Callaghan, *Shakespeare Without Women: Representing Gender and Race on the Renaissance Stage* (London and New York: Routledge, 2000), Ch. 1: '"And all is semblative a woman's part": Body Politics and *Twelfth Night*', and Ch. 2: 'The Castrator's Song: Female Impersonation on the Early Modern Stage'.

18. Belsey, 'Disrupting Sexual Difference', pp. 166–7, 190.

19. Different angles on the use of language in Shakespearean comedy and romance can be found in Howard Felperin, '"Tongue-tied, our queen?": The Deconstruction of Presence in *The Winter's Tale*', in *Shakespeare and the Question of Theory*, ed. Patricia Parker and Geoffrey Hartman (New York and London: Methuen, 1985), pp. 3–18; Malcolm Evans, 'Deconstructing Shakespeare's Comedies', in *Alternative Shakespeares*, ed. Drakakis, pp. 67–94, and *Signifying Nothing: Truth's True Contents in Shakespeare's Text*, 2nd edn (Hemel Hempstead: Harvester Wheatsheaf, 1989), pp. 50–68, 145–64; Katharine Eisaman Maus, 'Transfer of Title in *Love's Labor's Lost*: Language, Individualism, Gender', in *Shakespeare Left and Right*, ed. Ivo Kamps (New York and London: Routledge, 1991), pp. 205–23; Anne Barton, 'Leontes and the Spider: Language and Speaker in Shakespeare's Last Plays', in her *Essays, Mainly Shakespearean* (Cambridge: Cambridge University Press, 1994), pp. 161–81; and Patricia Parker, *Shakespeare From the Margins: Language, Culture, Context* (Chicago: University of Chicago Press, 1996), Ch. 2: 'The Bible and the Marketplace: *The Comedy of Errors*', Ch. 3: '"Rude Mechanicals": *A Midsummer Night's Dream* and Shakespearean Joinery', and Ch. 6: 'Dilation and Inflation: *All's Well That Ends Well*, *Troilus and Cressida*, and Shakespearean Increase'.

20. The significance of Philharmonus's prophecy is discussed more fully in Chapter 5, pp. 173–5.

21. *The Works of Thomas Nashe*, ed. R. G. McKerrow, 5 vols (Oxford: Blackwell, 1958), III, p. 312. See Kiernan Ryan, 'The Extemporal Vein: Thomas Nashe and the Invention of Modern Narrative', in *Narrative: From Malory to Motion Pictures*, ed. Jeremy Hawthorn, Stratford-upon-Avon Studies, second series (London: Edward Arnold, 1985), pp. 40–54.

22. *Samuel Johnson on Shakespeare*, ed. H. R. Woudhuysen (Harmondsworth: Penguin, 1989), p. 132.

23. Greenblatt, *Shakespearean Negotiations*, pp. 88–9.

24. *The Complete Works of William Hazlitt*, ed. P. P. Howe, 21 vols (London and Toronto: Dent, 1930), IV, p. 346.

25. Michel Foucault, *Discipline and Punish: The Birth of the Prison*, trans. Alan Sheridan (Harmondsworth: Penguin, 1977).

26. Leonard Tennenhouse, *Power on Display: The Politics of Shakespeare's Genres* (New York and London: Methuen, 1986), pp. 15, 157.

27. Foucault, *Discipline and Punish*, p. 201.

28. *Ibid.*, p. 200.

29. Jonathan Goldberg, *James I and the Politics of Literature: Jonson, Shakespeare, Donne, and their Contemporaries* (Baltimore and London: Johns Hopkins University Press), p. 239.

30. Richard Wilson, *Will Power: Essays on Shakespearean Authority* (Hemel Hempstead: Harvester Wheatsheaf, 1993), p. 126.

31. *Ibid.*, pp. 127–8.

32. A. C. Swinburne, *A Study of Shakespeare* (London: Chatto and Windus, 1880), p. 203.

33. *The Collected Works of Samuel Taylor Coleridge*, ed. Carl Woodring, 16 vols (London: Routledge; Princeton: Princeton University Press, 1990), 14: II, p. 62.

34. Walter Pater, *Appreciations* (London: Macmillan, 1889), p. 179.

35. *Ibid.*, p. 190.

36. *Complete Works of William Hazlitt*, ed. Howe, IV, pp. 347, 346.

37. See above, pp. 19–20.

38. See above, p. 100.

39. William Blake, *Complete Writings*, ed. Geoffrey Keynes (Oxford: Oxford University Press, 1972), p. 217.

40. Stephen Orgel (ed.), *The Tempest*, The Oxford Shakespeare (Oxford: Oxford University Press, 1987), p.10.

41. Frank Kermode (ed.), *The Tempest*, New Arden Shakespeare (London: Methuen, 1954), p. lxxxiii.

42. Quoted by Kermode, *ibid.*, p. lxxxiv.

43. D. J. Palmer (ed.), *The Tempest: A Selection of Critical Essays*, 2nd rev. edn (London: Macmillan, 1991).

44. Francis Barker and Peter Hulme, '"Nymphs and reapers heavily vanish": The Discursive Con-texts of *The Tempest*', in *Alternative Shakespeares*, ed. Drakakis, p. 204.

45. Paul Brown, '"This Thing of Darkness I Acknowledge Mine": *The Tempest* and the Discourse of Colonialism', in *Political Shakespeare: Essays in Cultural Materialism*, ed. Jonathan Dollimore and Alan Sinfield, 2nd edn (Manchester: Manchester University Press, 1994), pp. 48–71. There is now a formidable body of secondary literature devoted to political readings of the play. See in particular: Terence Hawkes, *That Shakespeherian Rag: Essays on a Critical Process* (London and New York: Methuen, 1986), Ch. 1: 'Playhouse–Workhouse'; Thomas Cartelli, 'Prospero in Africa: *The Tempest* as Colonialist Text and Pretext', in *Shakespeare Reproduced*, ed. Howard and O'Connor, pp. 99–115; Stephen Greenblatt, 'Martial Law in the Land of Cockaigne', in *Shakespearean Negotiations*, pp. 129–63; Annabel Patterson, *Shakespeare and the Popular Voice*, Ch. 7: '"Thought is Free": *The Tempest*'; Deborah Willis, 'Shakespeare's *Tempest* and the Discourse of Colonialism', *Studies in English Literature 1500–1900*, 29 (1989), 277–89; Howard Felperin, *The Uses of the Canon: Elizabethan Literature and Contemporary Theory* (Oxford: Clarendon Press, 1990), Ch. 2: 'Romance and Romanticism', and Ch. 9: '*The Tempest* in our Time'; John Gillies, *Shakespeare and the Geography of Difference* (Cambridge: Cambridge University Press, 1994), pp. 140–55; Howard Felperin, 'Political Criticism at the Crossroads: The Utopian Historicism of *The Tempest*', in *The Tempest: Theory in Practice*, ed. Nigel Wood (Buckingham: Open University Press, 1995), pp. 29–66; Martin Orkin, 'Whose Things of Darkness? Reading/Representing *The Tempest* in South Africa after April 1994', in *Shakespeare and National Culture*, ed. John Joughin (Manchester and New York: Manchester University Press, 1997), pp. 142–69; Jerry Brotton, '"This Tunis, sir, was Carthage": Contesting Colonialism in *The Tempest*', in *Post-Colonial Shakespeares*, ed. Ania Loomba and Martin Orkin (London and New York: Routledge, 1998), pp 23–42; and Callaghan, *Shakespeare Without Women*, Ch. 4: 'Irish Memories in *The Tempest*'.

46. A recent exception is David Norbrook's fine essay '"What cares these roarers for the name of king?": Language and Utopia in *The Tempest*', in *The Politics of Tragicomedy: Shakespeare and After*, ed. Gordon

McMullan and Jonathan Hope (London and New York: Routledge, 1992), pp. 21–54.

47. For a full psychological profile of Prospero as patriarch and discussions of gender and power in the play, see David Sundelson, '"So rare a wonder'd father": Prospero's *Tempest*', in *Representing Shakespeare: New Psychoanalytic Essays*, ed. Murray Schwartz and Coppélia Kahn (Baltimore: Johns Hopkins University Press, 1980), pp. 33–53; Coppélia Kahn, 'The Providential Tempest and the Shakespearean Family', *ibid.*, pp. 217–43; Lorie Jerrell Leininger, 'The Miranda Trap: Sexism and Racism in Shakespeare's *Tempest*', in *The Woman's Part: Feminist Criticism of Shakespeare*, ed. Carolyn Ruth Swift Lenz, Gayle Greene and Carol Thomas Neely (Urbana and London: University of Illinois Press, 1980), pp. 285–94; and Stephen Orgel, 'Prospero's Wife', in *Rewriting the Renaissance: The Discourses of Sexual Difference in Early Modern Europe*, ed. Margaret W. Ferguson, Maureen Quilligan and Nancy J. Vickers (Chicago and London: University of Chicago Press, 1986), pp. 50–64; Anne Thompson, '"Miranda, where's your sister?": Reading Shakespeare's *The Tempest*', in *Shakespeare and Gender: A History*, ed. Deborah E. Barker and Ivo Kamps (London and New York: Verso, 1995), pp. 168–77; Kate Chedzgoy, *Shakespeare's Queer Children: Sexual Politics and Contemporary Culture* (Manchester and New York: Manchester University Press, 1995), Ch. 3: 'Rewriting the Narratives of Shame: Women's Transformations of *The Tempest*'.

48. For further reflections on Caliban, see Peter Hulme, 'Prospero and Caliban', in his *Colonial Encounters: Europe and the Native Caribbean, 1492–1797* (London and New York: Methuen, 1986), pp. 89–134; Stephen Orgel, 'Shakespeare and the Cannibals', in *Cannibals, Witches and Divorce: Estranging the Renaissance*, ed. Marjorie Garber (Baltimore and London: Johns Hopkins University Press, 1987), pp. 40–66; Alden T. Vaughan and Virginia Vaughan, *Shakespeare's Caliban: A Cultural History* (Cambridge: Cambridge University Press, 1991); Marina Warner, '"The foul witch" and Her "freckled whelp": Circean Mutations in the New World', in *'The Tempest' and Its Travels*, ed. Peter Hulme and William H. Sherman (London: Reaktion Books, 2000), pp. 97–113; and Patricia Seed, '"This island's mine": Caliban and Native Sovereignty', *ibid.*, pp. 202–11.

49. Walter Benjamin, *Illuminations*, trans. Harry Zohn (London: Fontana, 1973), p. 258.

Chapter 5

1. See above, pp. 39–40.
2. Jerome McGann, 'The Third World of Criticism', in Marjorie Levinson, Marilyn Butler, Jerome McGann and Paul Hamilton, *Rethinking Historicism: Critical Readings in Romantic History* (Oxford: Blackwell, 1989), p. 97.
3. Quoted above, p. 66. See Ch. 2, note 32.
4. For illuminating queer perspectives on the story and Wilde's appropriation of Shakespeare, see William A. Cohen, 'Willie and Wilde: Reading *The Portrait of Mr W.H.*', *South Atlantic Quarterly*, 88 (1989), 219–45; Claude J. Summers, '"In such surrender there may be gain": Oscar Wilde and the Beginnings of Gay Fiction', in his *Gay Fictions, Wilde to Stonewall: Studies in a Male Homosexual Literary Tradition* (New York: Continuum, 1990), pp. 29–61; Lawrence Danson, 'Oscar Wilde, W. H., and the Unspoken Name of Love', *English Literary History*, 58 (1991), 979–1000; and Kate Chedgzoy, *Shakespeare's Queer Children: Sexual Politics and Contemporary Culture* (Manchester: Manchester University Press, 1995), Ch. 4: '"Strange Worship": Oscar Wilde and the Key to Shakespeare's *Sonnets*'.
5. *Complete Works of Oscar Wilde*, 3rd rev. edn (London: HarperCollins, 1994), pp. 312, 326, 339.
6. *Ibid.*, pp. 343, 344, 348, 349, 350.
7. *Ibid.*, pp. 1121, 1126, 1127.
8. *Ibid.*, p. 1130.
9. 'Preface to *The Dark Lady of the Sonnets*', in Bernard Shaw, *Selected One-Act Plays*, 2 vols (Harmondsworth: Penguin, 1965), II, p. 27.
10. Quoted above, p. 9. See Ch. 1, note 27.
11. Quoted above, p. 10. See Ch. 1, note 33.
12. Christopher St John (ed.), *Ellen Terry and Bernard Shaw: A Correspondence*, 2nd edn (London: Constable, 1931), p. 149.
13. Edwin Wilson (ed.), *Shaw on Shakespeare*, Penguin Shakespeare Library (Harmondsworth: Penguin, 1961), p. 245.
14. *Ibid.*, p. 73.
15. Quoted *ibid.*, p. 9.
16. Wilson (ed.), *Shaw on Shakespeare*, pp. 282, 285.
17. Bernard Shaw, *Three Plays for Puritans* (Harmondsworth: Penguin, 1946), pp. 33, 36.
18. Shaw, *Selected One-Act Plays*, vol. 2, p. 29.

19. *Ibid.*, pp. 13–14, 34, 32, 37, 25. Further views of Shaw's reception and appropriations of Shakespeare can be found in Ronald Mason, 'Shaw on Shakespeare', *The Shavian: The Journal of George Bernard Shaw*, 4 (1970), 46–51; Jerry Lutz, *Pitchman's Melody: Shaw about 'Shakespear'* (Lewisburg, PA: Bucknell University Press, 1974); and Sally Peters, 'Shaw's Double Dethroned: *The Dark Lady of the Sonnets, Cymbeline Refinished*, and *Shakes versus Shav*', in *Shaw: The Annual of Bernard Shaw Studies*, 7 (1987), 301–16.

20. James Joyce, *Ulysses* (London: Bodley Head, 1960), pp. 254, 259, 262. It is 'the quaker librarian' who reminds Stephen and his companions of the key part played by GBS in their nation's reception of Shakespeare: 'And we ought to mention another Irish commentator, Mr George Bernard Shaw' (*ibid.*, p. 251).

21. Edward Dowden, *Shakespeare: A Critical Study of His Mind and Art*, 9th edn (London: Kegan Paul, Trench, 1889), p. 126.

22. Djuna Barnes, 'James Joyce: A Portrait of the Man Who is, at Present, One of the More Significant Figures in Literature', *Vanity Fair*, 18:2 (April 1922), p. 65.

23. Jacques Derrida, *Specters of Marx: The State of the Debt, the Work of Mourning, and the New International*, trans. Peggy Kamuf (New York and London: Routledge, 1994), p. 37.

24. Joyce, *Ulysses*, p. 249. For further discussion of the role of *Hamlet* in *Ulysses*, see Martin Scofield, *The Ghosts of 'Hamlet': The Play and Modern Writers* (Cambridge: Cambridge University Press, 1980), Ch. 5: '"Methinks I see my father": Joyce's *Ulysses*', and René Girard, *A Theater of Envy: William Shakespeare* (New York: Oxford University Press, 1991), Ch. 29: 'Do You Believe Your Own Theory?: "French Triangles" in the Shakespeare of James Joyce'. A full-length study of Joyce's debt to Shakespeare is provided by William M. Schutte, *Joyce and Shakespeare* (New Haven: Yale University Press, 1957). See also Vincent Cheng, *Shakespeare and Joyce: A Study of Finnegans Wake* (Pittsburgh: University of Pennsylvania Press, 1984).

25. Donald H. Reiman and Sharon B. Powers (eds), *Shelley's Poetry and Prose* (New York: W. W. Norton, 1977), pp. 482–3, 508.

26. Mikhail Bakhtin, *Speech Genres and Other Late Essays*, ed. Carol Emerson and Michael Holquist, trans. V. W. McGee (Minneapolis: University of Minnesota Press, 1986), p. 165.

27. Dominick La Capra, *Rethinking Intellectual History* (Ithaca, NY and London: Cornell University Press, 1983), p. 14.

28. *The Complete Works of William Hazlitt*, ed. P. P. Howe, 21 vols (London and Toronto: Dent), IV, p. 232.

29. *The Collected Works of Samuel Taylor Coleridge*, ed. Carl Woodring, 16 vols (London: Routledge; Princeton: Princeton University Press, 1990), 14: II, p. 61.

30. T. S. Eliot, *Selected Essays* (London: Faber and Faber, 1932), pp. 145, 144, 146.

31. Heiner Müller, *Theatremachine*, trans. and ed. Marc von Henning (London: Faber and Faber, 1995), p. 100.

32. Frank Kermode, 'Cornelius and Voltemand: Doubles in *Hamlet*', in *Forms of Attention* (Chicago and London: University of Chicago Press, 1985), pp. 52, 59, 50. Kermode returns to the subject in his chapter on *Hamlet* in *Shakespeare's Language* (London: Allen Lane, 2000).

33. Terence Hawkes, *That Shakespeherian Rag: Essays on a Critical Process* (London and New York: Methuen, 1986), p. 94.

34. Herbert Marcuse, *The Aesthetic Dimension* (London: Macmillan, 1978), pp. 9–10, 72 (Marcuse's italics).

35. Jonathan Bate (ed.), *The Romantics on Shakespeare* (Harmondsworth: Penguin, 1992), p. 323.

36. Henry James, *Selected Literary Criticism*, ed. Morris Shapira (Cambridge: Cambridge University Press, 1981), p. 302.

Further Reading

I General Studies

Adelman, Janet, *Suffocating Mothers: Fantasies of Maternal Origin in Shakespeare's Plays, 'Hamlet' to 'The Tempest'* (New York and London: Routledge, 1992).

Atkins, G. Douglas, and David M. Bergeron (eds), *Shakespeare and Deconstruction* (New York, Bern, Frankfurt and Paris: Peter Lang, 1988).

Bamber, Linda, *Comic Women, Tragic Men: A Study of Gender and Genre in Shakespeare* (Stanford: Stanford University Press, 1982).

Barker, Deborah E., and Ivo Kamps (eds), *Shakespeare and Gender: A History* (London and New York: Verso, 1995).

Barker, Francis, Peter Hulme and Margaret Iversen (eds), *Uses of History: Marxism, Postmodernism and the Renaissance* (Manchester and New York: Manchester University Press, 1991).

Barton, Anne, *Essays, Mainly Shakespearean* (Cambridge: Cambridge University Press, 1994).

Bate, Jonathan, *The Genius of Shakespeare* (London: Picador, 1997).

Belsey, Catherine, *Shakespeare and the Loss of Eden* (London: Macmillan, 1999).

Berger, Harry, Jr, *Making Trifles of Terrors: Redistributing Complicities in Shakespeare* (Stanford: Stanford University Press, 1997).

Boose, Lynda E., and Richard Burt (eds), *Shakespeare, The Movie: Popularizing the Plays on Film, TV, and Video* (London and New York: Routledge, 1997).

Bradshaw, Graham, *Misrepresentations: Shakespeare and the Materialists* (Ithaca, NY and London: Cornell University Press, 1993).

Bristol, Michael D., *Carnival and Theater: Plebeian Culture and the Structure of Authority in Renaissance England* (New York and London: Methuen, 1985).

Bristol, Michael D., *Shakespeare's America, America's Shakespeare* (New York and London: Routledge, 1990).

Bristol, Michael D., *Big-Time Shakespeare* (London and New York: Routledge, 1996).

Bruster, Douglas, *Drama and the Market in the Age of Shakespeare* (Cambridge: Cambridge University Press, 1992).

Burt, Richard, *Unspeakable Shaxxxspeares: Queer Theory and American Kiddie Culture* (New York: St Martin's Press, 1998).

Callaghan, Dympna, *Shakespeare Without Women: Representing Gender and Race on the Renaissance Stage* (London and New York: Routledge, 2000).

Callaghan, Dympna, Lorraine Helms and Jyotsna Singh, *The Weyward Sisters: Shakespeare and Feminist Politics* (Oxford: Blackwell, 1994).

Charnes, Linda, *Notorious Identity: Materializing the Subject in Shakespeare* (Cambridge, MA and London: Harvard University Press, 1993).

Chedzgoy, Kate, *Shakespeare's Queer Children: Sexual Politics and Contemporary Culture* (Manchester and New York: Manchester University Press, 1995).

Cohen, Derek, *The Politics of Shakespeare* (London: Macmillan, 1993).

Cohen, Walter, *Drama of a Nation: Public Theater in Renaissance England and Spain* (Ithaca, NY: Cornell University Press, 1985).

Danson, Lawrence, *Shakespeare's Dramatic Genres* (Oxford: Oxford University Press, 2000).

de Grazia, Margreta, *Shakespeare Verbatim: The Reproduction of Authenticity and the 1790 Apparatus* (Oxford: Clarendon Press, 1991).

Desmet, Christy, and Robert Sawyer (eds), *Shakespeare and Appropriation* (London and New York: Routledge, 1999).

Dobson, Michael, *The Making of the National Poet: Shakespeare, Adaptation and Authorship, 1660–1769* (Oxford: Clarendon Press, 1992).

Dollimore, Jonathan, and Alan Sinfield (eds), *Political Shakespeare: Essays in Cultural Materialism*, 2nd edn (Manchester: Manchester University Press, 1994).

Drakakis, John (ed.), *Alternative Shakespeares* (London and New York: Routledge, 1985).

Dreher, Diane Elizabeth, *Domination and Defiance: Fathers and Daughters in Shakespeare* (Lexington: University of Kentucky Press, 1986).

Dubrow, Heather, and Richard Strier (eds), *The Historical Renaissance: New Essays on Tudor and Stuart Culture* (Chicago and London: University of Chicago Press, 1988).

Dusinberre, Juliet, *Shakespeare and the Nature of Women*, 2nd edn (London: Macmillan, 1995).

Eagleton, Terry, *William Shakespeare* (Oxford: Basil Blackwell, 1986).

Engle, Lars, *Shakespearean Pragmatism: Market of His Time* (Chicago: Chicago University Press, 1993).

Erickson, Peter, *Patriarchal Structures in Shakespeare's Drama* (Berkeley: University of California Press, 1985).

Evans, Malcolm, *Signifying Nothing: Truth's True Contents in Shakespeare's Text*, 2nd edn (Hemel Hempstead: Harvester Wheatsheaf, 1989).

Felperin, Howard, *The Uses of the Canon: Elizabethan Literature and Contemporary Theory* (Oxford: Clarendon Press, 1990).

Ferguson, Margaret W., Maureen Quilligan and Nancy J. Vickers (eds), *Rewriting the Renaissance: The Discourses of Sexual Difference in Early Modern Europe* (Chicago and London: University of Chicago Press, 1986).

Fiedler, Leslie, *The Stranger in Shakespeare* (St Albans: Paladin, 1974).

Garber, Marjorie, *Shakespeare's Ghost Writers: Literature as Uncanny Causality* (New York and London: Methuen, 1987).

Garber, Marjorie (ed.), *Cannibals, Witches, and Divorce: Estranging the Renaissance* (Baltimore and London: Johns Hopkins University Press, 1987).

Gillies, John, *Shakespeare and the Geography of Difference* (Cambridge: Cambridge University Press, 1994).

Goldberg, Jonathan, *James I and the Politics of Literature: Jonson, Shakespeare, Donne and Their Contemporaries* (Baltimore and London: Johns Hopkins University Press, 1983).

Grady, Hugh, *The Modernist Shakespeare: Critical Texts in a Material World* (Oxford: Oxford University Press, 1991).

Grady, Hugh (ed.), *Shakespeare and Modernity: Early Modern to Millennium* (London: Routledge, 2000).

Greenblatt, Stephen, *Renaissance Self-Fashioning: From More to Shakespeare* (Chicago and London: Chicago University Press, 1980).

Greenblatt, Stephen, *Shakespearean Negotiations: The Circulation of Social Energy in Renaissance England* (Oxford: Clarendon Press, 1988).

Greenblatt, Stephen (ed.), *Representing the English Renaissance* (Berkeley, Los Angeles and London: University of California Press, 1988).

Greenblatt, Stephen, *Learning to Curse: Essays in Early Modern Culture* (New York and London: Routledge, 1990).

Gurr, Andrew, *The Shakespearean Stage*, 3rd edn (Cambridge: Cambridge University Press, 1992).

Hall, Kim, *Things of Darkness: Economies of Race and Gender in Early Modern England* (Ithaca, NY: Cornell University Press, 1995).

Halpern, Richard, *Shakespeare Among the Moderns* (Ithaca, NY and London: Cornell University Press, 1997).

Hawkes, Terence, *That Shakespeherian Rag: Essays on a Critical Process* (London and New York: Methuen, 1986).

Hawkes, Terence, *Meaning By Shakespeare* (London and New York: Routledge, 1992).

Hawkes, Terence (ed.), *Alternative Shakespeares 2* (London and New York: Routledge, 1996).

Hendricks, Margo, and Patricia Parker (eds), *Women, 'Race' and Writing in the Early Modern Period* (London and New York: Routledge, 1994).

Hodgdon, Barbara, *The Shakespeare Trade: Performance and Appropriations* (Philadelphia: University of Philadelphia Press, 1998).

Holderness, Graham (ed.), *The Shakespeare Myth* (Manchester: Manchester University Press, 1988).

Howard, Jean E., *The Stage and Social Struggle in Early Modern England* (New York and London: Routledge, 1994).

Howard, Jean E., and Marion F. O'Connor (eds), *Shakespeare Reproduced: The Text in History and Ideology* (New York and London: Methuen, 1987).

Howard, Jean E., and Scott Shershow (eds), *Marxist Shakespeares* (London and New York: Routledge, 2001).

Hutson, Lorna, *The Usurer's Daughter: Male Friendship and Fictions of Women in Sixteenth-Century England* (London and New York: Routledge, 1994).

Jardine, Lisa, *Still Harping on Daughters: Women and Drama in the Age of Shakespeare*, 2nd edn (Hemel Hempstead: Harvester Wheatsheaf, 1989).

Jardine, Lisa, *Reading Shakespeare Historically* (New York and London: Routledge, 1996).

Joughin, John J. (ed.), *Shakespeare and National Culture* (Manchester and New York: Manchester University Press, 1997).

Joughin, John J. (ed.), *Philosophical Shakespeares* (London and New York: Routledge, 2000).

Kahn, Coppélia, *Man's Estate: Masculine Identity in Shakespeare* (Berkeley, Los Angeles and London: University of California Press, 1981).

Kamps, Ivo (ed.), *Shakespeare Left and Right* (New York and London: Routledge, 1991).

Kamps, Ivo (ed.), *Materialist Shakespeare: A History* (London and New York: Verso, 1995).

Kastan, David Scott, *Shakespeare After Theory* (New York and London: Routledge, 1999).

Kastan, David Scott (ed.), *A Companion to Shakespeare* (Oxford: Blackwell, 1999).

Kermode, Frank, *Shakespeare's Language* (London: Allen Lane, 2000).

Kettle, Arnold (ed.), *Shakespeare in a Changing World* (London: Lawrence and Wishart, 1964).

Knapp, Robert S., *Shakespeare: The Theatre and the Book* (Princeton: Princeton University Press, 1989).

Knowles, Ronald, *Shakespeare and Carnival: After Bakhtin* (London: Macmillan, 1998).

Laroque, François, *Shakespeare's Festive World: Elizabethan Entertainment and the Professional Stage* (Cambridge: Cambridge University Press, 1991).

Lenz, Carolyn Ruth Swift, Gayle Greene and Carol Thomas Neely (eds), *The Woman's Part: Feminist Criticism of Shakespeare* (Urbana, Chicago and London: University of Illinois Press, 1980).

Loomba, Ania, *Gender, Race, Renaissance Drama* (Manchester and New York: Manchester University Press, 1989).

Loomba, Ania, and Martin Orkin (eds), *Post-Colonial Shakespeares* (London and New York: Routledge, 1998).

Lupton, Julia Reinhard, and Kenneth Reinhard, *After Oedipus: Shakespeare in Psychoanalysis* (Ithaca, NY: Cornell University Press, 1993).

Maquerlot, J., and M. Willenis (eds), *Travel and Drama in Shakespeare's Time* (Cambridge: Cambridge University Press, 1996).

Marcus, Leah S., *Puzzling Shakespeare: Local Reading and Its Discontents* (Berkeley, Los Angeles and London: University of California Press, 1988).

Marcus, Leah S., *Unediting the Renaissance: Shakespeare, Marlowe, Milton* (London and New York: Routledge, 1996).

Marienstras, Richard, *New Perspectives on the Shakespearean World* (Cambridge: Cambridge University Press, 1985).

Marsden, Jean I. (ed.), *The Appropriation of Shakespeare: Post-Renaissance Reconstructions of the Works and the Myth* (Hemel Hempstead: Harvester Wheatsheaf, 1991).

Marx, Steven, *Shakespeare and the Bible* (Oxford: Oxford University Press, 2000).

Maus, Katharine Eisaman, *Inwardness and Theater in the English Renaissance* (Chicago and London: University of Chicago Press, 1995).

McDonald, Russ (ed.), *Shakespeare Re-read: The Texts in New Contexts* (Ithaca, NY: Cornell University Press, 1994).

McMullan, Gordon, and Jonathan Hope (eds), *The Politics of Tragicomedy: Shakespeare and After* (London and New York: Routledge, 1992).

Miola, Robert S., *Shakespeare's Reading* (Oxford: Oxford University Press, 2000).

Montrose, Louis, *The Purpose of Playing: Shakespeare and the Cultural Politics of the Elizabethan Theatre* (Chicago and London: University of Chicago Press, 1996).

Mullaney, Steven, *The Place of the Stage: License, Play, and Power in Renaissance England* (Chicago and London: University of Chicago Press, 1988).

Newman, Karen, *Fashioning Femininity and English Renaissance Drama* (Chicago: University of Chicago Press, 1991).

Novy, Marianne, *Love's Argument: Gender Relations in Shakespeare* (Chapel Hill and London: University of North Carolina Press, 1984).

Novy, Marianne, *Engaging with Shakespeare: Responses of George Eliot and Other Women Novelists* (Athens, GA and London: University of Georgia Press, 1994).

Novy, Marianne (ed.), *Women's Re-visions of Shakespeare: On the Responses of Dickinson, Woolf, Rich, H.D., George Eliot, and Others* (Urbana: University of Illinois Press, 1990).

Novy, Marianne (ed.), *Transforming Shakespeare: Twentieth-Century Women's Re-visions in Literature and Performance* (London: Macmillan, 1999).

Novy, Marianne (ed.), *Cross-Cultural Performances: Differences in Women's Re-visions of Shakespeare* (Urbana: University of Illinois Press, 1993).

Orgel, Stephen, *Impersonations: Gender and Performance in Shakespeare's England* (Cambridge: Cambridge University Press, 1996).

Orgel, Stephen, and Sean Keilen (eds), *Shakespeare: The Critical Complex*, 10 vols (London: Garland, 2000).

Parker, Patricia, *Shakespeare from the Margins: Language, Culture, Context* (Chicago: University of Chicago Press, 1996).

Parker, Patricia, and Geoffrey Hartman (eds), *Shakespeare and the Question of Theory* (New York and London: Methuen, 1985).

Patterson, Annabel, *Shakespeare and the Popular Voice* (Oxford: Blackwell, 1989).

Pechter, Edward, *What Was Shakespeare? Renaissance Plays and Changing Critical Practice* (Ithaca, NY and London: Cornell University Press, 1995).

Rozmovits, Linda, *Shakespeare and the Politics of Culture in Late Victorian England* (Baltimore and London: Johns Hopkins University Press, 1998).

Ryan, Kiernan (ed.), *Shakespeare: Texts and Contexts* (Basingstoke: Macmillan – now Palgrave, 2000).

Schwartz, Murray M., and Coppélia Kahn (eds), *Representing Shakespeare: New Psychoanalytic Essays* (Baltimore and London: Johns Hopkins University Press, 1980).

Shapiro, James, *Shakespeare and the Jews* (New York: Columbia University Press, 1996).

Shaughnessy, Robert, *Representing Shakespeare: England, History and the RSC* (Hemel Hempstead: Harvester Wheatsheaf, 1994).

Smith, Bruce R., *Homosexual Desire in Shakespeare's England: A Cultural Poetics* (Chicago: University of Chicago Press, 1991).

Smith, Bruce R., *Shakespeare and Masculinity* (Oxford: Oxford University Press, 2000).

Stockholder, Kay, *Dreamworks: Lovers and Families in Shakespeare's Plays* (Toronto: University of Toronto Press, 1987).

Sundelson, David, *Shakespeare's Restorations of the Father* (New Brunswick, NJ: Rutgers University Press, 1983).

Taylor, Gary, *Reinventing Shakespeare: A Cultural History from the Restoration to the Present* (London: Hogarth Press, 1990).

Tennenhouse, Leonard, *Power on Display: The Politics of Shakespeare's Genres* (New York and London: Methuen, 1988).

Thompson, Ann, and Sasha Roberts (eds), *Women Reading Shakespeare, 1660–1900: An Anthology of Criticism* (Manchester and New York: Manchester University Press, 1997).

Traub, Valerie, *Desire and Anxiety: Circulations of Sexuality in Shakespearean Drama* (London and New York: Routledge, 1992).

Vickers, Brian, *Appropriating Shakespeare: Contemporary Critical Quarrels* (New Haven and London: Yale University Press, 1993).

Wayne, Valerie (ed.), *The Matter of Difference: Materialist–Feminist Criticism of Shakespeare* (Hemel Hempstead: Harvester Wheatsheaf, 1991).

Weimann, Robert, *Shakespeare and the Popular Tradition in the Theater: Studies in the Social Dimension of Dramatic Form and Function* (Baltimore and London: Johns Hopkins University Press, 1978).

Weimann, Robert, *Author's Pen and Actor's Voice: Playing and Writing in Shakespeare's Theatre* (Cambridge: Cambridge University Press, 2000).

Wilson, Richard, *Will Power: Essays on Shakespearean Authority* (Hemel Hempstead: Harvester Wheatsheaf, 1993).

Wilson, Richard, and Richard Dutton (eds), *New Historicism and Renaissance Drama* (London and New York: Longman, 1992).

Zimmerman, Susan (ed.), *Erotic Politics: Desire on the Renaissance Stage* (New York and London: Routledge, 1992).

II Comedies

Adelman, Janet, *Suffocating Mothers: Fantasies of Maternal Origin in Shakespeare's Plays, 'Hamlet' to 'The Tempest'* (New York and London: Routledge, 1992), Ch. 4: 'Marriage and the Maternal Body: On Marriage as the End of Comedy in *All's Well That Ends Well* and *Measure for Measure'*.

Barber, C. L., *Shakespeare's Festive Comedy* (Princeton, NJ:Princeton University Press, 1959).

Belsey, Catherine, 'Disrupting Sexual Difference: Meaning and Gender in the Comedies', in *Alternative Shakespeares*, ed. John Drakakis (London and New York: Methuen, 1985).

Belsey, Catherine, *Shakespeare and the Loss of Eden* (Basingstoke: Macmillan – now Palgrave, 1999), Ch. 2: 'Desire in the Golden World: *Love's Labour's Lost* and *As You Like It*'.

Bradshaw, Graham, *Shakespeare's Scepticism* (Brighton: Harvester Wheatsheaf, 1987), Ch. 5: 'Tempering Mercy with Justice: *Measure for Measure*'.

Charlton, H. B., *Shakespearian Comedy*, 2nd edn (London: Methuen, 1938).

Cohen, Walter, '*The Merchant of Venice* and the Possibilities of Historical Criticism', in *Materialist Shakespeare: A History*, ed. Ivo Kamps (London and New York: Verso, 1995).

Cook, Carol, '"The sign and semblance of her honour": Reading Gender Difference in *Much Ado About Nothing*", in *Shakespeare and Gender: A History*, ed. Deborah E. Barker and Ivo Kamps (London and New York: Verso, 1995).

Coyle, Martin (ed.), *The Merchant of Venice: Contemporary Critical Essays* (London: Macmillan, 1998).

Dollimore, Jonathan, 'Transgression and Surveillance in *Measure for Measure*', in *Political Shakespeare: Essays in Cultural Materialism*, ed. Jonathan Dollimore and Alan Sinfield, 2nd edn (Manchester: Manchester University Press, 1994).

Dutton, Richard (ed.), *A Midsummer Night's Dream: Contemporary Critical Essays* (London: Macmillan, 1996).

Eagleton, Terry, *William Shakespeare* (Oxford: Blackwell, 1986), Ch. 3: 'Law: *The Merchant of Venice, Measure for Measure, Troilus and Cressida*'.

Elam, Keir, *Shakespeare's Universe of Discourse: Language Games in the Comedies* (Cambridge: Cambridge University Press, 1984).

Fineman, Joel, 'The Turn of the Shrew', in *Shakespeare and the Question of Theory*, ed. Patricia Parker and Geoffrey Hartman (New York and London: Methuen, 1985).

Freedman, Barbara, *Staging the Gaze: Psychoanalysis, Postmodernism and Shakespearean Comedy* (Ithaca, NY: Cornell University Press, 1991).

Freund, Elizabeth, '"Ariachne's Broken Woof": The Rhetoric of Citation in *Troilus and Cressida*', in *Shakespeare and the Question of Theory*, ed. Patricia Parker and Geoffrey Hartman (New York and London: Methuen, 1985).

Frye, Northrop, *A Natural Perspective: The Development of Shakespearean Comedy and Romance* (New York: Columbia University Press, 1965).

Goldberg, Jonathan, *James I and the Politics of Literature: Jonson, Shakespeare, Donne and Their Contemporaries* (Baltimore and London: Johns Hopkins University Press, 1983), Ch. 5: 'Social Texts, Royal Measures: Donne, Jonson, and *Measure for Measure*'.

Greenblatt, Stephen, *Shakespearean Negotiations: The Circulation of Social Energy in Renaissance England* (Oxford: Clarendon Press, 1988), Ch 3: 'Fiction and Friction'.

Hall, Jonathan, *Anxious Pleasures: Shakespearean Comedy and the Nation State* (Madison, WI and London: Associated University Presses, 1995).

Hartman, Geoffrey, 'Shakespeare's Poetical Character in *Twelfth Night*', in *Shakespeare and the Question of Theory*, ed. Patricia Parker and Geoffrey Hartman (New York and London: Methuen, 1985).

Hendricks, Margo, 'Obscured by Dreams: Race, Empire, and Shakespeare's *A Midsummer Night's Dream*', *Shakespeare Quarterly*, 47 (1996), 37–60.

Howard, Jean E., 'Renaissance Antitheatricality and the Politics of Gender and Rank in *Much Ado About Nothing*', in *Shakespeare Reproduced: The Text in History and Ideology*, ed. Jean E. Howard and Marion F. O'Connor (New York and London: Methuen, 1987).

Jardine, Lisa, *Reading Shakespeare Historically* (New York and London: Routledge, 1996), Ch. 4: 'Twins and Travesties: Gender, Dependency and Sexual Availability in *Twelfth Night*'.

Kastan, David Scott, '*All's Well That Ends Well* and the Limits of Comedy', *English Literary History*, 52 (1985), 575–89.

Korda, Natasha, ' "Judicious oeillades": Supervising Marital Property in *The Merry Wives of Windsor*', in *Marxist Shakespeares*, ed. Jean E. Howard and Scott Shershow (London and New York: Routledge, 2001).

Krieger, Elliot, *A Marxist Study of Shakespeare's Comedies* (London: Macmillan, 1979).

MacCary, W. Thomas, *Friends and Lovers: The Phenomenology of Desire in Shakespearean Comedy* (New York: Columbia University Press, 1985).

Malcolmson, Cristina, ' "What You Will": Social Mobility and Gender in *Twelfth Night*', in *The Matter of Difference: Materialist-Feminist Criticism of Shakespeare*, ed. Valerie Wayne (Hemel Hempstead: Harvester Wheatsheaf, 1991).

Marcus, Leah S., *Unediting the Renaissance: Shakespeare, Marlowe, Milton* (London and New York: Routledge, 1996), Ch. 4: 'The Editor as Tamer: *A Shrew* and *The Shrew*'.

Mason, Pamela (ed.), *Shakespeare: Early Comedies: A Selection of Critical Essays* (London: Macmillan, 1995).

Moisan, Thomas, '"Which is the Merchant Here? And Which the Jew?":
Subversion and Recuperation in *The Merchant of Venice*', in *Shakespeare
Reproduced: The Text in History and Ideology*, ed. Jean E. Howard and
Marion F. O'Connor (New York and London: Methuen, 1987).

Montrose, Louis, '"The Place of a Brother" in *As You Like It*: Social Process
and Comic Form', in *Materialist Shakespeare: A History*, ed. Ivo Kamps
(London and New York: Verso, 1995).

Montrose, Louis, *The Purpose of Playing: Shakespeare and the Cultural Politics
of the Elizabethan Theatre* (Chicago and London: University of Chicago
Press, 1996), 'Part II: The Shaping Fantasies of *A Midsummer Night's
Dream*'.

Nevo, Ruth, *Comic Transformations in Shakespeare* (London: Methuen, 1980).

Palmer, D. J. and Malcolm Bradbury (eds), *Shakespearian Comedy*, Stratford-
upon-Avon Studies 14 (London: Edward Arnold, 1972).

Parker, Patricia, *Shakespeare From the Margins: Language, Culture, Context*
(Chicago: University of Chicago Press: 1996), Ch. 2: 'The Bible and the
Marketplace: *The Comedy of Errors*'; Ch. 3: '"Rude Mechanicals": *A
Midsummer Night's Dream* and Shakespearean Joinery'; and Ch. 6: 'Dila-
tion and Inflation: *All's Well That Ends Well*, *Troilus and Cressida*, and
Shakespearean Increase'.

Patterson, Annabel, *Shakespeare and the Popular Voice* (Oxford: Blackwell,
1989), Ch. 3: 'Bottom's Up: Festive Theory'.

Pequigney, Joseph, 'The Two Antonios and Same-Sex Love in *Twelfth Night*
and *The Merchant of Venice*', in *Shakespeare and Gender: A History*, ed.
Deborah E. Barker and Ivo Kamps (London and New York: Verso, 1995).

Ryan, Kiernan, '*Measure for Measure*: Marxism Before Marx', in *Marxist
Shakespeares*, ed. Jean E. Howard and Scott Shershow (London and New
York: Routledge, 2001).

Snyder, Susan, 'Naming Names in *All's Well That Ends Well*', *Shakespeare
Quarterly*, 43 (1992), 265–79.

Traub, Valerie, 'Desire and the Difference It Makes', in *The Matter of
Difference: Materialist Feminist Criticism of Shakespeare*, ed. Valerie
Wayne (Hemel Hempstead: Harvester Wheatsheaf, 1991).

Waller, Gary (ed.), *Shakespeare's Comedies* (London and New York: Longman,
1991).

White, R. S. (ed.), *Twelfth Night: Contemporary Critical Essays* (London:
Macmillan, 1996).

Wilson, Richard, *Will Power: Essays on Shakespearean Authority* (Hemel
Hempstead: Harvester Wheatsheaf, 1993), Ch. 6: 'The Quality of
Mercy: Discipline and Punishment in Shakespearean Comedy'.

Wood, Nigel (ed.), *Theory in Practice: Measure for Measure* (Buckingham: Open University Press, 1996).

III Histories

Belsey, Catherine, 'Making Histories Then and Now: Shakespeare from *Richard II* to *Henry V* ', in *Uses of History: Marxism, Postmodernism and the Renaissance*, ed. Francis Barker, Peter Hulme and Margaret Iverson (Manchester: Manchester University Press, 1991).

Calderwood, James L., *Metadrama in Shakespeare's Henriad: Richard II to Henry V* (Berkeley: University of California Press, 1979).

Dollimore, Jonathan, and Alan Sinfield, 'History and Ideology: The Instance of *Henry V*', in *Alternative Shakespeares*, ed. John Drakakis (London and New York: Methuen, 1985).

Greenblatt, Stephen, 'Invisible Bullets: Renaissance Authority and Its Subversion, *Henry IV* and *V*', in *Political Shakespeare: Essays in Cultural Materialism*, ed. Jonathan Dollimore and Alan Sinfield, 2nd edn (Manchester: Manchester University Press, 1994).

Highley, Christopher, *Shakespeare, Spenser and the Crisis in Ireland* (Cambridge: Cambridge University Press, 1997).

Hodgdon, Barbara, *The End Crowns All: Closure and Contradiction in Shakespeare's History* (Princeton: Princeton University Press, 1991).

Holderness, Graham, *Shakespeare Recycled: The Making of Historical Drama* (Hemel Hempstead: Harvester Wheatsheaf, 1992).

Holderness, Graham, ' "What ish my nation?": Shakespeare and National Identities', in *Materialist Shakespeare: A History*, ed. Ivo Kamps (London and New York: Verso, 1995).

Holderness, Graham, *Shakespeare: The Histories* (London: Macmillan, 2000).

Holderness, Graham (ed.), *Shakespeare's History Plays: Richard II to Henry V* (London: Macmillan, 1992).

Howard, Jean E., and Phyllis Rackin, *Engendering a Nation: A Feminist Account of Shakespeare's English Histories* (London and New York: Routledge, 1997).

Kastan, David Scott, *Shakespeare and the Shapes of Time* (Hanover, NH: University of New England Press: 1982).

Kastan, David Scott, 'The King Hath Many Marching in His Coats', in *Shakespeare Left and Right*, ed. Ivo Kamps (London and New York: Routledge, 1991).

Knight, G. Wilson, *The Olive and the Sword* (Oxford: Oxford University Press, 1944).

Maley, Willy, ' "This sceptred isle": Shakespeare and the British Problem', in *Shakespeare and National Culture*, ed. John Joughin (Manchester: Manchester University Press, 1997).

McEachern, Claire, '*Henry V* and the Paradox of the Body Politic', in *Materialist Shakespeare: A History*, ed. Ivo Kamps (London and New York: Verso, 1995).

Mullaney, Steven, *The Place of the Stage: License, Play, and Power in Renaissance England* (Chicago and London: University of Chicago Press, 1988), Ch. 3: 'The Rehearsal of Cultures'.

Parker, Patricia, *Shakespeare From the Margins: Language, Culture, Context* (Chicago: University of Chicago Press, 1996), Ch. 5: ' "Conveyors Are You All": Translating, Conveying, Representing, and Seconding in the Histories and *Hamlet*'.

Patterson, Annabel, *Shakespeare and the Popular Voice* (Oxford: Blackwell, 1989), Ch. 4: 'Back by Popular Demand: The Two Versions of *Henry V*'.

Rackin, Phyllis, *Stages of History: Shakespeare's English Chronicles* (Ithaca, NY: Cornell University Press, 1990).

Rossiter, A. P., *Angels With Horns and Other Shakespeare Lectures* (London: Longman, 1961), Ch. 3: 'Ambivalence: The Dialectic of the Histories'.

Tennenhouse, Leonard, *Power on Display: The Politics of Shakespeare's Genres* (New York and London: Methuen, 1988), Ch. 2: 'Rituals of State: History and the Elizabethan Strategies of Power'.

Wood, Nigel (ed.), *Theory in Practice: Henry IV* (Buckingham: Open University Press, 1995).

IV Tragedies

Adelman, Janet, *The Common Liar: An Essay on Antony and Cleopatra* (New Haven: Yale University Press, 1973).

Adelman, Janet, *Suffocating Mothers: Fantasies of Maternal Origin in Shakespeare's Plays, 'Hamlet' to 'The Tempest'* (New York and London: Routledge, 1992), Ch. 2: ' "Man and wife is one flesh": *Hamlet* and the Confrontation with the Maternal Body'; Ch. 5: 'Suffocating Mothers in *King Lear*'; Ch. 6: 'Escaping the Matrix: The Construction of Masculinity in *Macbeth* and *Coriolanus*'; and Ch. 7: 'Making Defect Perfection: Imagining Male Bounty in *Timon of Athens* and *Antony and Cleopatra*'.

Barker, Francis, *The Culture of Violence: Essays on Tragedy and History* (Manchester: Manchester University Press, 1993).

Belsey, Catherine, *The Subject of Tragedy: Identity and Difference in Renaissance Drama* (London and New York: Methuen, 1985).

Belsey, Catherine, 'Cleopatra's Seduction', in *Alternative Shakespeares 2*, ed. Terence Hawkes (London and New York: Routledge, 1996).

Belsey, Catherine, 'The Name of the Rose in *Romeo and Juliet*', in *Shakespeare's Tragedies: Contemporary Critical Essays*, ed. Susan Zimmerman (London: Macmillan, 1998).

Belsey, Catherine, *Shakespeare and the Loss of Eden* (London: Macmillan, 1999), Ch. 5: 'Sibling Rivalry: *Hamlet* and the First Murder'.

Bradley, A. C., *Shakespearean Tragedy*, 3rd edn (London: Macmillan, 1992).

Burnett, Mark, and John Manning (eds), *New Essays on Hamlet* (New York: AMS Press, 1994).

Cavell, Stanley, '*Coriolanus* and the Interpretation of Politics', in *Shakespeare and the Question of Theory*, ed. Patricia Parker and Geoffrey Hartman (New York and London: Methuen, 1985).

Charnes, Linda, 'What's Love Got To Do With It? Reading the Liberal Humanist Romance in *Antony and Cleopatra*', *Textual Practice*, 6:1 (Spring, 1992), 1–16.

Charnes, Linda, 'The Hamlet Formerly Known as Prince', in *Shakespeare and Modernity: Early Modern to Millennium*, ed. Hugh Grady (London and New York: Routledge, 2000).

Coyle, Martin (ed.), *Hamlet: Contemporary Critical Essays* (London: Macmillan, 1992).

Drakakis, John (ed.), *Shakespearean Tragedy* (London and New York: Longman, 1992).

Drakakis, John (ed.), *Antony and Cleopatra: Contemporary Critical Essays* (London: Macmillan, 1994).

Eagleton, Terry, *William Shakespeare* (Oxford: Blackwell, 1986), Ch. 4: '"Nothing": *Othello, Hamlet, Coriolanus*', and Ch. 5: 'Value: *King Lear, Timon of Athens, Antony and Cleopatra*'.

Felperin, Howard, *Shakespearean Representation: Mimesis and Modernity in Shakespearean Tragedy* (Princeton: Princeton University Press, 1977).

Foakes, R. A., *Hamlet Versus Lear: Cultural Politics and Shakespeare's Art* (Cambridge: Cambridge University Press, 1993).

Frye, Northrop, *Fools of Time: Studies in Shakespearean Tragedy* (Toronto: University of Toronto Press, 1967).

Garber, Marjorie, *Shakespeare's Ghost Writers: Literature as Uncanny Causality* (New York and London: Methuen, 1987), Ch. 6: '*Hamlet*: Giving up the Ghost'.

Goldberg, Jonathan, *James I and the Politics of Literature: Jonson, Shakespeare, Donne and Their Contemporaries* (Baltimore and London: Johns Hopkins University Press, 1983), Ch. 4: 'The Roman Actor: *Julius Caesar, Sejanus, Coriolanus, Catiline,* and *The Roman Actor*'.

Goldberg, Jonathan, '*Romeo and Juliet*'s Open Rs', in *Queering the Renaissance*, ed. Jonathan Goldberg (Durham, NC and London: Duke University Press, 1994).

Greenblatt, Stephen, *Renaissance Self-Fashioning: From More to Shakespeare* (Chicago and London: Chicago University Press, 1980), Ch. 6: 'The Improvisation of Power'.

Greenblatt, Stephen, 'Shakespeare and the Exorcists', in his *Shakespearean Negotiations: The Circulation of Social Energy in Renaissance England* (Oxford: Clarendon Press, 1988).

Halio, Jay (ed.), *Shakespeare's Romeo and Juliet: Texts, Contexts and Interpretation* (Newark: University of Delaware Press, 1995).

Halpern, Richard, *Shakespeare Among the Moderns* (Ithaca, NY and London: Cornell University Press, 1997), Ch. 5: 'Hamletmachines'.

Hawkes, Terence, *That Shakespeherian Rag: Essays on a Critical Process* (London and New York: Methuen, 1986), Ch. 5: '*Telmah*'.

Jardine, Lisa, *Reading Shakespeare Historically* (New York and London: Routledge, 1996), Ch. 9: 'Conclusion: What Happens in *Hamlet?*'

Kahn, Coppélia, 'The Absent Mother in *King Lear*', in *Rewriting the Renaissance: The Discourses of Sexual Difference in Early Modern Europe*, ed. Margaret W. Ferguson, Maureen Quilligan and Nancy J. Vickers (Chicago and London: University of Chicago Press, 1986).

Kahn, Coppélia, *Roman Shakespeare: Warriors, Wounds, and Women* (London and New York: Routledge, 1997).

Kastan, David Scott, *Shakespeare After Theory* (New York and London: Routledge, 1999), Ch. 9: '*Macbeth* and the "Name of King"'.

Kerrigan, William, *Hamlet Perfected* (Baltimore and London: Johns Hopkins University Press, 1994).

Kettle, Arnold, 'From *Hamlet* to *Lear*', in *Shakespeare in a Changing World*, ed. Arnold Kettle (London: Lawrence and Wishart, 1964).

Kiernan, Victor, *Eight Tragedies of Shakespeare* (London and New York: Verso, 1996).

Marcus, Leah S., *Unediting the Renaissance: Shakespeare, Marlowe, Milton* (London and New York: Routledge, 1996), Ch. 5: 'Bad Taste and Bad *Hamlet*'.

Newman, Karen, 'Femininity and the Monstrous in *Othello*', in *Shakespeare Reproduced: The Text in History and Ideology*, ed. Jean E. Howard and Marion F. O'Connor (New York and London: Methuen, 1987).

Nuttall, A. D., *Timon of Athens* (Hemel Hempstead: Harvester Wheatsheaf, 1989).

Parker, Patricia, 'Fantasies of "Race" and "Gender": Africa, *Othello*, and Bringing to Light', in *Women, 'Race' and Writing in the Early Modern Period*, ed. Margo Hendricks and Patricia Parker (London: Routledge, 1994).

Parker, Patricia, *Shakespeare From the Margins: Language, Culture, Context* (Chicago: University of Chicago Press, 1996), Ch. 5: ' "Conveyors Are You All": Translating, Conveying, Representing, and Seconding in the Histories and *Hamlet*'.

Patterson, Annabel, *Shakespeare and the Popular Voice* (Oxford: Blackwell, 1989), Ch.1: 'Caviar or the General: *Hamlet* and the Popular Theater', and Ch. 5: ' "What Matter Who's Speaking?": *Hamlet* and *King Lear*'.

Rose, Jacqueline, '*Hamlet*: The Mona Lisa of Literature', in *Shakespeare and Gender: A History*, ed. Deborah E. Barker and Ivo Kamps (London and New York: Verso, 1995).

Ryan, Kiernan (ed.), *King Lear: Contemporary Critical Essays* (London: Macmillan, 1993).

Showalter, Elaine, 'Representing Ophelia: Women, Madness, and the Responsibilities of Feminist Criticism', in *Shakespeare and the Question of Theory*, ed. Patricia Parker and Geoffrey Hartman (New York and London: Methuen, 1985).

Sinfield, Alan (ed.), *Macbeth: Contemporary Critical Essays* (London: Macmillan, 1992).

Smith, Peter J., and Nigel Wood (eds), *Theory in Practice: Hamlet* (Buckingham: Open University Press, 1996).

Snow, Edward, 'Language and Sexual Difference in *Romeo and Juliet*', in *Shakespeare's 'Rough Magic': Renaissance Essays in Honor of C. L. Barber*, ed. Peter Erickson and Coppélia Kahn (Newark: University of Delaware Press, 1985).

Vaughan, Virginia Mason, *Othello: A Contextual History* (Cambridge: Cambridge University Press, 1994).

Wayne, Valerie, 'Historical Differences: Misogyny and *Othello*', in *The Matter of Difference: Materialist-Feminist Criticism of Shakespeare*, ed. Valerie Wayne (Hemel Hempstead: Harvester Wheatsheaf, 1991).

Weimann, Robert, 'Mimesis in *Hamlet*', in *Shakespeare and the Question of Theory*, ed. Patricia Parker and Geoffrey Hartman (New York and London: Methuen, 1985).

White, R. S. (ed.), *Romeo and Juliet: Contemporary Critical Essays* (London: Macmillan, 2001).

Williamson, Marilyn, 'Violence and Gender Ideology in *Coriolanus* and *Macbeth*', in *Shakespeare Left and Right*, ed. Ivo Kamps (New York and London: Routledge, 1991).

Wilson, Richard, *Will Power: Essays on Shakespearean Authority* (Hemel Hempstead: Harvester Wheatsheaf, 1993), Ch.2: '"Is This a Holiday?"': Shakespeare's Roman Carnival', and Ch. 4: 'Against the Grain: Representing the Market in *Coriolanus*'.

Wynne-Davies, Marion, '"The Swallowing Womb": Consumed and Consuming Women in *Titus Andronicus*', in *The Matter of Difference: Materialist-Feminist Criticism of Shakespeare*, ed. Valerie Wayne (Hemel Hempstead: Harvester Wheatsheaf, 1991).

Zimmerman, Susan (ed.), *Shakespeare's Tragedies: Contemporary Critical Essays* (London: Macmillan, 1998).

V Romances

Adelman, Janet, *Suffocating Mothers: Fantasies of Maternal Origin in Shakespeare's Plays, 'Hamlet' to 'The Tempest'* (London and New York: Routledge, 1992), Ch. 8: 'Masculine Authority and the Maternal Body: The Return to Origins in the Romances'.

Barber, C. L., '"Thou That Beget'st Him That Did Thee Beget": Transformation in *Pericles* and *The Winter's Tale*', *Shakespeare Survey*, 22 (1969), 59–67.

Barker, Francis, and Peter Hulme, '"Nymphs and reapers heavily vanish": The Discursive Con-texts of *The Tempest*', in *Alternative Shakespeares*, ed. John Drakakis (London and New York: Methuen, 1985).

Barton, Anne, '"Enter Mariners Wet": Realism in Shakespeare's Last Plays', in her *Essays, Mainly Shakespearean* (Cambridge: Cambridge University Press, 1994).

Belsey, Catherine, *Shakespeare and the Loss of Eden* (London: Macmillan, 1999), Ch. 3: 'Marriage: Imogen's Bedchamber', and Ch. 4: 'Parenthood: Hermione's Statue'.

Bergeron, David, *Shakespeare's Romances and the Royal Family* (Lawrence: University of Kansas Press, 1985).

Bristol, Michael D., *Big-Time Shakespeare* (London and New York: Routledge, 1996), Ch. 6: 'Social Time in *The Winter's Tale*'.

Brown, John Russell, and Bernard Harris (eds), *Later Shakespeare*, Stratford-upon-Avon Studies 8 (London: Edward Arnold, 1966).

Brown, Paul, ' "This Thing of Darkness I Acknowledge Mine": *The Tempest* and the Discourse of Colonialism', in *Political Shakespeare: Essays in Cultural Materialism*, Jonathan Dollimore and Alan Sinfield, 2nd edn (Manchester: Manchester University Press, 1994).

Callaghan, Dympna, *Shakespeare Without Women: Representing Gender and Race on the Renaissance Stage* (New York and London: Routledge, 2000), Ch. 4: 'Irish Memories in *The Tempest*'.

Cartelli, Thomas, 'Prospero in Africa: *The Tempest* as Colonialist Text and Pretext', in *Shakespeare Reproduced: The Text in History and Ideology*, ed. Jean E. Howard and Marion F. O'Connor (New York and London: Methuen, 1987).

Chedzgoy, Kate, *Shakespeare's Queer Children: Sexual Politics and Contemporary Culture* (Manchester and New York: Manchester University Press, 1995), Ch. 3: 'Rewriting the Narratives of Shame: Women's Transformations of *The Tempest*'.

Demaray, John G., *Shakespeare and the Spectacles of Strangeness: 'The Tempest' and the Transformation of Renaissance Theatrical Forms* (Pittsburgh: Duquesne University Press, 1998).

Felperin, Howard, *Shakespearean Romance* (Princeton: Princeton University Press, 1972).

Felperin, Howard, *The Uses of the Canon: Elizabethan Literature and Contemporary Theory* (Oxford: Oxford University Press, 1990), Ch. 9: '*The Tempest* in Our Time'.

Frye, Northrop, *A Natural Perspective: The Development of Shakespearean Comedy and Romance* (New York: Columbia University Press, 1965).

Greenblatt, Stephen, *Shakespearean Negotiations: The Circulation of Social Energy in Renaissance England* (Berkeley: University of California Press 1988), Ch. 5: 'Martial Law in the Land of Cockaigne'.

Greenblatt, Stephen, *Learning to Curse: Essays in Early Modern Culture* (New York and London: Routledge, 1990), Ch. 2: 'Learning to Curse: Aspects of Linguistic Colonialism in the Sixteenth Century'.

Halpern, Richard, *Shakespeare Among the Moderns* (Ithaca, NY and London: Cornell University Press, 1997), pp. 140–58: 'The Topical and the Transcendental: Shakespeare's *Pericles*'.

Hawkes, Terence, *That Shakespeherian Rag: Essays on a Critical Process* (London and New York: Methuen, 1986), Ch. 1: 'Playhouse–Workhouse'.

Hulme, Peter, 'Prospero and Caliban', in his *Colonial Encounters: Europe and the Native Caribbean, 1492–1797* (London and New York: Methuen, 1986).

Hulme, Peter, and William H. Sherman (eds), *The Tempest and Its Travels* (London: Reaktion Books, 2000).

Joughin, John J., 'Shakespeare, Modernity and the Aesthetic: Art, Truth and Judgement in *The Winter's Tale*', in *Shakespeare and Modernity: Early Modern to Millennium*, ed. Hugh Grady (London and New York: Routledge, 2000).

Kahn, Coppélia, 'The Providential Tempest and the Shakespearean Family', in *Representing Shakespeare: New Psychoanalytic Essays*, ed. Murray Schwartz and Coppélia Kahn (Baltimore: Johns Hopkins University Press, 1980).

Kastan, David Scott, *Shakespeare After Theory* (New York and London: Routledge, 1999), Ch. 10: '"The Duke of Milan and his Brave Son": Old Histories and New in *The Tempest*'.

Kay, C. M., and H. E. Jacobs (eds), *Shakespeare's Romances Reconsidered* (Lincoln: University of Nebraska Press, 1978).

Loomba, Ania, *Gender, Race, Renaissance Drama* (Manchester: Manchester University Press, 1989), Ch. 6: 'Seizing the Book'.

Marienstras, Richard, 'Elizabethan Travel Literature and Shakespeare's *The Tempest*', in his *New Perspectives on the Shakespearean World* (Cambridge: Cambridge University Press, 1985).

Markham, Simon (ed.), *The Tempest: The Critical Tradition* (London: Athlone, 2000).

Mowat, Barbara A., *The Dramaturgy of Shakespeare's Romances* (Athens, GA: University of Georgia Press, 1976).

Mullaney, Steven, *The Place of the Stage: License, Play, and Power in Renaissance England* (Chicago and London: University of Chicago Press, 1988), Ch. 6: '"All That Monarchs Do": The Obscured Stages of Authority in *Pericles*'.

Nevo, Ruth, *Shakespeare's Other Language* (London: Methuen, 1987).

Norbrook, David, '"What Cares These Roarers for the Name of King?": Language and Utopia in *The Tempest*', in *The Politics of Tragicomedy*, ed. Gordon McMullan and Jonathan Hope (London and New York: Routledge, 1992).

Orgel, Stephen, 'Prospero's Wife', in *Rewriting the Renaissance: The Discourses of Sexual Difference in Early Modern Europe*, ed. Margaret W. Ferguson, Maureen Quilligan and Nancy Vickers (Chicago and London: University of Chicago Press, 1986).

Orgel, Stephen, 'Shakespeare and the Cannibals', in *Cannibals, Witches and Divorce: Estranging the Renaissance*, ed. Marjorie Garber (Baltimore and London: Johns Hopkins University Press, 1987).

Palfrey, Simon, *Late Shakespeare: A New World of Words* (Oxford: Clarendon Press, 1997).

Patterson, Annabel, *Shakespeare and the Popular Voice* (Oxford: Blackwell, 1989), Ch. 7: ' "Thought is Free": *The Tempest*'.

Relihan, Constance C., 'Liminal Geography: *Pericles* and the Politics of Place', *Philological Quarterly*, 71 (1992), 281–99.

Richards, Jennifer, and James Knowles (eds), *Shakespeare's Late Plays: New Readings* (Edinburgh: Edinburgh University Press, 1999).

Ryan, Kiernan (ed.), *Shakespeare: The Last Plays* (London: Longman, 1999).

Skeele, David, *Thwarting the Wayward Seas: A Critical and Theatrical History of Shakespeare's 'Pericles' in the Nineteenth and Twentieth Centuries* (Wilmington: University of Delaware Press, 1998).

Sokolova, Boika, *Shakespeare's Romances as Interrogative Texts* (London: Edwin Mellen, 1992).

Sundelson, David, ' "So rare a wonder'd father": Prospero's *Tempest*', in *Representing Shakespeare: New Psychoanalytic Essays*, ed. Murray Schwartz and Coppélia Kahn (Baltimore: Johns Hopkins University Press, 1980).

Thompson, Anne, ' "Miranda, Where's Your Sister?": Reading Shakespeare's *The Tempest*', in *Shakespeare and Gender: A History*, ed. Deborah E. Barker and Ivo Kamps (London and New York: Verso, 1995).

Tobias, Richard, and Paul G. Zolbrod (eds), *Shakespeare's Late Plays* (Athens, OH: Ohio University Press, 1974).

Vaughan, Alden T., and Virginia Vaughan, *Shakespeare's Caliban: A Cultural History* (Cambridge: Cambridge University Press, 1991).

Warren, Roger, *Staging Shakespeare's Late Plays* (Oxford: Clarendon Press, 1990).

White, R. S. (ed.), *The Tempest: Contemporary Critical Essays* (London: Macmillan, 1999).

Wilson, Richard, *Will Power: Essays on Shakespearean Authority* (Hemel Hempstead: Harvester Wheatsheaf, 1993), Ch. 6: 'Observations on English Bodies: Licensing Maternity in Shakespeare's Late Plays'.

Wood, Nigel (ed.), *Theory in Practice: The Tempest* (Buckingham: Open University Press, 1995).

VI Poetry

Bate, Jonathan, 'Sexual Perversity in *Venus and Adonis*', *Yearbook of English Studies*, 23 (1993), 80–92.

Belsey, Catherine, 'Love as Trompe-l'œil: Taxonomies of Desire in *Venus and Adonis*', in *Venus and Adonis: Critical Essays*, ed. Philip C. Kolin (New York: Garland, 1997).

Berry, Philippa, 'Woman, Language, and History in *The Rape of Lucrece*', *Shakespeare Survey*, 44 (1992), 33–9.

Booth, Stephen, *An Essay on Shakespeare's Sonnets* (New Haven: Yale University Press, 1969).

Bowen, Barbara E., 'The Rape of Jesus: Aemilia Lanyer's *Lucrece*', in *Marxist Shakespeares*, ed. Jean E. Howard and Scott Shershow (London and New York: Routledge, 2001).

Chedzgoy, Kate, *Shakespeare's Queer Children: Sexual Politics and Contemporary Culture* (Manchester and New York: Manchester University Press, 1995), Ch. 4: '"Strange Worship": Oscar Wilde and the Key to Shakespeare's *Sonnets*'.

Cousins, A. D., *Shakespeare's Sonnets and Narrative Poems* (London: Longman, 1999).

Crewe, Jonathan, *Trials of Authorship: Anterior Forms and Poetic Reconstruction from Wyatt to Shakespeare* (Berkeley, Los Angeles and Oxford: University of California Press, 1990), Ch. 6: 'Shakespeare's Figure of Lucrece: Writing Rape'.

Donaldson, Ian, *The Rapes of Lucretia: A Myth and Its Transformation* (Oxford: Oxford University Press, 1982).

Dubrow, Heather, *Captive Victors: Shakespeare's Narrative Poems and Sonnets* (Ithaca, NY and London: Cornell University Press, 1987).

Felperin, Howard, *Beyond Deconstruction: The Uses and Abuses of Literary Theory* (Oxford: Oxford University Press, 1985), Ch. 5: 'Toward a Post-structuralist Practice: A Reading of Shakespeare's *Sonnets*'.

Felperin, Howard, *The Uses of the Canon: Elizabethan Literature and Contemporary Theory* (Oxford: Clarendon Press, 1990), Ch. 4: 'The Dark Lady Identified, or What Deconstruction Can Do For Shakespeare's *Sonnets*'.

Fineman, Joel, *Shakespeare's Perjured Eye: The Invention of Poetic Subjectivity in the Sonnets* (Berkeley: University of California Press, 1985).

Flores, Ralph, 'Metatheater as Metaphorics: Playing Figures in Shakespeare's *Sonnets*', in *Shakespeare and Deconstruction*, ed. G. Douglas Atkins and David M. Bergeron (New York, Bern, Frankfurt and Paris: Peter Lang, 1988).

Greene, Thomas M., 'Pitiful Thrivers: Failed Husbandry in the *Sonnets*', in *Shakespeare and the Question of Theory*, ed. Patricia Parker and Geoffrey Hartman (New York and London: Methuen, 1985).

Hulse, Clark, *Metamorphic Verse: The Elizabethan Minor Epic* (Princeton: Princeton University Press, 1981).

Jed, Stephanie, *Chaste Thinking: The Rape of Lucretia and the Birth of Humanism* (Bloomington and Indianapolis: University of Indiana Press, 1989).

Kahn, Coppélia, 'The Rape in Shakespeare's *Lucrece*', in *Shakespeare and Gender: A History*, ed. Deborah E. Barker and Ivo Kamps (London and New York: Verso, 1995).

Keach, William, *Elizabethan Erotic Narratives* (Brighton: Harvester Press, 1977).

Kerrigan, John (ed.), *The Sonnets and A Lover's Complaint* (Harmondsworth: Penguin, 1986), 'Introduction'.

Koppenfels, Werner von, 'Dis-Covering the Female Body: Erotic Exploration in Elizabethan Poetry', *Shakespeare Survey*, 47 (1994), 127–37.

Patterson, Annabel, *Reading Between the Lines* (London: Routledge, 1993), Ch. 8: 'Sleeping with the Enemy: *The Rape of Lucrece*'.

Roberts, Sasha, 'Editing Sexuality, Narrative and Authorship: The Altered Texts of Shakespeare's *Lucrece*', in *Texts and Cultural Change in Early Modern England*, ed. Cedric C. Brown and Arthur F. Marotti (London: Macmillan, 1997).

Sedgwick, Eve Kosofsky, 'Gender Asymmetry and Erotic Triangles' in her *Between Men: English Literature and Male Homosocial Desire*, 2nd edn (New York: Columbia University Press, 1992).

Vendler, Helen, *The Art of Shakespeare's Sonnets* (Cambridge, MA: Harvard University Press, 1997).

Vickers, Nancy, ' "The Blazon of Sweet Beauty's Best": Shakespeare's *Lucrece*', in *Shakespeare and the Question of Theory*, ed. Patricia Parker and Geoffrey Hartman (New York and London: Methuen, 1985).

Index